Some readers' comm

G000075180

J. P. Donleavy would be proud to have written this.

I love this. Not since *Confederacy of Dunces* by John Kennedy Toole have I been so amused. The characters are realistic and it makes you realise that the world really has gone mad.

I don't often LOL when reading, but Little Owl, swearing parrots and threatening cross-bow fire had me in hysterics. You have a level of acerbic wit that most of us can only dream of. Hilarious.

I rank this with the likes of David Sedaris. Perhaps even a bit more consistently funny than Sedaris. Like Sedaris, David Sherrington twists common, everyday things into a rare and hysterical perspective.

Age of Bewilderment is tremendous. Witty and acutely observed.

Oh heavens, I love it!

Brilliant. Your observations on modern society are spot on. Outstanding.

Absolutely love your work, hysterical, warm, funny, realistic, so genuine.

Witty, witty, witty. I loved this. Observations are spot-on and so cleverly made It's simply great.

I love your wit, love the nostalgia. This is a very enjoyable read.

David casts a caustic eye over what passes for normal life in this our 21st century and finds tiny pearls of humour in the most banal of clams.

This is a wonderful book, it made me laugh out loud many times.

Not only a great sax player, but a born storyteller.

Age of Bewilderment

Age of Bewilderment

David Sherrington

BwildR

A BwildR Publication
In association with Silverpark Associates Limited
www.BwildR.net

ISBN: 978-1-900217-01-9

Original cover image and author photo by John Sherrington
Cover painting by Robert Jacobson
Book design by Robert and Erik Jacobson
www.longfeatherbookdesign.com

For Sarah, Lisa, Daniel and Anna

If I had known I was going to live this long, I would have taken better care of myself.

—Eubie Blake 1887-1983

Follow your bliss and the universe will open doors for you where there were only walls.

—Joseph Campbell

Contents

Age of Bewilderment

Play in a Day

Monday:

A promising start to the week. I am, it seems, a valued customer of a major energy company and they are showing their deep and touching concern for the environment by encouraging us all to use less electricity. Taken to its logical conclusion, this looks like a Kamikaze business plan to me. Their slogan, "Saving today — Saving tomorrow", has a hollow ring to it, as does their claim that by merely turning off the standby light on my telly, curling tongs or whatever, I could save the planet. I wonder if they take the same hectoring tone with the perpetrators of the Blackpool illuminations, or Eric Clapton when he's giving it some welly.

I put out my laundry on the daisy-chain of multi-coloured bungee straps that passes for a washing line on my balcony. One end of the line is attached to a rusting lucky horseshoe on the wall and the other to an equally corroded satellite dish. I wince and cower as I do this, since I've heard that a flailing bungee strap could take one's eye out.

My tatty underwear faded T shirts and Dennis the Menace socks flap and bounce away on the bungee line, reminding me of a colourful Tibetan funeral site, without the vultures, prayer wheels and yak butter.

Tuesday:

Talking of Eric Clapton, I'm puzzled by why a lot of guitarists these days seem to pull such pained faces when they play. It's as if they are suffering paroxysms of extreme hemorrhoidal discomfort, or that some unseen hand is squeezing their privates. Bert Weedon never did this. He had a fixed grin when he played, as if he had just had it off with Alma Cogan, or Pet Clarke.

His *Play in a Day* book sold in its millions, so in theory there are probably a lot of guitarists out there who did just that and went no further, preferring perhaps to pull faces rather than moving on to the fourth chord on day two.

I go to the local mini-market, where Status Quo are blaring out of the in-store sound system. Perhaps Bert was one of their early, but quickly abandoned influences. I buy chicken Kiev, some bacon and a bottle of Fair Trade pinot grigot. The bacon has a "buy one get one free" sticker on it. I take just the one packet, since I'm trying to cut down on red meat. It can, apparently, make one aggressive, although I don't need bacon to make me feel that way some days, particularly in the football season or when captains of industry are on *Desert Island Discs*.

I go to the checkout where a girl, little more than an embryo with eyeliner and attitude, is discussing her love life on her mobile. I wait patiently through "it weren't were its", glottal stops and sentences that all seem to end in unnecessary question marks, until she decides to serve me. Feeling in quite good spirits and somewhat avuncular, I decide to have a little joke. Holding up the bacon, I say,

'This is the free one. I might come back next week and pay for the other one, or certainly when the winter fuel allowance kicks in.'

She stares at me as if I'm speaking Swahili and reaches down to press a buzzer that summons the manager, who appears to be only a little older than she. He talks very slowly to me, and over my protestations that I was only joking, carefully explains the philosophy behind BOGOF. Next up at the checkout is the pinot grigot. The Embryo holds it in the air between her thumb and forefinger, as if it's a paedophile's urine sample.

'Alcohol!' she shouts, making me flinch guiltily, as if a bungee had caught me behind the ear.

Wednesday:

After an unsettled night, during which I dreamt that I was an extra-terrestrial capable of seeing through women's clothing, I decide that a bacon sandwich and a mug of builder's tea will set me up for the day. As the tea over-brews nicely, the bacon sizzles in the frying pan and gives off alarming gangrenous white pus. I Google this and discover that it's water. Apparently, dead pigs are pumped full of it to fill out the meat and add weight.

As I recall, medieval brewers and bakers were hanged for adulterating their wares. I fantasise about the satisfying clunk of dislocating upper vertebrae as the mini-market manager takes the drop before a baying crowd of disgruntled shoppers. I eat the bacon sandwich anyway.

Thursday:

This evening the couple downstairs are having a row. They are both Antipodeans. She is called Chardonnay and he, Brent.

'Jeez Shards, give it a rest,' he whines.

'Give it a rest?' she screams. 'If I gave it a rest Brint, nothing would ever get done.'

And so on and on. It's like listening to an omnibus edition of *Neighbours*.

Bono, the squillionaire singer from U2, is on the telly berating us for ignoring poverty in the Third World and illegally sharing music files. I make myself laugh by thinking that he's an "i" short of a dog biscuit. I put the chicken Kiev in the oven, closing my eyes to avoid noticing that I have never cleaned it. I see from the packet that the Kiev is apparently made from "re-formed chicken". Maybe I'll have a little joke the next time that I'm in the mini-market. "Is this a previously delinquent hen?" I'll ask. Or, "Was this once a thuggish bantam?". I think better of it, remembering how poorly the bacon gag went down.

Friday:

An unsettled night, but potentially very productive. I think that I could be on to a winner. I dreamt of yellow no parking lines stretching as far as the eye could see. In fact, they encircled the earth and went out to the farthest reaches of the galaxy.

As I breakfast on a lightly boiled barn egg, I think hard about what this dream could mean. Then it dawns on me. All these yellow lines are unnecessary. They disfigure our towns and villages and the paint and labour involved must cost the nation a fortune. So, why not paint yellow lines only in those places where one *can* park? No yellow line — no parking. There could be enormous savings.

I believe this is called blue sky thinking, coming from left field, or thinking out of the box. Sir Richard Branson is famous for this, although I thought *Tubular Bells*, on the Virgin label, pedestrian and tediously repetitive. I decide to dash off a letter to the Department for Transport forthwith. There could be a gong in this.

Saturday:

Another barn egg for breakfast. What is a barn egg? The use of the term "barn" is clearly intended to summon forth images of a bucolic bygone age, where hay-chewing farmers leant on gates, yokels knew their place and Land Army girls frolicked in the hay as our brave boys wheeled overhead in their Spitfires. The true origin of these eggs is, I suspect, a depressing concrete bunker in Essex crammed with beakless hens frantically looking for the tiniest space to deposit their eggs. I might write an ironic letter to the mini-market asking for a tour of their barn.

Shards and Brint are planning to breed. I know this because today Shards had a loud telephone conversation with her mother back in Woop Woop, or wherever. I was checking that my laundry had sufficiently matured on the bungees, so I heard everything.

'Brint and I are going to start trying for a baby Mumsie,' she said.

This sounds vaguely combative, like planning a military campaign, or an arm wrestling contest. The thought of Brint and Shards adding to the gene pool has me weighing the merits of eugenics. I decide that an hour's saxophone practice might take my mind off this and perhaps temporarily dampen their ardour.

Sunday:

I Google Bert Weedon and discover that he's still alive. I bring my washing in. Unscathed.

Cyclops

Monday:

A quiet day. I walk into town. Over the old wooden river bridge, past the parish church and into the High Street. Woolworth's is boarded up, as are many other shops. All that's left is charity shops, bookmakers, take-aways, over-priced coffee shops and of course the blameless banks. I notice a New Age shop offering a special deal on American Indian ear candles and caffeine enemas. Despite all the Westerns I've watched over the years, I have absolutely no memory of ever having seen an Indian with candles in his ears, or indeed of anyone ingesting coffee other than by the usual route. But then my memory is not what it was.

I dread being introduced to someone new these days. If I have to remember *their* name, then I might have to jettison someone else's from the creaking data banks. I can imagine a situation where too much new input comes in and I'll forget how to perform basic functions like lifting the lavatory seat, or putting my underpants on before my trousers. When I'm introduced to someone new, I've taken to quietly humming the *Star Wars* bar music to distract myself. It gets me some funny looks, but at least I don't always hear their name. In the event that I do, then my brain begins a frantic internal shuffling, searching for an empty slot, or a piece of data to jettison. Recently, being introduced to a certain Deirdre Buntington-Smythe caused me to completely forget how to tie a Windsor knot.

Tuesday:

Before rising, I lie in bed listening to the shipping forecast. It sounds oddly like a recitation of school reports. " Portland, Bill — Good, occasionally moderate. Fitzroy — fair. Dogger — moderate, sometimes rough." And so on. I almost expect to hear "Fisher — could do better."

Wednesday:

Am I alone in disliking church bells? Every Tuesday night bell ringers practice at the parish church. To me, it's an insult to the ears. Who are these people? How is it that they can flood the whole town with this uninvited cacophony every Tuesday? Maybe they are all tone deaf hunchbacks merely seeking sanctuary. Not sure whether the term "hunchback" is PC these days.

Thursday:

My hearing has been shattered over the years playing pub gigs with Neanderthal guitarists. Consequently, at social gatherings, what some people might regard as a pleasant buzz of conversation, is like the Tower of Babel to me. Once at a dinner party, I was seated next to a muscular New Zealand woman and the combination of her accent and the background noise meant that I didn't understand a word she said. So I nodded and smiled. Imagine my surprise early the next morning when I was summoned from my bed by a loud knocking on my door. There she stood in full hiking kit with an ordnance survey map dangling from a lanyard round her neck.

'G'day', she said, cheerily punching my arm, 'ready to go for a tramp?'

I later discovered that going for a tramp is the Antipodean equivalent of hiking and not an attack on an itinerant, or a woman of dubious virtue.

Friday:

I will be attending a school reunion tomorrow. In the past, I've always avoided these, but I have resolved to get out more. I spend the day wondering what to wear and eventually decide to go for a sort of Johnny Cash look — all in black and slightly dangerous, but offset by white plimsolls. I also decide not to shave, thinking that a bit of designer stubble might add to the mean look that I'm after.

My P Reg Fiesta is playing up so I take it to the local garage. As I putter onto the forecourt, I can see the mechanics in their smoke-filled tea room, no doubt practicing the low whistles that they reserve for condemning old bangers. Eventually, one of them saunters out and looks under the bonnet. I'm spared the whistle as he casually re-attaches a sparking plug lead.

'There's your problem,' he says, swaggering back to the tea room.

'Thanks Dave,' I call after him.

I always call mechanics Dave — they seem to respond to that.

Saturday:

On entering the venue for the school reunion, I present my invitation to a big fronted woman at the door.

'You don't remember me do you?' she says.

I confess that I don't, whereupon she smacks me across the face with a clutch of invites.

'Bastard!' she sobs and several people turn around to see what the fuss is about.

A grizzled, burly figure emerges from the crowd and comes over to the door. I immediately recognise him as Grudgeon, the school bully and I have to say that my colon almost goes into evacuation mode as he approaches. However, he's wearing a dog collar and hugs me.

'Peace friend,' he intones.

My last memory of Grudgeon is of him pummeling my head with one hand while coolly puffing on a Woodbine with the other. He tells me that he is now a chaplain to the Queen. I'm tempted to ask which one, but decide against it.

I go to the bar and order a double scotch which I down in one and call for another. A woman's voice behind me says,

'I always knew you'd end up with a drink problem, big head.'

Under the folds of facial fat, blusher and a clown's mouth, I recognise her as a girl from my old class. I once dubbed her Cyclops, because she had glasses with sticking plaster over one lens. Her glasses now look like the bottoms of jam jars, so I presume the plaster patch didn't correct her problem. She tells me that she has had four children and I wonder how this glazed gargoyle could ever have been the object of anyone's desire. Looking me up and down she asks, 'Have you come from a funeral?'

'Yes,' I lie, 'my brother was killed in a circus accident. There wasn't much left after Zeppo's lions had finished with him. Charlie Cairoli was there — he makes that soprano sax talk.'

Behind the jam jar bottoms, her eyes spin like the ball bearings in those miniature pinball games one used to get at Christmas. The bearings settle into a beady stare and she stalks off.

I slink into a dark corner with my drink and watch as this room full of geriatrics bray and guzzle to a background of crappy Sixties music. I might have shared a sliver of history with them, but I can't feel any connection or fellow feeling with them now. They are frozen in time like the arrested drip of a Siberian standpipe. I decide to leave and as I edge toward an exit, a voice cackles across the decades, causing me to stop in my tracks.

'Hey you, come here.'

It's my old history teacher, Miss Vine. She's propped up by cushions in a corner seat, pointing a bony finger at me. I shuffle sheepishly toward her.

'So what have you done with yourself?' she demands.

She looks like Ursula Andress when she reverted to a wizened crone in the film, *She*. I proudly tell her that after a chequered career as a musician, I eventually read history at university.

She stares at me for some time, her rheumy eyes critically looking me up and down.

'Musician? Rubbish! Of course you didn't go to university. You became a plumber as I recall. You always were a fantasist. And why are you dressed like an undertaker's assistant? Stand up straight. I see that you haven't learnt to shave yet — and why are you wearing plimsolls?'

The room goes quiet and people begin to giggle and point. Amid the rising tide of laughter, I continue toward the exit and make my escape. Crossing the car park, I notice the Queen's chaplain and Cyclops locked in a passionate embrace against a Range Rover.

Sunday:

After last night's humiliations and to re-assure myself that I'm not indeed a plumber, I practise the saxophone and read a little Gibbon.

Ashes to Ashes

Monday:

I attend a funeral today at the local crematorium. It's not for some-one that I knew particularly well and he'd lived to a ripe old age. So no tragic circumstances or a premature death. Which is just as well as I do find funerals faintly comic and have to concentrate hard not to laugh out loud. For a start there is the plethora of platitudes.

"He would have wanted it that way". Or "At least he didn't suffer". And, "E's gone to a better place".

Standing in the Crem dutifully mumbling hymns and prayers, I en-tertain disturbing thoughts. Do they burn the stiffs in batches at the end of the day? If so, how do they sort out which ashes to put into which urns? And what about all the melted fat? Maybe the council siphons this off to fuel their bio-dustcarts — saves them pestering the local chippies I suppose.

Anyway, I'm willing to bet that pure human fat is superior to old chippie oil that has long hosted Mars bars, saveloys and questionable haddock. The other question that plagues me during the rituals is where all the surplus ash goes after they've randomly filled the urns. Maybe they store it up for the winter months and then sprinkle it on icy pave-ments outside old people's homes. A little old lady gamely picking her way to the mini-market in the depths of winter may not realise that her safe passage is courtesy of some of her dear departed husband's charred remains that she thought were entirely contained within the cherished urn on her mantelpiece.

Following the service, the mourners are invited to snacks and drinks at a local hotel. Drinking during the day has never been my forte, but I join the rest in quaffing down glasses of wine and ripping at chicken legs. I'm beginning to enjoy myself when, to my horror, I'm asked to say a few words about the deceased. Since I hardly knew the man, I find this difficult and waffle on about what little I can remember. Emboldened by the wine perhaps, I decide to round off with a little humour and speculate on what might happen if there were a *real* fire at the crematorium and it was in danger of burning down.

'Imagine the 999 call,' I chuckle. 'Fire at the Crem you say? Yeah, pull the other one mate.'

This is greeted with a stony silence and I realise, too late perhaps, that not everyone shares my sense of humour, or has achieved the same level of intoxication.

Tuesday:

An appointment at the blood pressure clinic. This is a bi-annual event during which the same silly questions about my lifestyle are asked and in response to which I invariably lie. The armband deflates with a satisfying hiss and the nurse unstraps it.

'How was it for you?' I ask.

She laughs, she actually laughs. I begin to believe that I haven't entirely lost my touch.

Wednesday:

A documentary on the telly about the Big Bang theory. A parade of scientists and geeks say that the universe began with an almighty bang and that debris flew off to form galaxies. So far so good. I can follow that, but what is not mentioned, or even questioned is what it was that went bang in the first place.

Just to confuse the issue, Brian May, the poodle-ish guitarist with Queen, appears. I'm impressed to learn that he has a doctorate in astronomy and I'm thankful that his contribution to the programme doesn't include any of his greatest hits.

Inevitably, Sir Patrick Moore is wheeled out. He seems to have experienced a quantum leap in weight over the years. I imagine that he must get his suits run up by a marquee manufacturer. Should he ever spontaneously combust, or go bang, the subsequent debris, splintered monocle and all, would probably form a whole new galaxy.

Thursday:

I awake late after an unsettled night. April, who lives in Number One, locked herself out of her flat at about two in the morning and started to howl and kick her door. She was once called Kevin, but is currently receiving medication prior to a sex re-assignment procedure. She still has a deep voice and is quite muscular. She wears heavy make-up and dresses in frilly diaphanous outfits and very high heels.

I went down and found her sitting on the stairs, mascara running and legs akimbo in an unladylike pose, looking like a stranded stag night victim. One of her high heels was stuck in a hole in the flimsy door. She told me that she'd had a dreadful evening. Her latest boyfriend has dumped her and now she can't get into her flat. As I consider having to offer her sanctuary, Reg the caretaker arrived on the scene. Reg, who is a devoted country music fan, lives in the basement flat and takes care of cleaning, wheelie bins and general maintenance, He has a yappy little dog called Patsy, apparently named after Patsy Cline the long deceased country singer. This brutish little cur has snapped at my heels on many an occasion. From my balcony, I've frequently watched her out on the lawn scanning the horizon like an anxious mariner, or a tortured guitarist, as she strains to evacuate her bowels. I've often toyed with the idea of bumping her off with a crossbow, or a vat of boiling oil.

Reg produced a bunch of keys and let April into her flat. I didn't know that he had keys to all the flats and resolved to get my lock changed. I don't like the thought of him rifling disdainfully through my CD collection, while Patsy scent marks my furniture.

April slumped wearily into her flat, but not before the dog dragged her shoe from the door and ran off with it.

'Thanks, Reg,' she said, 'I'll get the shoe in the morning.'

Despite my innate cynicism, I admire April. Most of us aspire to life changes, but to change one's body as well takes courage. April, would not, however, be my first choice of names. Sounds too much like a maiden aunt, or the alias of a call centre operative.

Friday:

I practice the saxophone in preparation for a pub gig on Saturday night. I'm interrupted in full flight by a banging at the door. It's Brint, the Antipodean from the flat below.

'Any chance of giving it a rest mate? Only Shard's a bit crook with a headache,' he says.

I commiserate and agree to "give it a rest", wondering whether Shard's headache is genuine, or an attempt at getting a little respite in the trying for a baby.

I recently saw an advertisement for a device claiming to enable sax players to practise silently. There was a picture of a man whose torso and arms were cocooned in what looked like a giant rice crispy. He had headphones on and was blowing down the business end of a sax, the rest of which was presumably within the cocoon. I could imagine falling over whilst so encumbered and, like an upturned beetle, being unable to get up, finally dying of dehydration and starvation. The funeral platitudes would of course include, "He died doing what he loved" and "He would have wanted it that way".

Saturday:

And so to the gig this evening at a local pub with a band called The Suicidal Gerbils. Their repertoire is a fairly undemanding mix of blues and r'n'b which they play with great gusto and very little finesse. My role, in between competing with the guitarist's determination to fill every gap, is to toot a bit and play a few solos.

The guitarist has at his feet a box with various buttons, each producing a different ear-splitting and largely unnecessary effect. Periodically, he stabs at this theatrically with his foot, like someone trying to stamp out a fire, or kill an adder. He behaves as though everyone has come to see him and the rest of the band are mere ciphers — perhaps we are. He has a towel with which to mop his fevered brow between numbers, after struggling manfully with three or possibly four chords and the stubborn refusal of his volume control to go beyond ten. His every histrionic solo is greeted with rapturous applause by a small bunch of groupies sporting "Gerbs Forever" T shirts.

I realised long ago that music is secondary to image and that in purely commercial terms, I chose the wrong instrument. It's difficult to look sexy or tortured with a sax stuck in one's face. Which is probably why I remain impoverished and groupie-less. I leave the pub with my ears ringing, but fifty quid better off. I'm beginning to think I prefer the church bells — or perhaps I need some ear candles.

Sunday:

A visit from our new community policeman, Jason.

'Just checking on seniors in the area sir,' he says.

Jason is wearing a hi-vis jacket and a stab vest and is bristling with technology. He's adorned with various mysterious attachments and a radio crackles on his lapel. I can't imagine that he could move very fast in all this kit and would be about as effective as a barnacle if he ever had to give chase.

'Hey, weren't you on the Gerbs gig last night?' he asks.

I confirm this, perhaps puffing out my chest a little.

'Cor, that guitarist played a real blinder,' he says.

Oh, Cordelia

Monday:

It's over a week since the school reunion, but I'm still smarting from the experience. It reminded me of how much I hated school. It seemed like a Dickensian madhouse to me. I was bewildered by the sheer tedium and the brutality of it all. Many of the teachers were ex-servicemen, with bits missing — either physically, or mentally and they were about as competent as George Formby's dentist. These psychopaths had survived the war, but were anything but unscathed. They seemed to regard the chalk-face as the equivalent of trench warfare. We children were the enemy, to be beaten into submission, either by physical abuse or boredom. Either way, I found it hell and longed for the holidays.

So, I started playing truant and faking sick notes from my mum. At first, it would be, "my son has had a heavy cold", or "a tummy upset". Being quite an imaginative little boy, I started giving myself more exotic ailments. I even went to the library to look them up. Before I was twelve, I'd had virtually every major disease, including yellow fever and trench foot. It says something for the competence of the school that this was never questioned.

My downfall came when my mum bumped into the headmaster in the street one day. He thanked her for her recent letter and commiserated over my epic struggle with a giant tapeworm. My mother, somewhat surprised to learn of this, accepted his condolences and assured him that from now on I would be in rude health. I spent the remainder of my schooldays staring out of the window like an estate agent. Hence, I know next to nothing about geometry, algebra, the Trojan Wars, photosynthesis, long division, woodwork, or who killed Cock-Robin. And I still can't tie my shoelaces properly, or use any kind of implement, apart from basic cutlery. As long as it's left-handed.

I dine on a frozen fish pie called "Bosun's Choice". I couldn't detect anything within resembling fish and conclude that this particular bosun is a strict vegan.

Tuesday:

No response as yet to my letter to the Department for Transport regarding my idea to virtually abolish yellow no parking lines. I imagine that this has probably gone beyond some faceless departmental lackey and on to ministerial level, so I'm not disappointed. If, as I fully expect, I am eventually invited to the Palace, I shall confess to Her Maj that I too keep my breakfast cereal in a Tupperware box. Not quite sure what I'll say to Phillip if he's about. I know next to nothing about Greece, carriage horses, or the pursuit of furry, or feathered animals.

Wednesday:

Still feeling cheated by the Bosun's pie, I decide to take advantage of the senior's lunch at my local chippy. A poster on the window states that this includes a generous portion of filleted line- caught Atlantic cod. If, as we're told, cod is becoming scarce, what difference does it make whether it's caught by rod and line or a net? I suppose the rod gives it a sporting chance. I picture nerdy suburban anglers perched precariously on their little fold-up stools on the deck of a bucketing trawler, gamely dipping their rods into the boiling Atlantic while cheerfully munching on cheese and chutney sandwiches that their indulgent wives have packed, glad to have the nerds out of their hair for an hour or two.

I sit among the seniors in the chippy, feeling a bit of a fraud, since I don't yet dribble, or cup my hand around my ear when addressed. Some of the women have bandaged legs, as if they're in the initial stages of mummification. The cod is rather good and I'm tucking in heartily when disaster strikes. I have a fish bone caught in my throat. I stagger to my feet, coughing and spluttering. The burble of senile chatter is silenced as I struggle to breath.

'Fish bone,' observes some cackling old crone. 'E oughta be more careful. Cod's funny like that.'

Fearing that one of the wrinklies, or worse still the spotty youth behind the counter, might wrestle me to the floor in a botched attempt at the Heimlich Manoeuvre, I flee from the chippy and race to my car. I arrive at the local casualty department in good time and within minutes suffer the indignity of having a camera shoved up my nose by a cheerful schoolboy in a white coat. After much probing, the cod bone is located and removed. It's Bosun's Choice from now on.

Thursday:

A new resident has moved in on the first floor. She looks to be a little younger than me and from a distance at least, very attractive. Reg, the caretaker, is helping her to unload her car and shamelessly flirting. I decide to saunter downstairs to get a better view.

She and Reg struggle with a large box. I offer to help, but Reg shoots me a territorial look. I introduce myself and she tells me that her name is Cordelia.

'Ah,' I say, giving a little bow, 'Lear's youngest daughter.'

'Oh yes, that's right,' she says, seemingly pleased that I know the Shakespearian connection.

She's about fifty-ish, very well preserved and definitely my type. She thanks Reg and closes her door. Reg looks peeved.

'You might know her dad,' he hisses through his teeth, 'but remember, I saw her first mate.'

Friday:

I check my emails. It's the usual junk. "Big Babes in your Area", "Bulk Viagra", "Enlarge your penis by 50% today" and so on. I fantasise that if I took advantage of the bulk medication and enlargement, I could give a local big babe a wicked time of it and run a swathe through the female population of my sleepy town.

There's also an email from a Nigerian princess, desperate to unlock her imprisoned father's millions. It begins with "Dearly beloved" and continues in this biblical vein to its conclusion, which naturally requests my bank details. I reply, offering the princess exclusive use of my handheld Universal Scratch Card Reader in return for ten thousand dollars up front. I tell her that the ability to find winning scratch cards *before* purchase will soon revive her family fortunes and obviate the need to send pathetic emails. I don't expect a reply.

Saturday:

In spite of the blood pressure clinic nurse's admonitions about cutting down on fat, I dine on a slab of Brie, crusty bread and Normandy butter — all washed down with a lively little Merlot. And no bones about it. It would have been nice to have shared this with a big, or an even modestly proportioned babe, but my bliss is nevertheless completed by listening to a Louis Jordan CD, which confirms for me, at least, one of the origins of rock 'n' roll.

Sunday:

A pub lunch with an old girlfriend. We once enjoyed gymnastic sex together, but now we're just a couple of old codgers sitting by a river, watching mayflies spin their dance of death, while shaven-headed Mars bar reps and IT managers play with their balls in their week-end track suit bottoms as they wait at the bar for pissy lager.

I get an enthusiastic email from the Nigerian princess asking for further details of the Universal Scratchcard Reader. Oh dear, I really must temper my sarcasm sometimes. She might have some unpleasant associates in this country who could track me down and torture me for the secrets of this non-existent device.

Ming the Merciless

Monday:

A letter from the Department for Transport saying that my communication regarding the virtual abolition of yellow no parking lines has been received and noted. I can see some overpaid, over-lunched Whitehall mandarin dismissively holding it between thumb and forefinger, telling an underling to file it under "cranks".

Maybe some day, when this mandarin's backside is on the line for underestimating tarmac quotas or whatever, he'll pull this out of the bag as his own idea to save his Oxbridge skin. I hope that this happens before I succumb to the embrace of the corporation barbecue, so I can sue his arse off. Then I might retire to Juan les Pins and ogle the beauties on the beach as I take an after dinner stroll along the plage. A harmless old man in a Panama hat.

Tuesday:

I'm having one of my peaky days. Lying in bed before rising, I can hear my heartbeat in my ear. For a time, it goes along quite nicely, but then seems to wander off track, skipping beats like a mediocre drummer. Maybe the Brie and Normandy butter that I gobbled down last Saturday night wasn't such a good idea.

This evening I listen to a radio programme about post-war advertising. The old Ovaltine song is played.

'We are the Ovaltineys, little girls and boys.'

I find this depressing. I'm reminded of warm school milk, Billy Cotton, cod liver oil, Max Bygraves, huge class divides and the whole mustn't grumble, glum, grey world of Britain in the early Nineteen Fifties. All this began to change in the middle of the decade with the coming of rock 'n' roll from America.

Lads up and down the land began buying guitars or drums and formed countless groups. Village halls, youth clubs, scout huts and the new coffee bars reverberated with the sound of these mostly dire bands. Rebellion was in the air and the new music and the counter-culture that grew up around it was condemned in pulpits, parliament and most of the press, but it was unstoppable and a movement began that would feed into the so-called Swinging Sixties in which I played a modest and largely unsung part.

Our laughable, homegrown response to the early American invasion was Tommy Steele, Cliff Richard and a snivel of wannabe Elvises and Eddie Cochrans. Cliff, in his early days looked like a tortoise without a shell trying to look mean and moody. One could imagine him practising his aggressive little poses in front of a mirror, looking about as menacing as a feather duster.

Wednesday:

I watch a TV programme about the possibility of life on other planets. The latest theory appears to be that if life does exist, it's likely only to be bacterial. Once the technology is in place, I suppose the race for space will be similar to the exploitative scramble for Africa in the Nineteenth Century.

I can see astronauts on far-flung planets negotiating with bubbling puddles of snot for mineral rights and suchlike. Where no response is forthcoming from the puddles, this will then be deemed to be a tacit agreement to the planting of a flag and the rape of the planet. A puppet government will be formed, comprising a few driblets of snot and a district commissioner. Missionaries might be sent to teach the puddles the error of their ways and how Jesus wants them for sunbeams.

If these intergalactic frontiersmen ever stumble across Flash Gordon's arch enemy, Ming the Merciless, however, they might find him less acquiescent than the snot. I've always had a soft spot for Ming. A man not to be sniffed at.

Thursday:

Out early for the newspaper. On my return, there's a note through the door saying that "Freddie the Fish Man" has called. I'm immediately reminded of a crappy B-movie called *The Creature from the Black Lagoon*, in which a scaly, half-man, half-pilchard terrorised the Florida Keys, or somewhere, ravishing scantily-clad young girls and generally making a nuisance of himself. It transpires that Freddie does a weekly delivery of fresh fish. I'm no marketing expert, but I think he might consider dressing up as a pilchard to create a bit of a frisson, but go easy on the ravishing.

Friday:

I perform some basic body maintenance; nose hair, nails, hard skin and ear drops. I watch a TV profile of the late, abrasive, but hugely talented Nina Simone and imagine her marooned on a desert island with a Sting, Bono or Cliff. I think the rescue mission would find only one survivor.

Saturday:

I take the old Fiesta to the car wash at the local petrol station. I insert a token in the machine, but nothing happens. Impatiently, I hoot the car horn and Harry, the proprietor, comes out of his kiosk and examines the giant brushes, giving one of them a good kick.

I realise that I should have pressed the "GO" button and proceed to do so. The machine springs to life and one of the brushes takes Harry for a short spin before throwing him off in a sea of foam. Despite the momentum, he manages to remain upright, scuttling across the forecourt like a fiddler crab. He shoots me a murderous look as he paddles back to the kiosk.

Sunday:

I succeed in shredding my chin with a cheap disposable razor. I emerge from the bathroom with several bits of loo paper stuck to my face to stem the blood. I notice that on the razor packet it says "dispose of responsibly". I'm glad I saw that, otherwise I might have been inclined to chuck a few over the wall of the local playgroup, or hide one among the pick 'n' mix sweets at the mini-market.

There's a knock on my door. It's Cordelia, the new resident, who I fancy like mad.

'Sorry to trouble you. Have you got any jump leads? My battery's dead.'

I go into chivalrous Mister Fixit mode, as if nothing could be easier and she's not to worry her pretty head about it. Outside, I align my old Fiesta with her quite impressive something or the other and connect the cables.

The symbolism of our two cars joined by a throbbing cable is not lost on me as I fantasise about what I could do to her given half a chance. Right now, I could drink her bath water, peel her a grape, or *even* go shopping with her.

'Shall we give it a go?' she asks.

I agree and she successfully starts her car. I do a kind of nonchalant John Wayne rolling gait to her window, narrowing my eyes as if searching for threatening Apaches.

'Anything else I can help you with today ma'am?' I drawl.

'Oh no, you've been most kind. Thank-you.'

I give her a lazy American cavalry salute and say she's right welcome. She's about to drive off when she asks,

'Have you been shaving in the dark?'

Little Owl

Monday:

Today, on the stairs, I bump into Buzz and Thelma from flat four. I recently discovered that they run the New Age shop in the town, where cut price ear candles and caffeine enemas are on sale. Their front door is festooned with stickers such as "Meat is Murder", "Smash Capitalism" and "Vegetables Have Rights Too". Buzz is an old Sixties hippy. Beads and a ponytail and faded jeans. He has a ring through an eyebrow and a tongue stud. Thelma is a big-fronted woman with a large arse. She reminds me of a centaur.

'Hey man, good to see ya,' says Buzz. 'We're having a little get together this Saturday — all the block's invited — eight o'clock. Nice vegan wine, good eats, wicked music.'

I find myself mesmerised by the tongue stud and agree to attend. Buzz and Thelma roar off in a newish BMW. Once capitalism is smashed, they will, presumably, be sharing the car with all of us in the block.

Tuesday:

I breakfast on a Fair Trade banana, crisp bread and low sugar marmalade. I reckon that if I can do this on alternate days, I might have a fighting chance of getting a free television licence and a telegram from the Queen. On the other hand, what's the use of living to a hundred if all one can do is watch crap on the telly in a dystopian wilderness, where Cliff is still warbling and pretending to be macho?

Wednesday:

After a day re-arranging the cobwebs and dust in the flat, I decide on an early night. I lie awake for some time, unable to sleep. A fox barks, an owl hoots. A car door slams. Laughter in the street and I feel unutterably alone. Out of time and place. I remember lost and unrequited love, being a mostly frightened little boy, thwarted aspirations, words and deeds I wish I could take back and the heartbeat in my ear has, if anything, become more erratic. Not one of my better days. Fortunately, I suppose, living *tout seul*, I don't at least inflict this sombre mood on anyone else. Only an indifferent universe.

Thursday:

Off to the mini-market to see if I can get a cheap chicken for the weekend. The in-store speakers are pumping out *Nineteenth Nervous Breakdown*, by the Rolling Stones. I have mixed feelings about The Stones. In their early days, they did much to popularise some of the neglected roots of rock 'n' roll and they had a rawness and energy that was a refreshing alternative to the general anodyne pap that was passing for popular music at the time. But as soon as I saw them, and particularly when I heard them speak, I knew they were from the other side of the tracks.

I could imagine nice teas after school, lots of Meccano, fitted carpets, stamp albums, pencil boxes and bedtime stories. They tried to hide their origins with glottal stops and dropped aitches, but I wouldn't mind betting that, Mick Jagger, the so-called 'bad boy of rock' was, unlike me, a good boy at school whose only misdemeanours were probably the occasional bouts of petulance over a snapped crayon, or a scuff on his plimsolls.

I actually met him in the Sixties. I was playing at a club on the Cromwell Road in London. During the interval I went to the gents. I was joined at the trough by Mick and we both stood peeing in that guarded way that men do, as if they're expecting to be attacked from behind. I'm not sure whether he washed his hands afterwards, but he did run them through his hair and check himself in the mirror.

'Gas band man,' he said and minced out.

Now he's Sir Mick, presumably for services to music or narcissism, while I'm still a commoner trying to buy a cut price chicken at the mini-market, where The Embryo with eye liner and attitude is on the till. She sullenly processes my purchases.

'You can only buy one packet of paracetamol at a time,' she tells me in a bored voice. 'Health and safety. You've got two 'ere.'

'I don't understand,' I say, 'why's that?'

She sighs.

'Because you could take an overdose I suppose. I dunno.'

'Oh what a shame,' I say, 'I wanted to kill myself *today*. There's nothing on the telly tonight and I've written the suicide note already. Couldn't you make an exception?'

I should have learnt from past experience that she has no sense of humour. She presses a buzzer to summon the manager who lectures me about health and safety. A tutting queue has built up behind me. As I'm leaving, a man shouts out,

'You could always jump under a train mate. It's cheaper.'

Friday:

I visit an optician for a free eye test. She fits a device to my head with lots of lenses in it, making me feel like a Borg from *Star Trek*. She invites me to read the test chart of jumbled letters. I imagine a Slav in the same position saying,

'Read it? Of course I can read it. It's my surname.'

After a lot of faffing about she tells me that I need vari-focal lenses. These sound suspiciously like bi-focals to me. About twenty years ago I had a pair of these and they caused me to over-estimate the actual size of my feet. When I looked down, it was as though I was wearing outsized clown's shoes. As a result I nearly fell down a flight of stairs. I dumped the glasses.

I get a prescription and tell her I'll think about it — which I probably won't.

Saturday

For Buzz and Thelma's do, I've decided to struggle into one of my old wedding suits, a white T shirt and my hand-tooled snakeskin boots. After a bracing scotch, I go down to the party. Buzz greets me at the door, looking me up and down.

'Hey, flares man, wicked. Grab some grub — it's all vegan and macro-biotic. Are those boots made from snake skin?'

When I proudly confirm that are, he makes me take them off and leave them outside in the hallway.

'Thelma would go ape if she saw those,' he says.

Their flat is bedecked with candles which give off a cloying scent, reminiscent of an up-market urinal. I notice Brint and Shards entwined together in a corner and wonder whether the "trying" has had any effect yet.

Also present are the couple from Flat Three, Adrian and Robin — the latter being female. Adrian is a VAT inspector and in my view suffers from obsessive compulsive disorder, which, given his job, might be considered an asset. On his way to work, he wipes his feet before leaving the flats and wipes them again with tissue before hopping awkwardly into his car. On several occasions, I've seen him wiping the banisters with antiseptic wipes as he descends the stairs. I imagine that pavement cracks must be a real challenge to him, but the double entry system is probably a doddle. Reg calls them VATman and Robin, which is quite witty coming from a country music fan.

I try some of the food which looks like dollops of dog turd on biscuits. It tastes like dollops of dog turd on biscuits. A short woman, heavily beaded and wrapped in an Indian blanket, introduces herself.

'Hi, I'm Little Owl,' she says. 'Thelma tells me you're a musician. What do you play?'

I tell her that I play the sax

'Ooh, I get all wet when I hear the sax,' she says.

The scotch and wine have begun to kick in and I look at her more closely. These days, my libido might be a little depleted, but I think I can still spot a prospect, even one that is blanketed, beaded and named after a bird of prey. She tells me that she puts in one day a week at the New Age shop doing colonic irrigation and caffeine enemas. Drunken ardour gets the better of incredulity and disgust, so I continue talking to her as if what she says makes any sense.

At one point, VATman and Robin make moves to leave leave, but Thelma, with her considerable bulk, blocks their way.

'Adrian's got a migraine,' says Robin.

Thelma wrestles him to a chair.

'I can do migraines,' she says, as she proceeds to massage his head.

He shrinks like a salted slug at her touch. He is out of his comfort zone; no wipes, no tissues and he is being pummeled by a centaur.

'I'm perfectly all right, really I am. Perfectly all right,' he squeaks, fleeing from Thelma's clutches. He backs out of the flat, wiping his feet as he goes.

The rest of the evening becomes a drunken blur of New Age nonsense, Buzz playing bongos, The Centaur singing and…

Sunday:

... I awake with a strange woman in my bed. I know that we didn't "do it", because I've still got my underpants and one of my boots on and she is fully dressed and snoring like a navvy. I double check that it isn't April, the transgenderist from Flat One and realise that it's Little Owl.

I am in desperate need of some caffeine, but would definitely prefer to ingest it through my mouth, so I'm very careful not to awaken her just in case she has her equipment with her. I dress quietly and search in vain for my other boot. I leave a note on the kitchen table saying, "Nice meeting you. I've been called away. Help yourself to coffee and please shut the door on the latch when you leave."

I spend most of the day aimlessly driving around. I have a pub lunch and sneak back home late in the afternoon. Thankfully, my overnight guest has departed.

As dusk settles, I go onto the balcony. half expecting to see Little Owl perched in a nearby tree, tubes at the ready. I look down to see Reg, the caretaker's yappy little dog, Patsy, on the lawn gnawing at my missing boot. She pauses in her labours and looks up, giving me a grin of doggy pleasure.

I look up crossbow prices on the internet.

The Old Forty-Niners

Monday:

I'm feeling a bit fragile after the weekend's events. I'm getting too long in the tooth for these shenanigans. Drinking too much, losing one of my cherished snake skin boots and finding myself in bed with a woman calling herself Little Owl, who earns her living performing caffeine enemas. It's hardly decorous for someone of my age.

Reg the caretaker returns my missing boot, which has been chewed up by his vile little dog, Patsy. I imagine he has, like the courtier in *Cinderella*, canvassed everyone in the block and they've all had a good laugh at my expense.

'Sorry mate,' he says, 'I dunno how Patsy got hold of it. She's a bugger for shoes'

I think to myself that she would have less of a footwear fetish if she were skewered to the lawn by a crossbow bolt.

I get a phone call from Little Owl saying how much she enjoyed Saturday night and that we must do it again. I'm non-committal and tell her that I've got a lot of gigs coming up. I rack my still befuddled brain as to what we could possibly have done that she'd like repeated. I must go ex-directory.

Tuesday:

A train journey to London to put my beloved Selmer Mark Six saxophone in for a mini overhaul.

I haven't always enjoyed a happy relationship with the railway. Back in the 1960s, I parked at the local station and boarded the train for London. On my return in the evening, I was confronted by a reptilian man who turned out to be a British Rail plain-clothes policeman. He pointed to a portable sign that indicated that parking tickets should be purchased at the ticket office.

I was convinced that this sign hadn't been there when I parked

in the morning and said as much in no uncertain terms. A "was —
wasn't" argument followed and after sarcastically calling into question
the policeman's parentage, I stormed off in the car, not paying the small
parking charge as a matter of principle. That told him, I thought.

The summons arrived about a week later. Aside from an illegal parking charge, I was also accused of several other archaic offences under
railway law, including something like using abusive or blasphemous
language likely to offend ladies and frighten livestock. This policeman
had obviously trawled the archives. I was incensed and wrote back stat-
ing my intention vigorously to defend the case.

My day in court arrived and the first setback occurred when I saw
that the chairman of the bench was my old geography master Mister
Watts. He and I definitely hadn't hit it off in my school days.

Under his baleful gaze, I laid out my case including a description of
the policeman's rude and bullying behaviour. Aside from the policeman, British Rail produced an aged employee whose job it was to put
the parking sign out each day. He was an amiable old duffer, a bit like
Godfrey in *Dad's Army*. I saw the chance of an easy victory by at-
tempting to prove that he might have been forgetful on this occasion.

'Oh no sir,' he said very respectfully, 'I do it religiously each morning before I have a brew up.'

I then asked if he had always worked for British Rail putting out
signs.

'Oh no sir, I used to be a locomotive driver,' he said with some pride.

I was about to suggest that he might therefore have become bored
with his present menial tasks after such an exciting career on the foot-
plate, when I was interrupted by Watts from the bench.

'What sort of engines did you drive?' he asked him.

'Well I started out on the old forty-niners sir,' the old duffer said.

Watts' eyes glazed over.

'Not the forty-niners with the cantilevered scuttle bucket?' he
queried.

'The very same sir. And then I moved on to the Fifty series.'

'I know,' said Watts, 'with the articulated congenital deflectors.'

The old man confirmed this.

Looking at Watts' rapturous expression, I knew I was doomed.
Thank God I wasn't charged with a capital offence, otherwise I could
see Watts donning the black cap while swapping train numbers with

Godfrey as I was led kicking and screaming to the gallows.

I had hoped to sum up, masterfully quoting from the Magna Carta and mentioning in passing the The Rights of Man, the Tolpuddle Martyrs and perhaps the Dreyfus case, but I asked no further questions and was immediately found guilty and fined twenty pounds plus costs. Subsequently, I felt somewhat vindicated by a banner headline in the local paper reporting the case which read, "BRITISH RAIL POLICE-MAN WAS TRUCULENT". That told *him*.

Wednesday:

I buy a new mobile phone. Not because I'm enamoured of them, but because my old phone has expired, having completed a wash cycle in the pocket of my jeans. I complain to the shop assistant that they all seem to have such small keys. In between painting her nails she tells me that Help the Aged can supply a phone for the partially sighted, but warns me that it doesn't have a camera, as if this is a life-changing loss.

Thursday:

I spend most of the day trying to figure out how my new phone works.

A pattern of behaviour has grown around the use of mobiles. People pace up and down and randomly kick car tyres, or litter as they speak. On my trip to London on the train, several people informed the ether that they were on the train, what time they would be home, what the latest sales figures were and so on. It would be amusing if the other passengers were loudly to echo their words like a Gilbert and Sullivan chorus.

'I'm on the train.'

(Sing) 'HE'S ON THE TRAIN.'

'I...got the sack.'

(Sing) 'HE'S GOT THE SACK, SACK, SACK.'

'I'm...I'm... leaving you.'

(Sing) 'HE'S LEAVING, HE'S LEAVING, HE'S LEAVING HER.'

Most mobiles appear to have an annoying facility called predictive text, where the phone tries to anticipate what one wants to write. Once I get the hang of my new phone after a few months, I might try texting some stream of consciousness stuff from Joyce, or perhaps the lyrics of *A Whiter Shade of Pale*, just to confound it.

Friday:

A quick visit to the mini-market this evening. Vivaldi's *Four Seasons* is blaring from speakers outside the shop, where a group of sullen teenagers is gathered. Once inside, I ask the manager why we're being treated to Vivaldi. He tells me that it is meant to deter teenagers gathering outside the shop. I remark that it doesn't appear to be very effective.

'Ah, you wait. I'll put the Wagner on in a minute,' he chuckles.

On leaving the shop, one of the teenagers asks me for a light. I ask him if he finds the loud music off-putting.

'Oh no, I find it quite restful,' he says

With that, *The Ride of the Valkeries* blares out. I notice the manager peering expectantly out of the shop window. The teenagers remain in place. I feel like suggesting to him that a little Stockhausen, or Phillip Glass might do the trick. I wonder if Vivaldi or Wagner could ever have dreamt that their music might one day be used as a deterrent to loitering teenagers. I wonder what music they might use if they were ever troubled by gangs of loitering war babies like me. Top of my list, would have to be Elvis Costello, who sounds like Melvyn Bragg, nasally tra-la-ing through a gas mask.

Saturday:

My weekly shop. As I trundle my trolley around the supermarket, Little Owl appears, perhaps from a perch in the rafters.. She doesn't have a trolley or a basket, so I immediately think this meeting is non-accidental. In the cold light of day she looks more like an ageing Geronimo rather than an owl, little or otherwise. To my astonishment, she starts rummaging through my shopping, making disapproving tuts

'You need looking after,' she tells me.

She gives me an ornate business card that trumpets her arcane specialities.

'You'll call, I know you will,' she says.

Play Misty For Me comes to mind as I watch her waddle away in a rattle of beads and a swirling blanket.

Sunday:

I'm probably getting a bit paranoid, but I've got a bad feeling about Little Owl. I'm sure that I'll get short shrift from the local boys in blue if I make a complaint.

'I see sir. Let me see if I've got this right. You're being stalked by an owl.'

Much mirth in the police canteen, while I'm being force-fed caffeine by Little Owl. Up the arse.

An Audition in Whitehall

Monday:

I listen to the *Today* programme on the radio this morning. I can only take so much of this, because it annoys me intensely when, in the absence of an informed interviewee on a particular topic, the reporters interview each other. The net result is pure speculation and we the listeners are no wiser. The reporters though have filled a space and justified their ridiculous salaries.

And who are these reporters — these so-called experts? Listening to them, they remind me of those smart-arsed kids at school who collected stamps or had moths and butterflies skewered in albums. They were the ones who put their hands up first when the teacher asked a question and they were often favoured monitors or prefects. They always had their gym kit, fountain pens and pencil boxes. One day, I'll get them all. At playtime

Tuesday:

I get a letter telling me that my GP has retired. I've been with him for over thirty years and he has good-naturedly tolerated my lies about what I drink and eat. I suspect that his underlying medical philosophy probably differs little from that of his medieval counterparts. One either gets better, or one dies and the latter is a certainty anyway.

Over the years, I've been comforted by the thought that should I be on my last legs, he might be relied upon to administer an unethical extra slug of morphine to ease the passage to the corporation barbecue. Now, I suppose that I'll just have to get used to an infant medic wagging a finger at my over-indulgence and suffer a lingering death.

I'm sure that it's only a matter of time before supermarket checkouts will automatically download precise details of one's purchases to an NHS computer. A visit to the GP will be like the Inquisition. Every little heresy — a smudge of Normandy butter, a sliver of Brie, a splash of Merlot, or the odd Eccles cake, could condemn one to a corrective lecture at least, or at worst a public denunciation before a jeering crowd of miserable joggers and emaciated weight-watchers.

Wednesday:

I read in the newspaper of a school where grades have been abolished and where every pupil, regardless of ability or achievement, gets a diploma. Since I took little part in my own schooling and hated every minute of it, I'm favourably inclined toward this idea. However, I do worry about this trend and imagine a future in which a kid who can run fast will be fitted with leg irons to allow the rest to keep up and where a girl who sings like an angel will be forced to gargle with Harpic, so as not to make her less talented peers feel inadequate.

Thursday:

A visit to the bank to pay in a cheque. As I'm standing in the queue, a spotty Herbert with a lapel badge identifying him as "Kingsley — Customer Liaison" approaches me.

'Could I have a word when you've finished at the counter, sir?'

It transpires that Kingsley is wondering whether I've made a will or not. He's obviously working from a memorised script, because I can't stop him. I try to tell him that I don't have enough in assets to worry about, but he ploughs on regardless, telling me that the bank can act as my executor in "the unfortunate event" of my demise. He finishes off his little spiel by telling me that prudence now means peace of mind tomorrow.

There are so many reasons why I find this irritating and I could easily lose my temper over any one of them. I look at Kingsley and wonder how he came to such a sorry pass, having to solicit probate business from old codgers like me. Did he never stare out of the window at school and dream of being Robin Hood, or having adventures in foreign parts and rescuing maidens in distress? Or was working in a sleepy town branch of a bank the pinnacle of his dreams? I decide not to lose my temper.

'Listen, Kingsley, I'd rather trust what little I have to the Kray twins, than let your bank get its sticky little fingers on it. You've been helping yourselves to my money for far too long as it is, with all your spurious charges.'

He looks crestfallen. He's probably never heard of the Krays. I think they're dead.

Friday:

Back to London to collect my sax. Having done so, I decide to take a leisurely stroll back to Waterloo via Whitehall. A noisy crowd is gathered outside the entrance to Downing Street and I pause to see what the fuss is about. It turns out to be a demonstration regarding teachers' pay, which interests me not a jot.

I start to walk away, but I'm confronted by a wall of high visibility yellow and, together with the bellowing pedagogues, I'm pushed up against some railings by a phalanx of riot police, banging their shields with their clubs.

'Fascist pigs,' screams a woman next to me who might have been a domestic science teacher for all I know.

Just as I'm beginning to think I'll be crushed against the railings, I'm snatched from the crowd by two particularly large officers and dragged some yards away. Thinking this was a noble rescue effort, I start to thank them, when I'm pushed up against a wall and my sax case is snatched from me and gingerly put down on the pavement.

'So what's in the case sunshine?' asks one of the cops.

I explain that it's a saxophone and that I was just passing when I was caught up in the demo. Ignoring me, he starts talking into his lapel about a potential firearm or bomb and the possibility of using a controlled explosion. I have a vision of my beloved sax going up in a puff of smoke. Bizarrely, I also remember that Whitehall is the very spot where Charles the First lost his head. Under different circumstances, I might have gained a house point from the corralled teachers for this bit of local knowledge. I offer to open the case and the police retire to a safe distance. I hold up the sax for them to see.

'Play it,' says one of them.

So, I piece it together and nervously tootle a little twelve bar blues.

'You could get work,' he says, pushing up his visor. 'On your way now and stay out of trouble.'

I hail a taxi.

Saturday:

Unbeknown to me, the Downing Street scrum was featured on the television news last night. I get a number of sarcastic phone calls, mostly from fellow musicians, asking why I was busking in Whitehall.

'I know the gig scene's bad,' says one, 'but I never thought I'd see you tootling in the middle of a demo.'

There are several more calls like this, so I let the answering machine take over.

Sunday:

I try out my newly overhauled sax. It's a bit petulant to begin with, as if sulking from the Whitehall farce. I can understand this. I found it humiliating too, having to audition for the riot squad.

I watch a Jools Holland programme on TV. He talks as if he's swallowed a kazoo and looks as if he's just headed a concrete football, but he's a very accomplished musician. In a dumbed- down future that prizes mediocrity, he'll probably be forced to wear lead-lined mittens when he plays the piano.

Even a Tiny Sparrow

Monday:

A visit to the local post office. This is run by two ancient spinster sisters and is like something out of Dickens. Its only nod to modernity is having electric lighting. They could be selling no end of things in the shop, but what shelves there are have only a curious assortment of things like balls of hairy string, brown paper, flypaper and hairnets. There's a long queue, which I join, watching as the two sisters, sitting side by side behind the counter like dusty bookends, slowly deal with their customers. Each one seems to present a problem and the sisters frequently consult each other, thus slowing down the whole process. I notice a tatty poster advertising advantageous rates on currency exchange and imagine how much the queue would be stalled if I asked for some Nepalese rupees, or Albanian leks.

I tut with impatience and the woman in front of me turns around. It's Cyclops from the school reunion, last seen grappling with a Queen's chaplain. I smile weakly and stare down at my feet, not wanting to be transfixed by the pin ball eyes.

'Oh, it's you, I might have known,' she says.

I nod and continue staring at my feet like a naughty schoolboy.

'Do you remember the Reverend Coot who used to teach us religious knowledge?' she asks.

I confirm that I do and she proceeds to tell me that he's still alive and living in a council home nearby.

'I went to see him last week. I'm sure he'd appreciate a visit from you.'

Since the Reverend Coot and I did not exactly hit it off all those years ago, I look up to see whether I can detect any irony in her expression. All I see are the pin balls orbiting the jam jar-bottomed glasses, like Torvil and Dean before they finally and triumphantly come together in the finale of Romeo and Juliet on ice.

In the afternoon, I have a new mattress delivered. The delivery men struggle up the five flights of stairs to my flat and I commiserate with them on the difficulty of trying to negotiate the twists and turns.

'Yeah,' says one, 'it's like trying to get a fat lady into a taxi.'

Tuesday:

Over breakfast I think about the Reverend Archibald Coot. I remember him as a stern, skeletal man with a small mouth that he frequently pursed, making it look like the knotted end of a party balloon. When he started coming to the school, I was about ten years old. I was in my post-tapeworm, staring out of the windows phase. In addition to this, I came from a deeply cynical, non-religious background, where disputation and opposition, purely for the sake of it, was a family sport. That is not to say, however, that I had hitherto engaged Coot in debate. I was generally far too timid and disinterested to do that.

On one particular day, Coot was droning on about the concept of omnipresence — the idea of God being everywhere all at the same time. As usual, I was staring out of the window as he laid out his case. Having recently seen Errol Flynn in *The Adventures of Robin Hood*, I imagined myself in Sherwood Forest, with a band of merry men, righting wrongs and giving the Normans a bad time. In the background I could distantly hear Coot going on about God even seeing a tiny sparrow fall. His monotonous voice became a lullaby and I drifted off to sleep, eyes closing, mouth gaping. My head flopped onto my chest and then snapped back up again several times in a pattern that Shards and Brint might these days call "bungee dozing".

Suddenly, I was being slapped about the head by Coot, demanding to know what he had just said. I told him that I didn't know.

'Of- course — you- don't- know,' he said, poking me in the chest with a bony finger, emphasising every syllable, 'you-were-as-leep weren't- you? Tell him class.'

'Godiseverywhereandevenseesatinysparrowfall,' they dutifully intoned without pause.

'He even sees a tiny sparrow fall.' Coot slowly repeated their words, with a faraway look in his eyes. 'Even a tiny sparrow.'

He made a dreamy fluttering movement with his hand and stared into the distance.

On that day, in that dreary classroom, all those years ago, something snapped within me. Until then, I had kept a low profile and dodged school whenever I could. When I was there, I did just enough to avoid the brutal retribution of the mainly psychopathic, war-wounded teachers. I was an apprehensive, ginger-haired, skinny little misfit, who still wet the bed and clung to his Mum, but the smug certainty of this sanctimonious stick insect poking me in the chest brought to the surface all the anger and frustration that I felt about school and my life in general. (Many years later, Margaret Thatcher would have the same effect on me.)

'I don't believe it,' I said, my blood rising

'What?' said Coot, incredulously.

'I *said*, I don't believe it. It's not possible for someone to be everywhere all at the same time.'

Coot made a wigwam of his fingers and his voice quietened to a confessional whisper.

'It is so because it is so,' he said, nodding his head at the weight and wisdom of his words.

'You can't prove it,' I said, beginning to cry with rage and frustration.

'I don't have to prove it. It is so because I say it is so and it is written here, in the Holy Scriptures,' said Coot, triumphantly brandishing a Bible in my face.

'Just because you say it's so and it's written in the Bible doesn't make it true. It's all rubbish,' I yelled.

Coot pensively pursed his lips, then said quietly,

'Come with me boy.'

He led me from the hushed classroom to the headmaster's office.

I was told to wait outside while Coot conferred with the Head. Through the closed door, I could hear muffled words and phrases like "insubordination", "heathen", "disruptive influence", "not want him in the class" and "... to be taught a lesson". I was called in to face the headmaster, a man with a wooden leg and a permanent wince on his face. I was expecting a beating, but instead, after berating me for being disrespectful to Coot, he told me that in future, instead of religious instruction, I would do Scottish country dancing with the girls from the year above my own.

So, every Monday morning for the rest of my time at the school, while my classmates were being treated to the intricacies of theology by Archibald Coot, I was swirling and twirling with a class of girls on the cusp of womanhood. I positively blossomed in my solitary male role, as I clumsily swooped and whooped among them, under arches of nubile arms, holding hands and, on occasion, having my arm around a pretty waist. I skipped and turned, reeled and wheeled, like a wild young Rob Roy and I fell in love with them all. Thanks to the Reverend Archibald Coot, my romantic spirit had been awakened. My love and admiration for the fairer sex, whom hitherto I had hardly noticed, had been kindled, never to die. I'll never know whether making me do the dancing was an act of enlightenment, or an attempt at humiliation on the part of the headmaster. There's no Billy Elliot ending though. I still can't dance.

Wednesday:

Brint has bought a guitar. I spot him bringing it and a little practice amp into the flats this morning.

'G'day,' he says, 'I thought I give the old guitar a go. Maybe we can jam together once I get the hang of it. A bit of the old rock 'n' roll stuff eh?'

I smile weakly and think that I'll be clinker before that happens. It takes me back again to those days in the mid to late Fifties when guitars were selling like hot buns and thousands of groups erupted faster than acne. Teenaged lads everywhere were strumming away and acting the part of their hero — Elvis, Eddie Cochran, Gene Vincent and Buddy Holly. Running alongside the rock 'n' roll revolution in Britain, was also skiffle and the revival of traditional jazz. These three camps were generally disdainful of each other, but in reality they shared common musical roots, albeit with different outcomes.

Behind the pretty white boys who were getting the hits and acclaim, there lay a long, largely unacknowledged tradition of African-American blues, gospel and jazz, that sprang from decades of poverty and oppression and the experience of being a reviled underclass. The raw rhythm of this music, particularly the driving boogie-woogie piano, bass lines and sax riffs, were shamelessly copied and earthy lyrics sanitized for mass consumption. The gutsy, sexy music of the ghetto became a neutered imitation, targeting angst-ridden white teenagers. That's not to say, however, that it was all bad. It wasn't. Far worse was to follow in the so-called Swinging' Sixties when pretension and posturing reached new heights and youth's dream of a more liberated and peaceful world were cynically manipulated and betrayed

I'm fairly sure that Brint would have little or no knowledge of the antecedents of "that old rock 'n' roll stuff", but then, to be fair, when it was all kicking off in the mid-Fifties, I perversely took up the ukelele and did George Formby impressions, which tickled my mum and dad no end. Should I ever hear Brint singing "Woke up this morning, had the blues..", though, I swear that he'll suffer the same fate that I plan for Patsy.

The cacophonous bell ringers are at it again this evening. I wonder what the range of a crossbow is.

Thursday:

I go to collect the newspaper. I normally walk to the newsagents, but as it's pissing down with rain, I take the Fiesta. Just as I'm about to enter the shop, a policeman appears from nowhere and tells me that I've committed an offence, by not having a seat belt on. I try a little humour and tell him that it's still in the car. He is not amused and proceeds to write out a fixed penalty notice. I remonstrate with him and say that it's surely my prerogative if I want to get mangled in a crash. I should have left it there of course, but I then go on to bemoan the nanny state and petty minded policemen.

'Why don't you go down to the mini-market and sort out the loitering Vivaldi fans?' I ask.

I throw the penalty notice on the pavement and jump up and down on it in my rage. I'm arrested and charged with littering and behaviour likely etcetera.

Back at the police station, I'm put in a cell. They actually put me in a cell, and remove my belt and plimsoll laces. I'm incandescent and shout myself hoarse about fascists and pigs. I take deep breaths and gradually calm myself down a bit. After an hour or so, the cell is opened and Jason, the community cop, enters. He pushes his hat back in that "now I'm off duty" way and tells me that he's managed to get the charges dropped.

'I should fucking hope so,' I shout. 'This is outrageous. It's a re-run of fucking Downing Street.'

Jason goes quiet.

'Downing Street?' he asks.

I start to tell him about me having been a suspected terrorist and he cautiously backs out of the cell, slamming the door. Another hour passes and then two plain clothes cops appear. They're wearing jeans and leather jackets, looking desperately casual. For some reason, one of them asks if I'm known by any other name.

'You'll have to ask my various wives that,' I joke, throwing caution to the wind, when in fact, I should have exercised it much earlier.

'I see, so you've got more than one wife have you?'

I can see where this is going and I'm tempted to claim a penchant for polygamy, sheep's eyes and camel racing, but I realise that I've got myself into belt-less, lace-less deep shit. Next stop, extraordinary rendition, an orange jumpsuit and water boarding, by knuckle-headed red necks in the Caribbean, when I should be safely at home wrestling with the crossword and chipping some mince out of the freezer.

Eventually, it's decided that I'm not a threat to national security, or the Bush family ranch and Jason runs me back to the Fiesta. On the way, he recommends an anger management course. Nothing could manage my anger at this point. The newsagent's has closed.

Friday:

After my day in the cells, with nary a biscuit or a cup of tea or coffee, I feel completely justified in having a full English breakfast. I ignore the snot coming off the bacon, but I do notice that the "be good to yourself" Lincolnshire sausages contain only fifty four percent meat. I imagine Bones in *Star Trek* holding it up and saying,

'It's a sausage, Jim, but not as we know it.'

What can the remaining forty six percent be? Recycled tampons, leper's underpants, surgical swabs or sawdust? Who knows? I can see a day when sausage labels might state "traces of meat", like Sixties music and much beyond might be described as having traces of rock' n' roll. But in negligible quantities.

Saturday:

I buy a Cornish pasty for my lunch. It was apparently made by some jolly yokel, since there is a picture of him on the wrapper. He's wearing a smock and smiling benignly at a doomed cow. As per instructions, I bite into the cardboard pastry and the gloop within and I am reminded of school dinners with disgusting mince full of gristle and snout, chalky scratchings on blackboards, Harold Macmillan, sweet rationing and Gracie Fields. I strongly suspect that the origins of this "Cornish" pasty lie further to the east, in a silo of reformed animal slurry on an industrial estate in Essex. Probably adjacent to the barn egg bunker. I bin it and have a Fair Trade banana. You know where you are with a banana.

Sunday:

This morning a dubious character looking a bit like George Cole's spiv in the *Saint Trinians* films, comes to my door trying to sell me an illustrated Bible. He flicks the pages to display garish pictures of the Nativity, the raising of Lazarus and the crucifixion.

'No thanks, I'm Jewish,' I lie.

Undeterred, he flicks the book open at a depiction of the parting of the Red Sea. 'Ere look,' he says. 'It's got your bit in it.'

I spend the evening composing death threats to Nigerian spammers.

The Big Bean Experience

Monday:

Robin, VATman's partner, calls round this morning…

'Adrian's been taken into hospital. I can't drive and I wondered if you could give me a lift over there,' she says.

I commiserate and agree to do so. On the way, she tells me that Adrian apparently tripped on a loose paving slab and has a broken ankle. I stare straight ahead as she tells me this, willing myself not to laugh. I can just see him obsessively stepping over cracks while missing the obvious. Aside from my fish bone visit to the casualty department recently, I haven't been in the main part of the hospital for years. Robin goes up to the ward where Adrian is currently reposing and I agree to wait for her.

I go into the reception area for a cup of tea. Expecting to see the WRVS ladies with their comforting tea urns and buttered tea cakes, I am instead confronted with what can only be described as a shopping mall, selling everything from flowers to neckties and toys to hamburgers. I'm surprised there's not a casino, or a massage parlour.

I eventually spot a place called The Big Bean and ask for a coffee. The girl behind the counter says nothing, but just points to a large board on which there is a bewildering array of "Coffee Experiences." I select a cappuccino.

'Golargefortwentypee?' she asks flatly.

I rifle frantically through the old data banks for the possible meaning of this word. *Collage for a centipede* is all I can come up with and I know that can't be right. I'm starting to feel hot around the collar and out of place and time. I ask her to repeat the question.

'Do you want to get a large one for twenty pence extra?' she says wearily, as if she's dealing with a retard.

I'm tempted to say that this is the best offer I've had all week, considering it's only Monday, but the penny drops and I settle for a regular coffee, which, when I smell it, is reminiscent of acorns and shitty nappies. The texture is like the foamy bile that precedes a full-blown vomit. It costs three pounds twenty. The receipt says "You are a valued customer. Thank-you for enjoying the Big Bean Coffee Experience."

As I wait for the coffee to get cool enough for me to pretend it's a smoothie, I look around at all the shops. I'm reminded of the money changers in the temple, or of a straw-strewn medieval market place with rogue clerics selling dodgy relics, pardons and novenas, among the dancing bears, cavorting fools and mendicant lepers. Maybe if I touch the Big Bean girl's apron, I'll be cured of scrofula, or learn to speak in tongues. Aneurin Bevan would have cast them all out.

After paying five pounds for the privilege of parking on public property, I drive Robin home. She tells me that Adrian will be in the hospital for about five days. I wonder how he'll cope without his wipes.

Tuesday:

I've begun to wonder whether I'm losing my grip. I don't mean the kind of affliction where one runs naked down the High Street, or starts flicking excrement pellets out of the window at passersby. No, I'm more concerned with the fact that what passes for normal daily life, seems increasingly to pass me by and appears alien and sometimes threatening.

In my worst moments, I worry that this might be the start of a downward slide toward senility and being spoon-fed minced up food by underpaid asylum seekers in a council nursing home. Yet apart from the odd memory lapse and a somewhat depleted libido, I think that I still have all my faculties. I'm aware that cultural shifts naturally arise between generations. I might mildly deplore some of these, as an old-ish person will, but there is something else that has taken place in the fabric of society that I find insidious, bewildering and difficult to pin down without appearing paranoid.

At its core is the way that capitalism is now called "the market economy". It's an artful euphemism that conjures up a benign picture of harmless yokels bartering turnips, rabbits and barn eggs in a place that Simple Simon might have been heading for to watch a spot of Morris dancing, or ferret juggling.

Alongside this little deception, is the notion that businesses are in some way altruistic, whose *raison d'être* lies only in serving the public and ensuring our future health and happiness. Hence, we have "Your M&S", "The listening bank", "Be good to yourself food", "Every little helps" and "Saving you money every day", among many other nauseating and meaningless platitudes that are clearly intended to lull us into thinking that we are in some sort of cosy partnership with supermarkets, banks and big business that is mutually beneficial. It's a bit like a piranha sweet talking a tiddler.

The apotheosis of this madness is the raising of the stock market to godlike status. How it will react to this or that event is endlessly discussed, as if it's a moody and fickle deity that mustn't be upset, otherwise it will send thunderbolts down from the heavens. Most worrying to me is the fact that all this bollocks seems to be accepted as perfectly normal by the majority of people. Foolishly perhaps, I've sometimes raised these issues at social gatherings and been regarded with pity, as if I've suggested that that the Tooth Fairy might not exist, or that Bambi actually died in the forest fire.

The paranoia kicks in when I wonder whether some sinister cabal of multi-nationals, hedge fund managers and sundry sleaze balls are putting something in the drinking water to induce a dreamlike state of blind acceptance among their victims. Or should I say "valued customers"?

The bell ringers are at it again this evening. Perhaps they are not as innocent as one might think. What appears to be a clanking cacophony could contain a cunning subliminal message for us all to support the status quo and continue to believe that the market economy is in our best interests.

I reject this idea as being too far-fetched and have an Ovaltine before retiring.

Wednesday:

A quiet day. I decide to have a spin in the old Fiesta out in the country to see whether I can find a genuine farm shop where I can buy some proper eggs and veg. After some time, I come across a hand painted sign at the bottom of a muddy track that says "fresh farm eggs". It looks just the ticket. The track twists and turns until eventually I come to a dilapidated shack amidst rusting agricultural machinery and a burnt out car. There's no sign of life, so I get out of my car and shout a hello. As if from nowhere, an evil looking dog races toward me snarling and slavering. I do the only thing possible under the circumstances and jump onto the bonnet of the Fiesta, fully prepared to get on the roof if necessary. Just then, the door of the shack opens and large red-faced man calls the dog off. My terror is unabated, however, since I notice that he's pointing a shotgun at me.

'What are you arter?' he asks, still leveling the shotgun at me. 'You from the social?'

I tell him that I just want to buy some eggs. His face creases with puzzlement as if I've suggested we might both dance a quadrille among the detritus of his farmyard.

'The sign,' I say, 'I saw the sign at the bottom of your drive.'

'*She* put that up and now she's gone taking the chicken with her. Good riddance I say.'

'Well, I'll just be going then, ' I say, clambering down from the car.

I notice that he's still got the shotgun pointed in my direction and for a moment I imagine that I'll die here, undiscovered in a shallow grave under a rusting turnip scraper or whatever. I bump back down the track and head for home.

On the way back I sneak into the mini-market, where the local lay-abouts are being treated to some Elgar. I buy some RSPCA approved eggs.

Thursday:

I wake up feeling very grumpy. I take a rubbish bag down to my designated wheelie bin. I hurl the bag in and it clatters with the sound of various empty bottles. As I turn to go back to the flat, Thelma, The Centaur, is right behind me wagging a pudgy finger.

'Sounds like bottles to me,' she says disapprovingly. 'You should be re-cycling those. Somebody's got to save the planet.'

Ordinarily, I would have agreed, making vague promises to heed her words, but there's something smug about her that annoys me.

'Tell you what, Thelma,' I say, 'when the government stops using uranium tipped shells to flak the shite out of nomads, when cows stop farting and Chelsea tractors are drawn by horses, I might think about it.'

'You need looking after,' she says over her shoulder as she clatters away on her sling backs. Her arse somewhat behind her front.

Friday:

VATman returns. I watch from my window as he is hoisted out of an ambulance, wincing at every touch of the paramedics as they endeavour to get him upright. He has a plaster cast on and I notice that one leg of his trousers has been cut off to accommodate it. His aversion to human contact is exacerbated by April who comes out of her flat and flutters around him like a mother hen, smoothing his brow and chucking him under the chin. Robin appears, looking somewhat flustered and I wonder why she wasn't with him, or at least there to greet him when he arrived.

Saturday:

I'm awoken by Brint practising his guitar. I think he might have learnt a chord. It's too early to say for certain, but I think I detected what might have been E in the first position. It can only get worse.

I practice the sax and dine on an omelette of the RSPCA approved eggs, washed down with a bottle of Sicilian red country wine. On the label, it's described as being a robust rustic wine. I suspect this might be yet another example of artful marketing, since it has a vague taste of cough linctus and Woolworth's lipstick. I drink it anyway.

Sunday:

I think that I might have solved the mystery of Robin's late and flustered appearance at Adrian's return from hospital. I went down to the basement to check my electricity meter and saw her coming out of Reg the caretaker's flat. She was buttoning up her shirt and stuffing what looked like her panties in the pocket of her jeans.

Bitter Banana

Monday:

I buy a job lot of frozen minced beef. My plan is to turn this into tasty shepherd's pies, lasagnes, bologneses and meatballs. "This is the way to save money", I think, as I bear it home like a triumphant falcon returning to its nest with a stoat. However, it's all in one great iceberg lump, so if I'm to cook all these goodies, I'll have to defrost it in one go and slave over the oven for hours. So, I put it in the freezer to join the Aunt Matilda's Lancashire Hot Pot, Harry Lauder's Highland Haggis, Bob Marley's Down Home Curried Goat and various long-forgotten tubs of unidentifiable gloop.

Tuesday:

I killed a cock pheasant today. It wasn't intentional. I was on my way to to visit a friend who lives out in the sticks, when it ran across the road in front of me. I braked and swerved and the bird ran this way and that like Bruce Forsyth on speed. Alas, Fiesta and pheasant collided. I stopped the car and went back to see if it might have survived. It hadn't. These birds can fly and it could easily have escaped by taking to the air, but I guess centuries of being shot on the wing by mindless Hooray Henries and corporate shooting parties has taught them that scuttling along the ground is safer.

I picked it up and laid it on the grass verge. It was such a lovely bird with beautiful coloration. Oh well, I guess it will make a nice surprise supper for a fox, or an impoverished yokel.

As I returned to the car I saw a drab looking hen pheasant pecking at the opposite verge. She occasionally looked up scanning her surroundings, presumably looking for her now deceased mate. I imagined her thoughts.

'He's off gallivanting again. Probably gone to try his luck with that flighty tart in the turnip field. He'll be back. Then I'll play hard to get.'

Wednesday:

I go to the minmarket and buy some croissants and a lottery ticket. I'm not convinced that the lottery isn't a massive fraud. Do any of us know anyone who has won a substantial amount, or been invited to select the balls or the draw machine? And who are those shadowy men with clipboards standing in the wings when the numbers come up? They look like accountants, but they could just as easily be international criminals. I'm sure that altruism alone can't be the only reason that Richard Branson and others of his ilk have long sought the lotto concession.

Thursday:

I watch a Rod Stewart concert on the television. Rod is a fervent supporter of all things Scottish, particularly independence. One could be forgiven for thinking that he must therefore have originated in the Gorbals, or a crofter's cottage, in a lantern-lit delivery by Doctor Finlay. ("More hot water, Morag") However, I understand that he was born in Highgate and currently lives in Epping.

In his performance, he has the irritating habit of continually grinning at the wings between phrases, as if he's sharing a private joke with someone we can't see.

Friday:

Buzz waylays me on the stairs this morning.

'Hey man. What's up?' he says. 'You should give Little Owl a call you know, particularly after, you know, what like happened. She's very sensitive.'

"Very sensitive" is not a phrase that springs to my mind when I think of her. Brick shit house, blanketed manatee and beaded harridan, seem more appropriate. I humour Buzz, but I'm miffed by his moralistic tone. He might look like a hippy and a tongue-studded rebel, run a New Age shop, burn incense and fuck around on the bongos, but I think a grasping little capitalist conformist lurks just below the surface.

Saturday:

The local rag carries a front page story about a skeleton being found on a town centre building site. This makes a welcome change from cattle auctions, cake sales and sensational headlines like "Cyclist admitted rear light flickered", or "Panties stolen from washing line". Disappointingly, the local museum confirmed that the skeleton was hundreds of years old and foul play is not suspected.

I've always had an aversion to this same museum since my discovery of a Roman centurion's helmet in a stream. I was about ten years old at the time. I was bunking off school, probably with a bad case of malaria or suchlike and skulking round the back lanes of the town. I stopped at a little stream and saw something glinting in the water. I pushed through some bushes and managed to hook it on the end of a stick. It was definitely a helmet of some kind with a visor that lifted up and down. Of course, it was rusted up and covered in slime, so I cleaned it off in the water and could hardly contain my excitement as I ran to the museum which was just up the road. I could already see my picture in the local paper, or even the national press.

"Schoolboy finds invaluable centurion's helmet in a stream. Archeologists amazed. Substantial reward."

When I arrived at the museum and climbed the stairs, I could hear the clinking of glasses and a buzz of chatter. As I entered the upstairs room clutching my priceless find, I saw that it was full of local worthies, supping wine and nibbling on snacks. The mayor was there in his chain of office, as was the town mace bearer in a ridiculous outfit of breeches and a tricorn hat. I had clearly interrupted a civic function of some kind.

As I entered the room, a scruffy, short-trousered, socks-to-the-ankle, dirty-faced waif from the council estate , an awkward silence fell among the worthies. The curator stepped forward, smiling indulgently, as if he got no end of Roman centurion's helmets brought to him every day. He was a wizened little man with a beard and bushy eyebrows.

'What have you got there then boy?'

'Well sir, I think it's a Roman centurion's helmet.'

'Do you now," he said taking my priceless find from me. He looked around the room, tipping a knowing wink to the mayor and his lady wife.

He turned it around, held it up to the light and pondered, stroking his chin as if trying to recall perhaps exactly which legion its original owner might have served in. He passed it to the mayor, a local builder made good on Jerry-built council houses and unnecessary bus shelters. He turned it over in his chubby, never done a day's work hands and expressed his bafflement.

'This lad thinks this is a Roman centurion's helmet. Anyone got any guesses as to what it really is?' said the curator.

He held my find aloft. The assembled worthies shook their heads in puzzlement.

"No? Well I'll tell you," he said triumphantly, 'it's the nozzle off the end of the hose on the corporation water cart. That's what it is. They dip it in the stream to suck up water which they later use to flush out cesspits. Your boys should take better care of their equipment Mister Mayor, otherwise I can see another tuppence on the rates.'

A general braying and snorting arose from the assembled worthies. A cheap laugh for the curator at the expense of an urchin.

I shuffled away, humiliated, my eyes stinging with tears. Thus was born a bitter banana.

Sunday:

Despite my hatred for Reg's dog Patsy, I do like dogs and miss having one, as I did for many years. I'm thinking of getting a Chihuahua. Because of its diminutive size, it would probably view my balcony as a vast expanse, like the pampas and wouldn't feel claustrophobic in the least. It might never leave the flat, yet feel that it occupied a galaxy. I'll probably call it Conchita and feed it tamales and fierce chilli peppers. Its subsequent small bore, but lethal droppings can then be flicked at Jehova's Witlesses and local Tories.

Angel of the Morning

Monday:

Returning from the paper shop, I find Shards sitting on the stair outside her flat. She has been crying and her mascara has run down her face making her look like a melting panda. She has locked herself out and Reg, who has keys to the flats, is nowhere to be found. Brint is apparently on his way with a key. I invite her to wait in my flat.

While she is sending Brint a text, I make her a coffee. It's the first time that I've been able to see her close up. She isn't bad looking in a rugged sort of way. She's still crying and I'm tempted to give her a fatherly hug, until I notice that she has arms like Desperate Dan and that reciprocation, or repulsion by her might involve some personal injury.

As she noisily sips her coffee between snivels, she opens her heart to me. Apparently Brint has told her that as soon as he gets the hang of the guitar, he might go off to join a rock 'n' roll band and tour the world. I think this unlikely, since he is still struggling with one chord. Then I remember The Troggs.

'You're a man of the world,' she says, looking at me as if I were Methuselah. 'Why can't men settle down?'

Why, indeed, I think, remembering my past follies

'After all, I married a tree surgeon, not a pansy muso,' she concludes.

Tuesday:

I've been asked to do a recording session on the clarinet next week. As I haven't played it in years, I'm a bit nervous about this. I began learning when I was twelve years old after a long spell in hospital. After some years of inventing ever more serious illnesses to escape school, I actually got one for real.

When I was eleven, my right knee would periodically swell up for no apparent reason and the pain was excruciating. This would be accompanied by a fever and high temperature, but would go away after a few days and then I'd be okay until the next episode. The doctors appeared to be baffled by this and I spent a lot of time at the hospital as a day patient being poked and prodded. On my twelfth birthday I was at the hospital on my own for yet another appointment. My usual doctor was unavailable and I was seen by a locum who appeared to me to be about a hundred years old.

'Are you feeling okay?' he asked.

I replied that I felt a bit hot and tired having waited a long time to be seen. He felt my head and took my temperature, something that up until then nobody had thought to do. I was admitted immediately and arrangements were made to inform my parents.

One might imagine that I would have felt bad about this, particularly as it was my birthday. However, even though I had no idea what was the matter with me, I was thrilled, because I could envisage a lengthy and legitimate absence from school. I was put into a room of my own within a men's ward. My parents visited that evening and I remember my mother being in tears. Indeed, every time she visited she was in tears, which, for a time, I found puzzling. Within a day or two, my whole leg was put in a plaster cast and I was confined to bed. Weights were attached to my leg to keep it straight.

Apart from being immobile, I liked being in hospital. I was in no pain, I wasn't at school and I got a lot of attention from the nurses. Although I was in a room that was isolated from the rest of the ward, I still got visits from some of the other patients and learned to play chess and a variety of card games. Each day my bed was wheeled out onto a balcony and I was able to look down and watch the hustle and bustle of the hospital and the town beyond.

On one such day, I was munching on my favourite snack of Kraft cheese triangles and biscuits. It was a beautiful sunny day and I felt quite at peace with the world, thinking of my hapless schoolmates and thanking my lucky stars.

For some reason, I decided to try to have a look at my chart which hung at the foot of my bed. After some squirming, during which the weights on my leg swung wildly, I managed to get hold of it. There was a graph showing my daily temperatures and other stuff about bowel movements and blood tests. I was about to put the chart back on its hook when I saw at the foot of the page, under the heading of diagnosis, a word that made my world stop; "Tuberculosis". It actually said, "tuberculosis of the knee", but it might just have well have said *doomed* as far as I was concerned.

In those days, TB was often a death sentence, despite advances in antibiotics. My godmother had died from it at a very early age and I knew of neighbours who had succumbed. For my mother, TB seemed to be both a thing to be dreaded and also somehow to have a stigma attached to it, like leprosy or VD. Now I knew why she was in tears every time she came to visit. Now I knew why I was allowed any number of Kraft cheese triangles and why everyone was so indulgent. I was going to die.

Wednesday:

After a frugal breakfast, I take my old clarinet out of its case. I've kept the wood oiled over the years and it's still in reasonable condition. I piece it together and have a tentative blow. It takes me some time to remember that the fingering is slightly different from the sax, but eventually I get a passable sound out of it.

When I read that dreaded diagnosis on my hospital chart all those years ago, I went into a state of shock. I was paralysed by fear, but I could confide in no one, because I was ashamed of having looked at my chart and I didn't want anyone to confirm that I was doomed. Every little kindness thereafter seemed to me to be an act of pity. My mother's tears were like premature mourning.

I started wetting the bed again and developed sores on my bum, for which I was rubbed down each day with something that smelt like petrol and stung like crazy. The fevers returned and my appetite for food, even the cheese triangles, disappeared. Consultants and housemen would gather at the foot of my bed on their daily rounds and their mumbled words sounded to me like noises off in a play in which I was already a corpse. I was a frightened, bed-ridden, piss-soiled little boy with no one to turn to. I went into an almost catatonic state, in which I spurned the best efforts of the other patients and the nurses to cheer me up.

One day, a cheery woman came to my room with the paraphernalia for basket weaving. I flung it across the room and she beat a hasty retreat. During the day, whether I was out on the balcony, or in my room, I just lay there in bed, weighed down in every sense. Waiting to die.

Thursday:

I continue to practice on the clarinet. It's a coquettish and fickle instrument. At one moment it can be seductive, with a rich and mellow tone and at another, given to capricious squeaks and petulance. I persevere and gradually begin to get back some of my old technique.

I didn't die. Weeks turned into months in the hospital. I was x-rayed so often it's a wonder that I didn't glow in the dark and I was given numerous injections and pills to take. Christmas arrived and the ward was decorated. On the day itself, my bed was wheeled into the main ward and a group of jolly nurses gathered around a Christmas tree to warble carols. Presents were handed out and I got a box that I couldn't be bothered to open. My mother came for an extended visit, during which she sobbed for longer than usual, cheering me up no end.

That night, back in my room, I lay awake listening to the sounds of the hospital. Ambulances arriving, cars driving in and out and the moans and coughs of the men in the ward. I was still awake in the early hours of the morning when the door to my room opened and a vision of loveliness came in. It was a young nurse that I hadn't seen before. She didn't look much older than me and she had the most beautiful face that I had ever seen. She was wearing the dark blue outdoor cloak that nurses wore in those days. She sat beside my bed and stroked my forehead and asked how I was feeling. I made my usual sullen responses that I was okay I supposed. Her eyes never left mine and for the first time, in all the months of fear and isolation, I began to cry. I told her that I knew that I had TB and that I was going to die. She held me in her arms and told me that I had been very brave to have suffered in silence and that I no longer had the disease and was certainly not going to die for a very long time. She asked me about school and laughed when I told her of my career as a serial fibber about illnesses.

'You should open your present,' she said finally, gliding from the room. I opened the parcel. In it was a plastic, gold-coloured toy clarinet. I never saw the young nurse again and I was discharged from the hospital a few weeks later, but not before I had driven the ward mad by my incessant tootling on the clarinet.

I spent the next six months in a plaster cast, hobbling around on crutches. My mother bought me a real clarinet and I began having lessons. In all, I'd had a year off school, but thereafter I never invented an illness again. To this day, even the sight of a Kraft cheese triangle makes my stomach churn.

Friday:

A letter from the local council informing me that I'm now entitled to a bus pass. I recently read accounts of oldies who have traversed the whole of the British Isles for nothing, using various bus routes. Since I did this in the back of a transit van in the Sixties, I have no desire to repeat the experience, even if it's free.

Saturday:

I go out for my dreaded weekly shop. Reg, the caretaker, waylays me on the stairs to tell me that April has gone away to have the gender re-assignment operation. I wince as he spares me no detail about what this involves.

As I'm pulling away in the Fiesta, I see Little Owl coming toward me on a bicycle. Only the wheels are visible under her bulk and the flowing blanketry. She waves frantically, wobbling from side to side. I stare straight ahead, pretending not to have seen her. Once past her, I look in the rear-view mirror and see that she has crashed into some bushes.

Sunday:

I decide to go for a walk before breakfast. I take an old path around the back of the town that I used when I was a paper boy. It backs on to the council estate where I grew up. I take a detour through a small gap in a fence to look for my old house. Nothing much has changed, but now some of the houses have smart driveways, neat gardens and imposing porches and front doors. No doubt a result of the sell-off of council homes by Thatcher in the Eighties. I spot the house in which I used to live. It has not been smartened up. There are a couple of broken windows and the front garden is full of junk and a rusty car that's going nowhere.

As I look around, I fondly remember games of street cricket, swapping cigarette cards and comics, bonfire nights and roller skating. I conveniently forget that for most of my childhood I felt like a fish out of water here. I get my mobile phone out and try to take a picture of the house. The front door opens and a shaven headed man emerges.

'Wass your game mate? You from the council?' he shouts.

I tell him that I used to live in the house.

'Well you don't now, so fuck off,' he says, advancing toward me.

I scuttle away and head for the path again. Just as I'm squeezing back through the fence, I'm greeted by a man of about my own age. I don't recognise him, but he seems to know me.

'Hello mate. Haven't seen you in years. You still playing the clarinet?' he asks.

'Sometimes,' I say, heading home for breakfast.

The Hindenburg Hallucination

Monday:

Further practice on the clarinet. When I began learning at twelve years old, my teacher was called, appropriately enough, Ernest Doe. He was not unlike the Reverend Coot — skeletal and humourless, but he was an excellent teacher. I practised diligently, but one tune that I couldn't master to begin with was the *Sailor's Hornpipe*. Bill, our next door neighbour, worked at night, so while he was trying to sleep during the day, he would be tortured by my fumbling efforts at the hornpipe.

Toodle-oop-poop-poop-too…(squeak) Toodle (squeak)-oop-poop-poop-toodle-oop… And so on.

One day, in exasperation, Bill came to our door and told my mother that he would *join* the fucking navy if I didn't get it right soon.

Within a year or so, and whilst still at school, I began playing in a semi-pro dance band called The Orpheans Dance Orchestra. The band was run by Ernie Hunt, a cadaverous man who looked as though he had fallen into a vat of cement powder. His hair was a powdery grey, matched by his complexion and the dandruff which seemed a permanent fixture on his shoulders. He played no instrument, but handed out the music from a little table at the back of the band.

His son, also called Ernie, played the accordion and was blind. Sometimes young Ernie's enthusiasm would get the better of him and he would stand up to take a solo, swaying and weaving like a fakir's snake, his sightless eyes gyrating wildly in their sockets. He would punctuate this by randomly kicking out one leg like a demented can-can dancer. Sadly, because of his disability, he would often lose his bearings and end up some distance from his chair with his back toward a usually indifferent audience.

The drummer had a huge bass drum, on the front of which was painted a desert island scene with a scantily dressed Polynesian girl to the fore. Each time he hit the drum with his foot pedal, the girl would bump and grind seductively. While this might have been appropriate during up-tempo, or Latin American numbers, it was in poor taste during a slow waltz, as the girl appeared to be in the last throes of a particularly satisfying orgasm. Any concern that the public might be offended by this was eventually resolved one night when Ernie junior, in the course of a particularly ecstatic solo, kicked his way through the front of the drum. After the gig, Ernie's dad docked me five bob for going into hysterics over this, which he said was "unprofessional".

Tuesday:

Church bells again this evening. I sit on my balcony and try to imagine what it is that annoys me so much about them. The sound itself is unpleasantly cacophonic, but there's something else that gets to me. It's the whiff of piety and worthiness — an all's well with this sceptred isle smugness; and in its incompetence, a glorification of the plucky amateur. A couple of glasses of chardonnay and I've got it. They're Tory bells. Morris Men are equally incompetent and laughable, but I think they're more left-leaning.

Wednesday:

As I'm doing the recording session today, I have a light breakfast and make final checks on the clarinet. Like a woman wronged, it can be unforgiving, so I want to make sure everything is right. I take it from its case and check that there no keys sticking or failing to work. Like most musicians, I'm ridiculously superstitious and one of my little peccadilloes is never to practice on the day of a performance if I can possibly avoid it. So I don't know whether the clarinet will be a bitch or an angel until I start to play in the studio.

I've done countless recording sessions over the years and the uninitiated might be forgiven for thinking that they are a simple matter of recording performances, mixing the subsequent sounds and going to the pub. Nothing could be further from the truth, particularly if a group rather than a solo performer is involved. A solo performer might have used session musicians at various stages, most of whom will have had no emotional or professional stake in the process, apart from doing their job as well as they can. The soloist might have a manager or producer, but generally they will be in agreement regarding what they want the finished product to sound like. Groups are a different matter entirely.

For a start, there are several egos, who, long before I arrive, might have been locked in an internecine struggle, each having their own agenda and scores to settle. Recording studios are strange, windowless places that tend to amplify tensions and expose shortcomings. They are also viewed by many groups as places in which to posture, bring their wives, girlfriends, hangers-on, dealers and even their roadies. It doesn't stop there though. These hangers on will also have differing allegiances and agendas. So, it's often against the backdrop of petulant posing, musical differences and indifference and a committee of the aggressively ignorant that the session player has to work and is judged.

I arrive at the studio in good time and find that it is indeed a group that I'll be working with. They are draped around the control room in poses of nonchalance or pique and none of them look a day over ten. A couple of girls huddled in a corner start giggling as I enter with my little black case.

'Christ, it's Jack the fucking Ripper,' I hear one of them say.

I'm introduced to all present and make a real effort not to remember their names. They play me the track that they want the clarinet on and for the life of me I can't imagine why.

'What we sort of want is like a demented solo running in the background,' says one of the band.

'Yeah.' Like, you know, some old geezer who's pissed and can't be stopped,' says another

The engineer, with whom I've worked before, raises an eyebrow ever so slightly, but enough to let me know that he's had enough of these bozos, having been cooped up with them for God knows how long.

I piece together the clarinet and go into a small booth in the studio. I put on the cans and ask them to run the track. I tootle along, sussing out the sequence, which is soon done as there are only four chords. Now it's just me and the engineer, who knows exactly what I'm trying to do and just keeps the track running, allowing me to feel my way and come up with some improvisation. I know that he'll be recording all the time I'm doing this and will save anything promising.

Every now and then through the cans, I can hear a debate going on in the control room. The committee has swung into action. Over the years, I've learnt to ignore this and rely on the engineer's judgment as he tries to filter out the inanities of the assembled brains trust. After half an hour or so, I've got it down and I know that given the miracles of modern technology, the engineer can paste and patch if necessary to make it coherent and/or demented.

As I collect my fee, the group are still arguing amongst themselves. The girls give a last giggle as I exit with enough cash for a month's groceries. The clarinet behaved impeccably. I give her a respectful rub down when I get home.

Thursday:

April has returned from her gender re-assignment. As I go for my morning newspaper, I see her emerging from a taxi. She's dressed as if she's going to Ladies' Day at Ascot. A frilly pink dress and a broad-brimmed hat with what looks like pieces of fruit stuck to it. The taxi driver holds the cab door open for her and then follows with her suitcase as she sashays into the flats. I wish her a good morning and when she replies it's in a voice about half an octave higher than her pre-op register. It still sounds mannish to me and I think she'll need to work on this.

Friday:

This morning, there's a furious row on the stairs between VATman and Robin. His leg is still encased in plaster, but he has managed to hobble down to the basement. I can't resist a bit of scandal, so I saunter down as if I'm going to my car.

'How could you?' shouts VATman to Robin. 'How could you, with that creep.' Here he points at Reg the caretaker who has a "what me guv?" look on his face.

'Listen to me Adrian, there's nothing going on. We were just chatting,' says Robin.

'Just chatting?' shouts VATman. 'Is that why your bra's sticking out of your pocket? Do you normally undress for a chat?'

'You've got it all wrong mate,' says Reg.

I'm nearly at the bottom of the stairs, but I slow my pace not wishing to end up in the middle of the fracas, but wanting to hear more. April emerges from her flat just as Reg is protesting his innocence. She surveys the scene below.

'Men!' she says contemptuously and flounces back into her flat. I wonder whether her re-alignment also included a bit of women's lib indoctrination.

I've almost reached the basement when I see VATman take a swing at Reg. He misses and does a pirouette before crashing to the floor. At this point, Patsy, Reg's yappy little dog, flies at his plastered foot, clamping her spiteful little teeth on it and biting and chewing for all she's worth. VATman screams and Robin screams, while Reg tries to get the dog off. I retreat back up the stairs. Some time later, I hear Robin helping VATman to hobble back to their flat. I await further developments.

Saturday:

My usual weekly shop. No sign of Little Owl thank goodness. With my new found wealth from the session fee, I foolishly buy some tequila, grenadine and orange juice. Weather permitting, I shall sit on my balcony this evening sipping a tequila sunrise.

Later, I do just that, but I do more than sip and before long I've nearly gone through a bottle of tequila. I'm feeling no pain as I watch a massive flying bug cruise toward me. It looks like the Hindenburg and I imagine that through its portholes I can see a decadent art-Deco cocktail bar. Marlene Dietrich is draped on a grand piano singing something in German and Peter Lorre is dealing cards to a bunch of swinish Nazis with dueling scars. The next thing I know it's pitch dark and three in the morning. I grope my way to bed vowing never to to touch tequila ever again.

Sunday:

Despite a fearsome hangover and trembling hands, I go for a pub lunch with an old friend who is gay. He's an American who has lived in the UK for years. He makes me laugh when he tells me that when he was planning to come here, his friends in San Francisco told him that he would have a good time because ten out of nine Englishmen are queer.

I find the flying bug on the balcony. It's dead. No sign of portholes, Marlene, Peter, or the Nazis.

Mystery Bags

Monday:

After the tequila episode and the Hindenburg Hallucination, I've decided that a week of abstinence is called for. I go to the mini-market and stock up on Fair Trade orange juice. The label says "not from concentrate", which I assume is a Pidgin English way of saying that the oranges were picked in a leisurely manner with no particular purpose in mind.

I notice that line-caught haddock, unsold at the weekend, has been reduced to fifty pence. I snap up three packets. I envisage a succulent fish pie, with parsley sauce and a modest cheesy potato topping. The girl at the checkout tells me that she often buys out of date fish for her cat. When I get home, I put the haddock in the freezer to join the other body parts and bargains that I'll probably never eat.

This evening, I get an email from someone who is writing a book about the UK music scene in the Sixties. Just from the tone of his enquiry, I can tell that he's an anorak, who probably knows the matrix numbers of every crappy record and the personnel of every crappy band, but will never know, or understand how vibrant, yet ultimately disappointing that whole era was. I'm not sure whether it's his email or the dubious fish purchase, but I break my vow of abstinence and finish off the tequila mixed with some of the orange juice. During the night, I have a recurring dream in which I'm pursued by a posse of caterwauling moggies singing Cilla Black's greatest hits. Deeply unpleasant. What's in tequila?

Tuesday:

That's it. I'm definitely going for the health kick. I have a boiled egg for breakfast with plain Ryvita rather than soldiers. I resolve to chew everything twenty five times, thus hopefully reducing my intake.

If the Bedouin goatherd who discovered the Dead Sea scrolls had taken a nibble out of them, I imagine it would have been a similar experience to that of eating Ryvita. Dry, tasteless and crumbling to dust.

Fruit for lunch, washed down with sparkling spring water. The label on the water bottle informs me that the contents come from deep in the Welsh mountains. I'm not going to be cynical about this. I'm really not, because I need to believe in all this crap for a while so that I can put up with the miseries of abstinence.

The Tory church bells ring out again this evening as I dine on a skinless chicken breast and a few branches of broccoli. My resolve is not helped by Brint and Shards, who are having a balcony barbecue below. I can smell meat being charred and the glug of wine being poured. I lean out from my balcony as far as I dare and see that they have company. From the snatches of conversation that I pick up, it transpires that Shard's mum and dad are over on a visit from Woop Woop or wherever.

'Care for another mystery bag Mumsie?' I hear Shards say.

'Don't mind if I do,' says Mumsie.

I Google "mystery bag" and discover that it's Antipodean slang for a sausage. After my slender repast, I could die for one of these — whatever it contained and however charred.

Wednesday:

On the way out to get my paper, I see Brint and Shards emerge from their flat with Shards' parents in tow. They are all wearing shorts and carrying various bags. Brint is clutching some flimsy looking picnic chairs and has a backpack on. I'm introduced to the parents who are called Dave and Mave (short for Mavis she tells me) Dave has a bone-crushing handshake and pumps my arm up and down as if he's cracking a whip.

'We were thinking of going to Stonehenge today,' says Shards. 'Is it worth a look?'

I tell her that I think it is and also advise them that nearby Avebury is also an interesting place to visit.

'After that,' Shards says, 'I thought we might swing by Land's End.'

I tell them that this might be a little ambitious for a day trip.

'Jeez mate,' says Dave, 'the missus here thinks nothing of doing a five hundred mile round trip just to get her highlights done.'

Thursday:

Another email from The Anorak, asking whether I had received his previous communication regarding the Sixties. It seems that he wants to interview me at some point and attaches a list of questions that he thinks are pertinent, but which to me appear completely irrelevant. I played such a minor part in the so-called Swinging Sixties and I can't imagine why he's pestering me. I look further at the questions. Who played the sax solo on such and such a record? Did the guitarist de-tune for this recording? Who was the sound engineer on..? And so on. Not a single question about what it was like to be in a band on the road. And not a single question about sex. Leaving this out is like ignoring the importance of steel, iron and steam in the Industrial Revolution.

I send him an email back purporting to come from my secretary, one Fenella Front-Buttock, in which she says that I'm currently in re-hab in New Mexico and will get back to him at sometime. The fact that in reality I couldn't afford the fare to New Malden is neither here nor there. I just hope that this shuts him up.

Friday:

A day of inexplicable aches and pains. I also feel grumpier than usual. I assume this is the result of my eating less and laying off the alcohol. I guzzle the sparkling Welsh water at breakfast lunch and dinner, trying to imagine that it's doing me good. I have a ready supply of raw carrot and celery to hand which I munch on throughout the day.

In the evening, I sit out on my balcony, still guzzling the water and munching on the rabbit food. Below me, I can hear the Aussies having their evening meal. A clatter of plates and the hiss of beer cans being opened. I'm feeling quite sorry for myself. It's not easy being a Puritan.

When the pain first starts, it's on my right side, just above my hip bone. I try to ignore it, but it gradually spreads across my lower abdomen and intensifies. I'm not a complete hypochondriac, but I can recognise the symptoms of appendicitis. I try to remain calm.

I'll pack a bag with a toothbrush and electric razor. I'll dig out my old pajamas and make sure that my underwear is clean. I'll leave a note for the milkman cancelling my milk and then I'll calmly call an ambulance.

Just as I'm about to carry out these sensible tasks, I let go with a fart of such magnitude that the cheeks of my arse fibrillate like Mick Jagger blowing a raspberry. The fart goes on and on, finally ending after about thirty seconds with a series of stuttering fartlets. The pain immediately subsides and I realise that I've been over-filling my innards with gassy water and roughage for the past few days. From below, Dave shouts up,

'Did Krakatoa just explode, or did someone drop a fart? Better out than in mate.' This was followed by laughter and a round of applause. I bin the rabbit food and Welsh water.

Saturday:

Brint calls round this morning saying that they are having a barbie on the lawn this evening and everyone's invited. I casually mention that there's a new resident on the first floor, just in case he doesn't know. I starve myself during the day so that I can at least eat some real food tonight and perhaps have a drink or two.

Another email from The Anorak in which he thanks Fenella for hers, but peevishly points out that to his certain knowledge I was seen recently playing in a local pub with The Suicidal Gerbils. This is starting to feel like persecution rather than genuine enquiry. This man clearly has no sense of humour and even addresses his email to Ms Front-Buttock. Fenella emails him back to say that I did indeed recently do a gig with The Gerbs, but the experience left me so traumatised that I have sought professional help.

From my balcony, I gaze down on the lawn as Brint and family busy themselves setting up the barbecue. Just as I'm about to go back inside the flat to get ready, I spot Buzz and Thelma wheeling a portable barbecue on to the lawn. I also see the unmistakable shape of Little Owl trailing behind them carrying a tray of something or other.

I decide to go for the Johnny Cash look again, because I remember reading that wearing black has a slimming effect. As I make my way downstairs, I'm joined by April who is wearing a sort of safari suit and very high heels. As we cross the lawn, Dave looks up from stoking the coals.

'Christ, it's Indiana Jones and the Grim Reaper,' he whoops. 'Grab a beer guys. Grub up in a mo.'

Thelma is wearing a T shirt with "Meat is Murder" emblazoned on the front. She, Buzz and Little Owl have set up a meat-free barbecue and are piously putting various bits of veg and what looks like miniature cow pats on it. VATman and Robin are sitting on the grass holding hands, so I assume reconciliation has occurred. Reg is chatting to Cordelia, who is looking very attractive. Little Owl casts a venomous look in my direction.

I sink a couple of beers in quick succession and feel light-headed, since I've not eaten anything all day. Dave has a vast array of meat ready to put on his barbie and I'm looking forward to tucking in. In the meantime, Thelma persuades me to try a veggie burger. I bite into it and I'm immediately reminded of Ryvita and the Dead Sea Scrolls. I put it behind my back and drop it into some bushes. It's immediately retrieved by Reg's dog Patsy, who drops it at Thelma's feet. I look skyward.

A couple more beers and I'm looking for an excuse to chat up Cordelia, who seems to be monopolised by the lecherous Reg. I ask Dave what he thought of Stonehenge.

'To tell you truth mate, I was disappointed. It looked like a builder's yard in the middle of nowhere. I can't see what all the fuss is about.'

From the corner of my eye, I see Little Owl bristle. She strides over to Dave flinging her blanket around herself.

''Stonehenge is one of our most sacred sites,' she shouts. 'If you didn't stuff yourself full of harmless animals, you'd be better able to appreciate the spirituality and re-connect with the feminine.'

Dave looks her up and down, which doesn't take long since she's all of four feet ten.

'I'm not sure about the feminine my love. I'm just saying it was a let down. If you want to see something really awesome, go and have a look at Ayers Rock.'

He flips a few mystery bags and bastes some chicken thighs. I can tell that he's up for a bit of banter. Undeterred, Little Owl stands her ground.

'And what about your treatment of the indigenous Australian people, the keepers of the dream? It's a disgrace.'

The assembled company falls silent. Dave tips me a crafty wink and takes a big bite out of a chicken thigh, wiping the juice from his chin with the back of his hand.

'Oh you mean the Abbos,' he says. 'We hardly ever see them from one year to the next.'

'That's because you've wiped most of them out,'

'Funny you should say that,' says Dave thoughtfully, 'I think I might have run one over one night when I was coming back from the hotel. Either that, or it was a bloody big possum, or maybe a Pom. I thought I heard it say "Oh fuck" as my back wheels bumped over it. Can't be sure though 'cos I'd sunk a few.'

Little Owl snorts and she, Buzz and Thelma retreat some distance away under a tree. Buzz starts playing his wretched bongos. We all tuck in to Dave's fare and I have a few more beers. Reg has brought out a portable CD player and treats us to a selection of country and western. I try to have a conversation with Cordelia, but I don't trust my hearing or my level of intoxication, so I keep it brief, not wishing to queer my future prospects.

During a break in Reg's music, I suggest to Dave that Australia doesn't really have a national anthem apart from *Waltzing Matilda*. He corrects me on this saying that they have something called *Advance Australia*, to which nobody knows the words, or hardly ever sings. I suggest that we compose one. In a flash of inspiration I sing,

'Australia, Australia,

Land of the kangaroo.'

Furrowed brows all round. No one can come up with the next line. I sing it again. There's a slight pause and Mave, in a little girlie voice pipes,

'And the duck-billed platypus too-oo.'

Sunday:

Back to the Ryvita.

A Quiet Wedding

Monday:

A man comes to service my old gas boiler. He's quite out of breath, having climbed four flights of stairs with his toolbox.

'Cor,' he says, 'those stairs are like the north face of the bloody Eiger. I wouldn't want to have to go up and down them too often.'

I agree with him, but say that it does have its compensations and show him the view from my balcony. He surveys the town below and the hills beyond, but doesn't seem convinced. I make him a cup of tea.

'Ere, didn't you used to be a sax player?' he asks.

I confirm this and say that I'm still playing. He then reels off the names of a number of bands that I've played with over the years.

'My son's always wanted to play the sax. Do you give lessons?'

'Only one,' I say. 'Buy the best sax you can afford then stick it in your gob and blow like a bastard.'

This seems to amuse him and he repeats it several times as he takes the boiler to bits and slurps his tea. One little thing that he does amuses me. He leaves the teaspoon in his mug as he drinks. He puts it in the twelve o'clock position and then tips the mug to drink. The spoon inevitably slides round to the six o'clock position on his upper lip. He tuts impatiently as if the spoon has a mind of its own and he then goes through the same procedure again.

Relieving me of eighty pounds, he tells me that the boiler is good for another year and takes his leave. Going down the stairs he laughs and repeats my lesson.

'Stick it in your gob and blow like a bastard. Ha ha. I like that. Blow like a bastard.'

I wonder if I'll be good for another year.

Tuesday:

I'm a little out of practice with courtship, but I'm determined to have a crack at Cordelia. I ponder on the best strategy and decide that perhaps a slightly bookish, thoughtful demeanour on my part might be attractive. I wouldn't want her to discover my little eccentricities too soon. With hindsight, the John Wayne impression was clearly a mistake.

Wednesday:

I collect my newspaper and read that the government wants kids to stay in full-time education until they are eighteen. I left school with a sigh of relief aged fifteen and began work in a local music shop. It was here that I met a guitarist called Doug Logan whose mother managed the shop.

He was a treacherous psychopath who seemed to hate everyone and harboured many grievances- mostly imaginary. His anger was particularly targeted toward the emerging rock and roll which he hated. He would sit in the shop playing tricky Django Reinhardt riffs and scowl menacingly at the young lads coming in to try out guitars. He would often deliberately trip them up, so that he could then pick a fight with them for being clumsy. He and I joined Pete Brown's Jazz Band, which was quite a good semi-pro band. Pete was an effete old Etonian, given to wearing a hanky dangling from his cuff and saying things like "Wizard" and "Top hole".

Logan had a long-suffering girlfriend and they decided to get married and asked me to be the best man. The service was to be at a local village church, followed by a reception at the Women's Institute hall nearby, with entertainment provided by the Pete Brown Jazz Band.

The bride was almost an hour late arriving at the church and Logan was becoming more psychotically unstable by the minute, pacing up and down the aisle, his bulging eyes swiveling around the congregation like a jackal searching for prey.

The two principal families had begun arguing with each other, when the bride finally entered, sobbing her heart out. She was accompanied by a scrum of muscular bridesmaids, who, despite being dressed in fluffy pink, looked like Ukrainian wrestlers in drag. There was also a scary little page boy who swaggered like Al Capone and looked as though he'd done a bit of boxing.

The vicar came to the altar, whispered a prayer and turned to face the congregation. He'd aged a little, but it was none other than my old theological sparring partner from school, The Reverend Archibald Coot. As his eyes rested on me and recognition dawned, his look was one of undisguised venom. He no doubt held me responsible for the fractious atmosphere in the church, the late arrival of the bride and the recent famine in Ethiopia. When I handed him the ring, he took it from me as if it was a scorpion.

Coot foolishly decided it would be a good idea to deliver a little homily or two before finally joining the happy couple in holy wedlock. He droned on about this and that and one became aware of some faint dissenting background noise from the pews. At first nothing more than an occasional muted "hrrumph", or sigh, but when Coot said that he hoped the happy couple would bring their children up as Christians, the dissenter gave full voice and stood up to say, 'Yeah, but 'ow many buggers do, that's what I should like to know?'

'Shut up Cyril, you're drunk', cried a woman in a silly hat.

Several members of the congregation chuckled, but were soon hushed when Logan turned from the altar and pointed his finger at them, nodding menacingly.

The WI hall was as one might expect it to be. Photographs of happy rambling ladies in twin sets and framed samples of needlework adorned one wall. The opening words to *Jerusalem* were set in tiles on another. Substantial and sensible tea urns and rickety trestle tables in the kitchen. A vague whiff of piety and carbolic.

We all went in with a palpable sense of collective relief, as if we had undergone an ordeal, but were now safe. People began smiling, shaking hands and socialising. The bride had stopped sobbing, food was consumed and drink taken. However, in the psychotic broth that was Logan's brain, the disjointed and generally aimless synapses were beginning to find allies in others of a darker nature. Critical mass was imminent. He spoke very little and had a fixed and menacing smile as we set up our gear to play.

Pete Brown, our band leader, had been attending another wedding and was due to arrive as soon as he could. In the meantime we played a few blues. Cyril, the church heckler, decided it would be a good idea to shake hands with Logan, presumably to make amends for his outburst. I spotted him early on, weaving his way toward us grinning inanely, one hand outstretched in a gesture of reconciliation.

He seemed to do a little dance, swaying to the music as he approached

Logan. It took some time, because he took a few steps forward, then swayed back a step or two. It was a like watching a tipsy hamster flirting with a cobra. When he was finally within striking range, Logan felled him with a single, but effective, blow with his guitar and Cyril crumpled to the floor. Logan now moved among the crowd flailing his guitar indiscriminately in all directions. Table loads of sausage rolls and suspect sandwiches were overturned, women screamed and children cried in terror. I took refuge in the kitchen, where Al Capone, the page boy, gave me a knowing wink as he rifled through the pockets of the guests' coats.

At this point, the old Etonian, Pete Brown, entered, clearly from a very different kind of wedding. He was wearing a topper and tails and playing a jaunty version of *When the Saints Go Marching in* on the trumpet. The tune sputtered out when he saw the scene of carnage and he was flung against the Jerusalem wall in the fracas. His top hat was trampled underfoot, as the crowd, like frenzied wildebeest, stampeded in an effort to escape Logan's flailing guitar. Order was only restored when the muscular bridesmaids formed a circle around the bride, who stood on a chair and screamed,

'Stop it!'

Eventually, things calmed down, wounds were dressed and we played some more. Cyril was taken home, whimpering.

The time then arrived for the happy couple to depart for a romantic honeymoon in Scotland. At the time Logan had a bubble car and the two lovebirds squeezed into it with their luggage and were bid a fond farewell by those of us still able to walk unaided. We waved and cheered as the little car wound its way up the hill out of the village.

There was a little smoke coming from it, but that was only to be expected from a crappy two stroke engine. At the top of the hill, the little smoke became a huge black billow and the engine disintegrated onto the road in a puddle of oil and pistons. My last memory of the day is of Logan on the horizon kicking the bubble car. The marriage lasted a surprising nine days. The band broke up after this. None of us could face working with a psychopath anymore.

Thursday:

In remembering Logan's wedding, I also recall that some weeks ago, Cyclops, she of the jam jar glasses, told me that The Reverend Coot was still alive and living in a local council home. On an impulse, I give the home a call to ask about visiting.

'Eventide,' says a bored sounding girl with a Slavic accent.

I ask about visiting times and in particular seeing Coot.

'Is OK between ten and three any daytimes. Tell us when you come. No bring food, cigarette or booze. Fruit OK, but no pipes,' she tells me.

'Pipes?' I query.

'Yes, pipes. They get stuck in dentures.'

I realise that she means "pips". I arrange to visit next Monday. I make a mental note to buy some bananas.

Friday:

I listen to *Desert Island Discs* on the radio. The guest is some boring mogul, knighted for his services to industry and the ruthless exploitation of workers and punters. It's amazing how many of these nabobs all seem to have started out with nothing, selling apples or sheep's innards from a market stall in the Old Kent Road, until they began their meteoric rise to fame and fortune. This remains a mystery until Kirsty Young, the presenter, asks what it was like to be at Eton, or mentions how a loan from old uncle Bob got them started.

To my knowledge, no one has ever chosen an inflatable sex toy, or a solar powered dildo as their one allowable luxury on the desert island.

Saturday:

This morning, I spot Cordelia sitting on the lawn reading a book. This is very promising and confirms for me that perhaps my bookish strategy might be on the button. I cast about for a suitably intellectual book and settle on Gibbon's *Decline and Fall of the Roman Empire*. Clutching this weighty tome, I saunter downstairs and onto the lawn.

'Oh hello,' I say as if surprised to see anyone there. 'Good book?'

'Oh, just a potboiler, nothing too weighty,' she says. 'What about you?'

'Nothing special,' I say. 'Just a quick read.' I cover up the tome hoping that she won't see what it is.

'Car OK now?' I ask, just to remind her of my chivalrous deed.

Before she can answer, a young man bounds across the lawn and she rise to greet him with obvious delight.

'All ready?' he asks after they have embraced.

'Yes, all ready,' she says, looking swept up and delighted.

'Enjoy your read,' she says as they leave arm in arm.

Drats and buggeration, she's got a fucking toyboy. This is going to be harder work than I thought. I trudge back upstairs and fling Gibbon in the bin.

Sunday:

A quiet day. I notice that the toyboy has spent the night with Cordelia. I see him go off mid-morning in a flashy looking car. I ponder on the possibility of loosening his wheel nuts the next time he visits, but think better of it as I don't think I could survive on prison food should my crime be discovered. I bet there's no chicken Kiev, barn eggs or Fair Trade wine in Pentonville.

Eventide

Monday:

Clutching a bunch of bananas, I set off for the Eventide Home to visit the Reverend Coot. I don't know why I'm doing this. I barely know him and the two occasions when our paths crossed nearly half a century ago were hardly happy ones. I'm convinced that he won't know me from Adam.

On arrival, I'm shown into a day room by one of the assistants. There are several old people slumped in chairs and a television with the sound off flickers in a corner. A woman with a plastic daffodil in her hand dances around to music only she can hear. I ask the assistant where Coot is and she points to a big winged armchair with its back to the room and facing a window.

As I approach the chair, I try to second guess which way the dancer is going to twirl. I get it wrong and we collide for a moment.

'Cheeky boy,' she says coquettishly and swats me with the daffodil before twirling off again.

I don't know why, but I'm feeling really nervous. Coot must be nearly ninety and is probably ga-ga. He won't know me. I'll give him the bananas, chat about the weather and leave. Yet I feel as if I've got an appointment with Moses.

I reach the window, and there he is, a tiny figure engulfed by the chair. He's reading a book and doesn't look up until I cough politely. He's completely bald and painfully thin. He looks like The Mekon from the *Dan Dare* comics. I notice that he's not wearing a dog collar. I tell him my name and he stares at me for what seems a very long time. Eventually, he smiles benignly, beckoning me to sit down.

'Ah, the classroom dissenter,' he says with a chuckle. 'Are you still a rebel I wonder?'

I'm completely taken by surprise and can't believe that he can really remember me and that he's being so amiable.

'Well, it was a long time ago, sir, 'I say. 'I think I might have mellowed a little over the years. Are you sure that you remember me?'

'Oh, I remember you well dear boy. In front of the whole class you questioned the concept of God's omnipresence and challenged me to prove it, which of course, I couldn't. You were punished for your insolence by being made to do country dancing with the girls as I recall.' He chuckles. 'Did you enjoy it? Much more fun than listening to me drone on, I should think.'

This isn't at all how I saw our meeting going. He's not ga-ga and he does know me from Adam. Far from being a somewhat scary figure from my distant past, he's more like Ebenezer Scrooge after his overnight conversion.

'I suppose I was a rude little boy,' I say, 'but I've always had a problem with certainty and I've never been able fully to subscribe to any kind of ideology, religious or political.'

'Quite right too,' says Coot. 'Certainty or dogma have been responsible for the most appalling atrocities over the centuries. I've seen some at first hand.'

The woman with the daffodil twirls in front of us singing.

'There's none so fair as little Alice in all the land they say, And I'm to be Queen o' the May, mother, I'm to be Queen o' the May,' she warbles, waving the daffodil in our faces like a fairy godmother's wand.

'You won't be queen of anything Alice unless you behave,' says Coot. 'Give her a banana.'

I offer her a banana and she takes the whole bunch, dancing off with them held aloft like an offering to the gods.

'I could have gone to a clerical rest home you know, ' says Coot, 'but can you imagine the sanctimonious bilge and smug piety that prevails in such a place? No, I prefer this.'

'Have you lost your faith then?' I ask.

'Bell, book and candle. Lock, stock and barrel. And I can tell you it's such a pleasure being relieved of the burden of certainty. When I see the deluded happy-clappy, so-called born-agains and Creationists these days, I feel nothing but pity and contempt.'

'But surely you still believe in the human spirit, in an underlying force for good.' I say

'Here's what I believe,' he says. 'You're born, you live and you die. If you're lucky, you won't get raped, murdered, tortured, or succumb to some unspeakable disease. There will be moments of happiness and others of gloom and despair. It's not written in the stars, or pre-ordained by some benign figure in the sky. It is so because it is so. There's a thin veneer of what we are pleased to call civilisation, but beneath it humans are vicious, kind, or indifferent, depending on what suits their purposes at the time.'

'But what about mankind's achievements in science and the arts?' I counter. 'Surely these attest to something, some sort of progress, a shaping of the world for the better.'

'They attest to man's creativity and intelligence, I grant you that. But they don't necessarily signify a force for good. Hiroshima was a product of science and ingenuity and Auschwitz the result of dogma. Don't forget that Hitler was an artist, albeit an indifferent one, before he took up as a homicidal maniac. I believe Churchill dabbled with the brushes too. '

'But what caused you to lose your faith?'

'It wasn't a single event, but a combination of factors over many years. I worked as an army chaplain in Northern Ireland and saw the results of the bombings. I saw guts and limbs being shovelled into bin bags. I don't think the universe gave a fig whether they were Catholic or Protestant guts and limbs. I've seen people starving to death in Africa for want of a few pence worth of grain, while their leaders and some of ours swung past in their bullet-proof limousines. I've listened to the weasel words of politicians as they send young men and women to their deaths in pointless wars. Does God look the other way sometimes, do you think?'

I'm shocked by all that he says. Not because I think he's wrong, but because for years I've only remembered him as the dogmatic cleric from my schooldays.

'I can't disagree with what you say, but over the years I've come to think that there might somehow be a spiritual dimension to life, something other,' I say.

'Prove it,' he says with a sly smile.

One of the slumbering inmates, a man in a dressing gown, suddenly sits bolt upright and shouts,

'Steady the Buffs. Who won the fucking war?'

A stream of piss flows down his leg onto the tiled floor, forming a steaming yellow puddle around his slippered feet. The woman with the daffodil dances through it, before one of the care assistants comes in with a bucket and mop and swabs the floor.

'Now, now Bertie,' she says not unkindly, 'you be naughty boy again. Yes? No make pee-pee in pants. Ring bell. OK?'

She turns to Coot.

'Is time for tea time, Archie. I got your favourite cake. '

I can see that it's time to leave. I shake Coot's hand

'Do come again,' he says warmly; 'I've so enjoyed our little chat.'

Tuesday:

As I was struggling with The Times crossword this morning, a parrot landed on my balcony. A real parrot. I couldn't believe my eyes. It seemed quite tame, so I started making tweeting and clucking noises at it. It didn't seem to be in any hurry to leave, so I gently threw some Fair Trade cornflakes in its direction. The parrot looked down at these with very little interest and began preening its feathers and scratching itself — one leg at time of course.

I was tempted to go into a Tony Hancock-as -Robert Newton- as- Long John Silver routine, tucking one leg behind me and saying "Ah Jim lad. Pieces of eight, pieces of eight", but felt that this reference might be lost on the bird and make me look foolish. Instead I tried the "who's a pretty boy then?" option. The parrot stopped it's preening and scratching and cocked its head from side to side, looking at me quizzically. I moved a bit closer and repeated the question. It fluttered up onto the balcony railing and before launching itself skyward, distinctly told me twice to "fuck off." My first rebuff of the week.

I Google parrots and discover that the one on my balcony was an African Grey. Apparently, it's estimated that there are some ten thousand stray parrots in England, many of them occupying the trees surrounding a rugby ground near Esher. Perhaps this is where they pick up their bad language. Had it been a cricket ground, then my visitor might have said "Owzat", or "Well bowled, sir" before flying off.

Wednesday:

I decide to give the flat a good clean, starting with a thorough hoovering. As I'm sailing round, the hoover picks up something metallic and there's a rattling noise as whatever it is courses down the tube. The hoover gives a couple of gurgles like an emu swallowing a money box and then conks out. Bugger, bugger, bugger. I sometimes feel that machines conspire against me.

I detach the pipe and hold it up to my eye to see if I can see the mystery object. I'm rewarded with a cascade of dust, house mites, dead wasps, postman's red elastic bands and other crap. I stagger, half-blinded to the bathroom and wash my eye out. I know it might seem fanciful, but I think that the hoover looks smug as it sits on the carpet acting the innocent. I disembowel it and discover that the object in question is a miniature replica of the Eiffel Tower. I have absolutely no recollection of ever having owned such an object. My mistrust of machines deepens.

Thursday:

VATman is out of plaster. I see him hobble gingerly to his car to go off to work. He wipes his feet before getting into the car. He is seen off by his wife, Robin. She pecks him on the cheek and waves fondly as he drives down the road.

I wait a decent interval and then go down to Reg the caretaker's flat to ask him for the key to the communal storeroom. He takes some time coming to the door and when he does, he's red faced and I can hear some whining country music. He pulls the door behind him, but not before I spot Robin flitting across the lounge in the altogether.

Just as I thought. More trouble afoot methinks.

Friday

Freddie, the Fish Man calls.

'I've got some nice fresh 'alibut on the van,' he tells me.

I'm such a sucker. I feel sorry for him having had to traipse up five flights of stairs. He's only trying to make a buck after all. I agree to buy a halibut and he returns with it wrapped in paper.

'Poach it in water or milk,' he advises me. 'But don't overcook it. Lovely stuff.'

I unwrap the fish in the kitchen. It's got two beady little eyes that protrude from its flat head and which seem to stare up at me with reproach, as if I'm responsible for its current predicament. In my heart I know that I'll never be able to poach, fry, grill, or otherwise prepare this denizen of the deep, so I chuck it in the freezer to join the rest of the stuff I'll probably never eat.

Saturday:

Another pub gig. This time, it's not with the Gerbils, but with a band that I enjoy playing with. The guitarist is not of the histrionic face-pulling tendency and they play some good stuff. In the interval, I'm approached by the type of person I dread at gigs. The saxophone expert.

'I see you've got a Selmer Mark Six,' he says. 'Has it got the articulated G sharp key?'

'I'm not sure,' I reply.

And I'm really not sure. I just play it. Maybe I'm missing something, but I've had this conversation many times and I know that its sole purpose is to display this nerd's superior knowledge of the instrument and my ignorance. In fact, some of the most knowledgeable people about saxophones that I've ever met can't play for toffee.

'I see that it has been re-lacquered,' he says sniffily. 'Ruins the tone you know. Much better to have kept the original finish.'

'Is that right?' I say, as if a couple of microns of lacquer could possibly affect its tone. It's all bollocks, but I'm still being polite. I take a closer look at him as I get my pint. He's like a little stoat. Pinprick eyes and an overbite of yellowish teeth.

'What reeds do you use?' he asks and before I can be bothered to answer, he's already telling me which ones I *should* use. I now deliver my standard response to such nerdery.

'Tell you what,' I say, 'why don't you get up for the first number in the next set and play my sax, then you can tell me where I've been going wrong for the last forty five years. Otherwise, fuck off.'

I'll never be a diplomat. The stoat scuttles away with a hurt expression — if that's possible with protruding teeth.

As I'm leaving the gig, a figure emerges from the shadows of the pub car park.

'I hope things worked out OK for you in New Mexico,' he says, somewhat sarcastically. 'I really would like to interview you regarding the Sixties. Please give me a call.'

He hands me a card with his contact details and slips back into the shadows. Christ, it's The Anorak. Stereo nerds in one night.

Sunday:

A note through the door from Thelma and Buzz. They are apparently going to hold a psychic fair on the lawn next weekend. They promise that it won't cause any disruption and I'm cordially invited to attend. Perhaps I'll get an answer to the mystery of the Eiffel Tower.

Chief Running Bear

Monday:

In keeping with my occasional nods toward a fitness regime, I decide to get my old bike out and cycle into town. I have to pump up the tyres and I find this quite an effort and ponder on how many calories I might have burnt up already.

The ride into town is one of unmitigated terror. For a start, I'm a bit wobbly on the old bike, but also cars and trucks whizz past me at great speed and the back draught (if that's what it's called) makes me wobble even more. This in turn causes motorists to honk their horns and in some cases hurl abuse at me. A vicious cycle is then created wherein I wobble, they honk. I wobble more, they shout. I wobble more and so on. Eventually, I decide to push the bike on the pavement.

Jason, the community cop pulls up on his bike. He's wearing his normal regalia of stab vest, hi-viz jacket and various gadgets. This is topped off by what looks like a Thunderbirds spaceship on his head. I suspect that this is a crash helmet, but for all I know might be some sort of mind control device plugged into GCHQ, or the CIA.

'You should get one of these mate,' he says, tapping the spaceship. 'Trouble with your bike?'

No,' I say, 'I'm just taking it for a walk. I used to have a dog, but it got run over by a speeding squad car on its way to the police canteen.'

Jason studies my face for a few moments and then re-mounts his bike.

'You've got an attitude problem. Do you know that?' he says over his shoulder as he wobbles off.

Tuesday:

What might have been a pleasant evening sitting on my balcony watching the sunset, is completely ruined by the bloody Tory church bells. If only they played a recognisable tune, or there was the faintest scintilla of melody, it wouldn't be so bad. But no, it's just cascade after cascade of cacophony.

I Google the parish church and find that it has a website and an email address for the vicar. I decide to send him an email from a specially created screen name.

FROM: O-Rotter
TO: Rev@Saintegberts.net
SUBJECT: A bellyful of bells.

Dear Rev,

I like to consider myself a charitable person, but every Tuesday evening my patience is sorely tried by the inept fumbling of your bell ringers. The racket that emanates from the church is nothing less than noise pollution. I assume that Tescos have not yet bought the vicarage, so you must still live close by. How you stand it is a mystery.

I imagine that there must be some mighty egos at work in the belfry, because your cloth-eared bell ringers seem to be competing with each other to play at the same time. Could you not persuade them to take it in turns, so that their efforts might at least have a simple ding-dong quality, rather than sounding like a fleet of competing ice cream vans?

My late husband, Ifor, occasionally played the swanee whistle, particularly after a glass or two of elderflower wine. I'm telling you this so that you'll see that I'm not an intolerant person. I believe there should be give and take in a marriage, although I did draw the line at "talking dirty" during sexual congress.

Yours,
Ophelia Rear-Otter (Mrs)

I await a reply and further fun.

Wednesday:

I think Brint might have moved on to a second chord on the guitar. Worse still, I hear Shards humming as he struggles with this musical mountain. Could this be the beginnings of a world-beating double act? I find this thought infinitely depressing and feel compelled to open a bottle of Fair Trade Rustic Red. It's so rustic that my eyes water as I sip it. There are undertones of silage, pig swill and fumbled incest in the top meadow about it. The aftertaste is redolent of acid drops and an old wine gum found at the back of the sofa. With so much character and lyricism, it's quite a bargain.

Thursday:

An email from the vicar:

Dear Mrs. Rear-Otter,

Thank you so much for your email regarding the church bells. I'm sorry to hear that they might have disturbed you. I have prayerfully considered your comments and would like to say that from time immemorial church bells have been used to herald or celebrate great events, as well as funerals and marriages.

Our bell ringers are considered by some to be the finest in the area and are drawn from all walks of life. In order to maintain their high standard however, they do need to practice. May I respectfully suggest that on Tuesday nights you close your windows and perhaps listen to the wireless? If you attend our church, perhaps you would like to make yourself known to me after a service.

Yours in Christ and Peace,
Rev. David Jones.

So much here to work on that I hardly know where to start.

Friday:

I email the vicar.

Dear Reverend Jones,,

Thank you for your prompt reply. I was interested in your invention of a new (to me anyway) adverb: PRAYERFULLY. Is English your second language by any chance? Your name sounds perfectly ordinary.

I don't see why I should have to cower in my own house of a Tuesday night, like Anne Frank, dreading the doorbell — or in this case the abysmal efforts of your belfry clods. If they are considered to be the finest in the area, I shudder to think what the rest must be like. I rarely listen to the wireless, as you quaintly call it. Too much smut for my liking and pagans on Thought for the Day.

No, I don't attend your church. I am Welsh by birth and was brought up as strict Chapel. I passed by the church recently as a service was turning out and was shocked to see semi-feral children with painted faces, men in T shirts and flibbertigibbets in scanty frocks emerging.

Were you by any chance the grinning man in the toga and sandals shaking their hands as they left?

I won't let this matter rest and fully intend to ask the council to install some sort of device to monitor the sound level of the bells. I know that they do this at boogie-woogie concerts and I see no reason why it couldn't be used in an ecclesiastical context. If an acceptable sound level is exceeded, I imagine that a cattle prod or taser could be used to keep your clanging egotists on their toes.

Yours, hoping for some peace,

Ophelia Rear-Otter (nee Parry)

Next!

Saturday:

And so the day of The Centaur's psychic fair arrives. From my balcony, I see a number of people setting out their stalls on the lawn. Reg, the caretaker an avid country music fan, is setting up some sort of sound system with speakers in the trees. I do hope it's not going to be a day of whingeing cowboy songs.

I saunter down around midday and there are a fair number of people in attendance. There are tarot readers, Feng-shui masters, palmists, homeopaths, psychics, spiritual healers and others whose specialities I've never heard of. Innocuous New Age music, which to me never ever seems to get anywhere, wafts from the speakers. I have to say that it's all rather pleasant and as far as I know harmless.

The fragrant Cordelia is in attendance and I arrange to bump into her.

'Oh, hello,' she says with a winning smile, 'are you going to try out anything that's on offer?'

I immediately think that I wouldn't mind trying her out for a start. That's the trouble with the male mind, even one as old as mine. There's always this little voice in one's head that persistently contradicts one's best efforts at being civilised and decent. The last thing I want is for Cordelia to see that I'm consumed with lust.

'Well, not yet,' I say. 'I'm keeping my options open.'

(Little Voice: 'She's got a lovely pair of tits.')

'I'm not sure that I believe in any of it, but I might try the fortune teller,' she says.

'Oh yes,' I say, 'can't be any harm in that.'

(Little Voice: 'And a nice bum. Wouldn't mind getting my hands round that.')

'You live in the top flat don't you?' she asks.

'Yes right at the top. I've got a lovely view from the balcony.'

(Little Voice: 'And a big double bed where I could give you a right seeing to.')

'Are you OK?' she asks. 'You look a bit feverish.'

(Little Voice: 'Just think of the foreplay. Slowly undressing her...')

I just wish these thoughts would stop so that I can have a proper conversation with her. But no, on they go.

(Little Voice: 'Nice legs too. Imagine those wrapped around you...')

'Oh shut up,' I blurt out before I can stop myself.

'I beg your pardon,' she says, looking surprised and offended.

'Yes, all shut up,' I stammer. 'Hammersmith Palais. All boarded up. Quite a shame really. I passed it on my way to the dentist the other day.'

'You have a dentist in Hammersmith?' she asks, looking at me as if I'm demented.

I *am* feverish now, desperately trying to get myself out of this ridiculous hole that I'm digging. I can feel a prickly heat on my back and my cheeks are burning.

'Oh yes, it's well known for dentists. You know like Hatton Garden for diamonds, Smithfield for meat and..er..er.. Arbroath for kippers.'

'I think you need some shade,' she says and floats away.

She looks over her shoulder once at me with what looks like a mixture of bemusement and pity. Bugger, bugger, bugger. Blown it again.

I see that The Centaur, has a tent set up with a sign outside saying "Thelma — Spiritual Healer and Sensitive" It's little more than a Wendy House and being large of frame, Thelma occupies most of it. She sits at a little camping table and is wearing an elaborate robe embroidered with dragons and unicorns. I'm about to go in to see whether she can cast any light on the mystery of the miniature Eiffel tower that I found in my hoover, when I notice that she already has a client. None other than Jason the cop sitting on a little stool in front of her. He's wearing shorts and trainers with black socks pulled up almost to his knees. He looks decidedly embarrassed and I can't resist peeking in.

'How can I help?' asks Thelma.

'Well, I get very itchy sometimes. You know, like a prickly heat kind of thing. I know I wear a lot of clobber when I'm on duty, but even at home I itch. My mum thinks it might be chives.'

'Hives,' Thelma corrects him. 'No, I don't think it's that. I think your itching could represent your existential angst, your yearning to be at one with the cosmos, your desire to connect with the feminine, your inner child, your warrior spirit.'

Jason looks totally bemused at this torrent of gobbledygook.

'Or,' continues Thelma, 'you might have an excess level of toxins in the lower intestine. Have you considered colonic irrigation?'

'Ooh, is it painful?' asks Jason drawing his chubby knees together defensively.

'No, but it can be a bit messy,' says Thelma. 'In your case though I think it might be helpful to consult my spirit guide, Chief Running Bear.'

'Chief Running Bear?' queries Jason.

'Chief of the Cherokee Nation. He died with honour at the Battle of Wounded..er.. Pride in 1873. Now, please be completely silent.'

Thelma takes a series of deep breaths and her eyes roll up so that only the whites are visible. Then her head lolls forward and she appears to be in a deep coma. Jason fidgets and seems uncertain as to what's coming next. Thelma eventually raises her head and begins intoning in a ridiculous cod American Indian voice.

'As the buffalo roams and the eagle soars,

As the Squirrel... squirrels and the mighty river roars...

Why have you awakened me from my slumbers white eyes?'

'Well, chief, er' stammers Jason

'Running Bear.'

'Well, Chief, I've got this itch,' says Jason. 'It's a bit embarrassing really. As I was telling..er'

'Thelma,' says Thelma helpfully in her normal voice.

'As I was telling Thelma, I've got...'

'Silence, or you will burn in our fires,' says the Chief

'Ooh, sorry,' says Jason nervously scratching his crotch.

The Chief makes a series of elaborate hand signals and continues.

'You wiped out the buffalo, stole our lands, raped our womenfolk and polluted our sacred rivers. You sold us rotgut whiskey and plague-infested blankets. You drove us ever further west to the parched and barren lands of Arizona and Nevada. And as we marched, with heavy hearts, bellies bloated with hunger, you picked us off like rabbits with your fire sticks. You have much to answer for, pink skin.'

"Ere, hang on a minute, Chief,' says Jason indignantly, 'you can't pin all that on me. I've not been to America. The nearest I ever got was joining the Mickey Mouse fan club when I was a kid.'

'Silence!' shouts the Chief, making Jason jump. 'You speak with forked tongue. You have angered the Great Spirit. Before many moons pass, you must be cleansed. The inner man must be purged with the healing waters of the mountain stream.'

He pauses and cups a hand to his ear.

'The beaver calls. I must return to my teepee. As the buffalo roams and the...'

Thelma's head slumps forward and snaps back up again as if she's awakening from a dream.

'He's gone. Was that any help?'

'Oh yes,' says Jason, rising from the stool and starting to back out of the tent.

'Well it looks like a thorough cleansing with colonic irrigation is the answer for you, or perhaps a caffeine enema,' says Thelma. 'I've got someone here who can carry it out.'

'Well, I'll certainly give it some thought,' says Jason, continuing to back out, alternately covering his bum and his nethers with his hands.

I just manage to dodge out of the way as he makes his exit. I take a few paces away and can't help laughing. As I'm doing so, I see Cordelia looking at me from across the lawn and she still has that bemused and pitying look.

I wait a few moments then go in to see Thelma. I show her the miniature Eiffel tower and explain how it buggered up my hoover and that I have no idea where it came from.

She takes it in her hands and taking deep breaths, closes her eyes. For a minute I think I'm going to meet the Chief, but she spares me this.

'I sense loneliness and alienation,' she says. 'Cynicism and despair. An obstinate unwillingness to acknowledge the spiritual, or honour the feminine.'

I can see where this is going. It'll be my supposed mistreatment of Little Owl and my chucking bottles into the wheelie bin next.

'Yes, yes,' I say impatiently, 'but where did it come from?'

She holds it up to her eye, then bangs it down on the table.

'Taiwan,' she says and sweeps out of the tent.

Sunday:

The fair on the lawn continues. I mingle for a while before I go for my weekly shop. I'm stopped in my tracks by the appearance of Little Owl on stilts. She's wearing a sort of medieval outfit with a long skirt covering her real legs and a conical hat perched on her head. She looks like some grotesque wading bird. She has a long feather in her hand which she uses to get people's attention by tickling the back of their heads. When they turn around, she hands them a business card. Quite enterprising really. New Age marketing in action.

Standing in the centre of the lawn and slugging extra-strong lager from cans are a couple of shaven-headed local yobs. They belch noisily and have that aggressive way of continually pushing their heads backward and forward like foraging chickens. They have clearly not come for a consultation with the Chief.

Little Owl approaches from behind and playfully tickles one of them with her long feather. He turns round slowly with a menacing look.

'Fuck off, weirdo,' he shouts, giving her a mighty shove.

She teeters off sideways like a tipsy crane fly, before crashing to the ground in an undignified heap. The next thing I see is the yobbo's legs whipped from under him and Cordelia standing over him with her foot on his neck.

'My, you're brave aren't you? she says. 'Shouldn't you be at Sunday school?'

His mate is already backing away as she lets the yob stagger to his feet, rubbing his neck.

'Now piss off,' she says through clenched teeth and the pair scurry away.

Christ! Who is this woman? If I had really caused her offence yesterday, I could have ended up in a neck brace and traction.

The Vacuum Chamber

Monday:

Work has begun on a new building site next to the flats. I watch from my balcony as the preliminary groundwork is started. It reminds me that during a lull in gigs in the Sixties, I worked on a building site and found it a demoralizing experience.

The whole site was bedeviled with periodic flooding and no one could figure out where the water was coming from. Experts were called in, bore holes sunk and ambitious drainage schemes undertaken. All to no avail. The water still kept coming and in places the site was a dangerous swamp. Enter Mister Peacock, a new site agent with ideas of his own about the mysterious source of the water. Peacock was a very small man with ill-fitting glasses that he had to keep pushing back up the bridge of his nose whenever he spoke. Notebook in hand, he strode around the site in huge galoshes several sizes too big for him.

On one occasion, despite a shouted warning from the foreman, he strode purposefully toward the centre of the site — known to us as The Pit. It was the deepest point of the morass and had achieved near mythic status by almost swallowing a bulldozer whole. Undaunted and ignoring the shouts from the periphery, Peacock strode resolutely on. As he got nearer to the menacing centre, he faltered a little. We held our breath.

He didn't sink as quickly as we had anticipated, but rather majestically like a tired old trawler, fatally holed. He looked pleadingly toward us, pushing his glasses up with his remaining free hand. The morass bubbled in anticipation of a live sacrifice. I think he might have whimpered something, but I was convulsed with laughter. Finally, the foreman shouted, 'Throw him a fucking rope, quick!'

After a considerable struggle, we dragged Peacock from the swamp, less the outsized galoshes. The morass gave a disappointed burp as it digested his footwear and settled back for the next victim.

Peacock didn't appear for a day or two after this, presumably trying to regain his dignity. When he did, however, it was with renewed zeal for the task of solving the water problem. He became convinced that the site was surrounded by some old Victorian water pipes which were leaking. He made our lives a misery, making us dig exploratory holes (which of course filled with water) to unearth the mystery pipes. He would peer down into the water- filled trench as we fished around for the pipes.

'Anything?' he would ask.

'Nothing', came the reply.

And so on to the next bloody trench with Peacock peering down expectantly. This went on for days until I could stand it no longer. Reaching down into yet another water filled hole, I said,

'Ah ha!'

Peacock pushed his glass up and nearly fell into the pit in eager anticipation of the vindication of his theory.

'What is it?' he asked

'Wait', I said and fished around some more.

'Can you feel a pipe?' asked Peacock, hardly able to contain himself

'No,' I said, 'but I think I've got my hand up a mammoth's arse.'

Tuesday:

I live near a famous and very traditional public school. I often see the boys going to and from their lessons and I've occasionally watched cricket matches there. I'm struck by how many of the pupils appear not to be from these shores. Many look to be the sons of Russian oligarchs, Middle Eastern nabobs and Asian potentates. This does credit to the school's marketing department, but I imagine there must be many instances of a clash of cultures.

'Toast me another muffin, Mitsubishi, there's a good fellow. Remember, the jam goes on after the butter.'

'No, no, Azul. It was not acceptable to lop off young Carrington-Smythe's hands merely because he stole your tuck.'

'Oh, well thrown Molotov Minor. Well thro...'

Of course, once the conquest of space gets underway, no doubt the ever-resourceful marketing department, impelled by their Squeers-like headmaster, will go into warp drive to attract pupils from alien cultures. This, in turn, could lead to further misunderstandings.

My Dear Ming the Merciless, Master of all you Survey, Sublime Methane Breather, OBE,

Your son, Ruthless Little-Sh-it, was justifiably beaten for incorrectly parsing a Latin sentence and tweaking a Vulcan's ear. Whilst I can understand your natural desire to protect your son and heir, I do believe that your response in demolishing the school chapel with a death ray was perhaps a little disproportionate, particularly as evensong was in progress at the time. I look forward to seeing you at Sports Day. Will Mrs Merciless be attending?

Headmaster:' Is young Quantum Anomaly attending all lessons?'

Teacher: 'We can't be entirely certain Headmaster. He never seems to be in the same place twice. And when he is, he is often to be seen somewhere else at the same time. Most perplexing'…

Another email from The Anorak, trying to set up an interview. I wouldn't mind if I had been a celeb in the Sixties, but I was an also ran, a mere footnote in history at most. But I know this is not the point for an obsessive like him. He wants me pinned down and collected regardless of my status. I find it quite scary. Makes me feel like a moth.

Church bells again tonight and as jarring as ever.

Wednesday:

I have my hair cut. The hairdresser, who's as camp as Catterick, suggests that it would look better if it were cut really short.

'It would take years off you,' he says. 'I could give it a bit of colour too if you like.'

I agree to the cut, but not the colour. I quite like my pepper and salt look. He proceeds to scalp me and then rubs gel into what hair I've got left, making it stick up. I look as though I've just stuck my finger in the mains.

As I leave the shop, I nearly collide with a kid on a skateboard.

'Hey, look where you're going,' I shout.

'Fuck off coconut head,' he shouts back over his shoulder as he whizzes away.

I bump into the fragrant Cordelia as I'm going into the flats. She looks at my head a little quizzically.

'Mmm, very drastic,' she says. 'Are you thinking of joining a boy band?'

Thursday:

An email from the Reverend Jones:

Dear Mrs Rear-Otter,

I feel bound to say that I find some of your comments a little un-charitable. The bell ringers are a fine group of men and women who work for no money — except a small fee for weddings and funerals — and who strive to enrich and uplift our lives to the greater glory of God.

Before becoming vicar of this parish, I served as an army chaplain in several war zones and witnessed at first hand man's inhumanity to man. That our dedicated bell ringers should be attacked by council operatives with cattle prods or tasers is therefore utterly abhorrent to me and, if I may say so, positively Orwellian. I feel sure that this was a macabre little joke on your part.

As you say you are troubled by the church bells, I assume you that live locally, yet none of my parishioners knows of you — which is un-usual in such a small community. May I once again invite you to one of our services. I think you would enjoy the free and easy atmosphere.

Yours in Christ and Peace
Rev. David Jones.

It looks as though the vicar might suspect a wind-up, but I'll fire one more shot across his bows and call it a day.

Dear Padre,

I was interested to learn that you have served in several war zones, since I think this might go to the heart of the matter. Is it possible that as a result of your proximity to combat, that you may have perforated ear drums and are therefore not fully able to appreciate how awful your bell ringers are? There's no shame in being tone deaf. Look how well Bob Geldof has coped.

Thank -you for your invitation to attend the church, but I think I'll stick to the morning service on the long wave if you don't mind. The thought of the happy-clappy hysteria in a free and easy atmosphere makes me shudder. It is precisely this lack of decorum that has allowed a gang of cloth-eared yokels to take over your belfry of a Tuesday night and torment the town with audio terrorism.

Finally, my name is not known in the parish, because I changed it by deed poll some years ago following my husband Ifor's mysterious demise. He was found garroted by a washing line in a neighbour's garden. The police jumped to the spurious conclusion that he was responsible for a spate of thefts of women's underwear locally, solely because he was clutching a corset and had a pair of floral knickers in his pocket at the time. I still miss his swanee whistle.

Yours,

Ophelia Rear-Otter (Mrs)

I'm beginning to like Ophelia.

Friday:

A windfall in the post. I've won twenty five pounds on a twenty pound premium bond that I bought thirty years ago. My elation is short-lived however when I calculate that this represents a 0.0000001 percent return on my investment. Talk about a con. Where has all the money gone?

When I was at school, at the dawn of the so-called atomic age, I remember a science teacher telling us that before long electricity would be so easily and cheaply produced using nuclear something or the other, that it would hardly be worth sending out any bills. I might get Ophelia to instigate an ironic correspondence with my electricity supplier on this subject. But then what's the point? They're all robber barons anyway.

And while I'm in rant mode, what about water charges? We live on an island that has more than its fair share of rain. Most of it can be easily captured before it runs into the sea. Yet we're charged the earth for it.

Air will be next. Rapacious capitalism knows no bounds. If you don't pay your air bill, you'll be forced to enter a government approved vacuum chamber and join other miscreants struggling for a last gasp like stranded goldfish, as fat cat Harley Street quacks eagerly check your compulsory organ donor card and charity shops squabble over the threadbare clothes that you probably bought from them in the first place because you've been impoverished by utility bills.

With these happy thoughts in mind, I practice the sax.

Saturday:

Another pub gig with the dreaded Suicidal Gerbils. The guitarist has added a second layer to the box of tricks that he periodically stabs at with his foot. I can't discern any difference in his playing, or the sound. It's all awful.

Shards and Brint are in the audience.

'Jeez man, what a player,' says Brint, buying me a welcome pint. 'Do you think I could ever get to play like that?'

I know that he's not referring to my masterly sax work, but to the guitarist's histrionics.

'Only if you're not careful and stuff play dough in your ears,' I tell him.

I return home, ears ringing and sit out on the balcony with a glass or two, breathing air while it's still free.

Sunday:

I watch an "in-depth" interview on TV with a famous footballer and his pop star wife. I'm amazed at how dim they seem, but also how they speak a form of English that is almost incomprehensible. "You know" , "like" and "know what I mean", feature prominently in their discourse.

They are fabulously wealthy and one could never imagine that they might ever have to resort to buying jobs lots of suspect mince, or end up in the vacuum chamber. I'll bet they can buy any amount of paracetamol, but regrettably will never oblige us by topping themselves.

Balancing Dogs

Monday:

Wash day. I load my ancient washing machine and for the umpteenth time puzzle over which knobs to press and how much powder to put in. Finally, I make my usual random selection in the hope that my clothes won't be shredded or shrunk to nothing. The machine seems to hesitate for a few moments as if it's not sure what to make of my selection, then begins to whirr and chortle reassuringly.

I set about *The Times* crossword with my usual optimism. I've run out of bread, so I have to be content with the dreaded Ryvita with my boiled egg. However hard one may try, one can't make soldiers out of Ryvita. Shards, or bits of mosaic maybe — soldiers, no.

The washing machine falls silent and I stare at it, willing it to life. Nothing. I do what I often do when cocky machines conspire against me. I kick it. It gives a few truculent clicks and then goes into its spin cycle. *'There, that showed you,'* I think as I return to the crossword.

As I continue to struggle with one across, I can hear the machine spinning away in the background. I actually solve three clues before I become aware that the machine is still spinning at an ever increasing rate. Suddenly, it breaks from its moorings and starts jitterbugging round the kitchen like a demented Dalek. Dirty water is pumping from its pipes and starting to head for the lounge. My first thought is to unplug it, but I have no idea where the plug is. My second thought is that if I'm standing in the water and the wires are jerked out of the back of the machine, I'll be toast, or even Ryvita. I rush to the meter cupboard and turn the power off. The machine convulses and twitches like a laboratory frog, before coming to rest in the middle of the kitchen, still spewing water.

Mop and bucket, mucket and slop. Not an auspicious start to the week. I feel like the sorcerer's apprentice. I call an engineer who cheerfully tells me there's a seventy-five pounds call out charge. Of course, when he arrives he condemns the machine outright.

'Not worth even opening her up,' he says. 'I can do you a new one for three hundred and I'll waive the call out charge and get your dirty washing back.'

Bang goes my dream of upgrading the Fiesta.

Tuesday:

A rare event for this little town. A visit from the Latvian State Circus. Why we should be so honoured is a mystery, but posters advertising this have been up for some time on many of the derelict shops in the High Street. I wander down to the municipal park where they have set up their tatty marquee and buy a ticket for Thursday night's performance. I don't especially like circuses, never have. I find clowns scary rather than funny and I do worry about being crushed by a disgruntled elephant or trampled on by a stampede of bullied camels or whatever. But I do need to get out more, so I'll grit my teeth and try to enjoy it. It could be a cultural experience since I have no memory of ever having seen any Latvians in the flesh.

While I'm in town, I decide to buy a new cartridge for my printer, because I've been sending out letters in barely visible sepia for some months. I'm astonished to discover that the cartridge costs half of what I paid for the printer. The lad behind the counter drags himself away from slaying dragons and goblins on a games console to inform me that I can have a refilled cartridge for half the price.

'Are they OK?' I ask

'Oh yeah,' he says, 'we sell loads of 'em.'

Back home I install the refilled cartridge. I feel quite proud of myself for having done this. I print out a letter to my home insurance company regarding the washing machine incident. It comes out in a rather fetching violet colour. I try again and this time it's sort of purple-ish. I imagine that it's excitedly working its way through the visible spectrum before reluctantly settling on boring old black. I'll give it time to settle down before I kick it.

Wednesday:

From my balcony, I spot Cordelia and Toyboy sitting on the lawn. They are in earnest conversation and at one point, she throws her arms around him and gives him a big hug. I imagine that he's just proposed and I'm filled with senseless jealousy. I'm pretty sure that if I hadn't stupidly blown it a few times, I could have got off with Cordelia.

I go down to collect my morning paper and the Fiesta won't start. I turn the engine over and the starter motor, or whatever it is that does this, seems to go '*Oh, no,no,no,no,no...ick.*' I try again. Same thing only slower and slower. I lift the bonnet as if I know what's under it and jiggle a few tubes and wires. No deal. Same refusals followed by an "ick".

April sashays out, dressed and made up to the nines. She's twirling a silly parasol.

'Got a problem?' she asks in a throaty voice.

I'm tempted to deny this and say that on the contrary I'm just tuning the engine, but I admit that I can't start the car.

'In a previous life I used to be a mechanic. I'll have a look,' she says.

I watch helplessly as she fiddles around under the bonnet. I notice that her hands, although well manicured, are still very masculine and large. Short of limb replacement, I can't see how gender re-assignment can ever get round this problem.

'Try it now,' she says.

I give it a go and the old banger springs into life, or at least its stuttering version of it.

'Loose battery terminal,' she says. 'Have you got any wipes?'

Thursday:

And so to the circus on a stormy rain-lashed night. I feel quite excited as I approach the not so big top. Before going in the tent, I throw caution to the wind and buy a cola, a giant bag of popcorn and a toffee apple. A clown is collecting tickets at the entrance.

'Happier days, ha ha, happier days,' he says in a thick accent as he collects the tickets.

Just as I'm about to hand my ticket over, there's a great commotion to one side. Thelma (*aka* The Centaur), Little Owl and a few others that I remember seeing at the fair on the lawn are waving placards and shouting. Thelma is at the forefront with a placard saying "Don't watch the balancing dogs." Others read, "Animals are not for fun" and "Homeopaths against cruelty". Little Owl, blanketed as usual, is pacing the periphery with her placard which says "Run Away from the Circus". This makes me smile, but I can't imagine that she thought of this herself, or intends it to be humorous. I spot Buzz, but he's hovering in the background taking no part in the picket.

Once inside, I settle on a long wooden bench seat. I take a big bite of the toffee apple. A thousand memories come flooding back; days at the seaside, donkey rides, candy floss, kiss-me-quick hats and all the fun of the fair. When I try to detach my mouth from the apple, I find that my upper teeth seem to be stuck. As I struggle with the apple, spilling popcorn and cola all around me, Cyclops pushes past with two myopic children in tow. She looks at me pityingly as I try to say hello with an apple on a stick in my gob.

'Big baby,' she snorts.

I manage to free myself from the apple and drop it discreetly behind me. Maybe Latvians use mastic or dental fixative instead of real toffee.

A band strikes up. Accordion, clarinet and drums. The musicians look thoroughly disreputable, as if they might have sold black market penicillin at one time. The show begins with the ticket-collecting clown being sprayed with a water pistol, doused in flour and generally humiliated by a rather attractive girl in a skimpy sequined outfit. It's utterly boring and predictable, but the children, who make up the bulk of the audience, seem to enjoy it.

A ringmaster appears, looking even more disreputable than the band. He has a pencil-thin moustache and dabs at his mouth with a frilly hanky between announcements. He informs us that next up is Tolstoy's Amazing Poodles. This act is presumably the subject of The Centaur's wrath.

The band plays some cod French music and a dour looking Slav leads on a variety of poodles, from very small to quite large. All are immaculately quaffed, like suburban hedges. They jump through hoops of fire, do somersaults and generally bore the pants off me. I'm beginning to remember all the reasons that I dislike circuses. Then Tolstoy, who doesn't look as though he ever had a book in him, lines all the poodles up at one side of the ring. The drummer starts a slow roll, the lights dim a little and the ringmaster appears.

'Ladeez and gentlemen, boys anda girls. Pleeze. Monsieur Tolstoy, who has performed before the crowned heads of Europe and the Maharaja of Jodhpur, will now attempt to recreate the pyramid at Gaza with a living, breathing, wall of poodles. Complete silence is essential. Monsieur Tolstoy.'

Tolstoy clicks his fingers and the largest of the dogs form a line. More finger clicks and the next size down spring onto their backs and so on until the tiniest poodles are at the top of a quivering edifice. One minute poodle remains to top off the triumph. Tolstoy goes into a bit of shtick trying to coax it up the slopes of the pyramid. "Ohs" and "ahs" from the audience as it coyly backs away from his beckoning fingers. Will it? Won't it? Eventually it springs forward and clambers over its colleagues to the top. Ta-ra! — A cymbal crash and long G from the band.

At this moment, Thelma and her band of protesters enter the tent with their placards, shouting and screaming.

'Don't watch the balancing dogs,' they cry, as they make their way to the centre.

The pyramid quivers and collapses in a heap of poodles. They then scatter in all directions, pursued by a frantic Tolstoy. General mayhem ensues, with the ringmaster blowing a whistle and cracking a whip. The band for reasons best known to themselves go into a selection Viennese waltzes , while Thelma and friends parade triumphantly round the ring. A chorus of boos and hissing is directed at them together with a shower of popcorn cartons and other missiles. I see Little Owl being slapped by the sequined girl and a homeopath's leg being rogered by one of the larger poodles. I haven't laughed so much in years. The tears stream down my face and I'm in fear of busting something internally. Suddenly, the noise diminishes. The band splutter to a halt and then there is almost complete silence. The melee in the ring has become static, like a tableau. I wipe my eyes and look to see what has caused this.

It's a lion. It surveys the assemblage with a noble, but weary look, like a bored judge hearing yet another false alibi.

'Nobodies move,' hisses the ringmaster through his teeth. 'Remain all completely still, pleeze.'

The lion paces around sniffing at the frozen figures. It finally stops before Thelma and then paces around her sniffing the air. She has turned ashen and I notice that the placard she is holding is shaking. The lion circles her again and I wonder if it perhaps has a folk memory of being hunted by centaurs in ancient times. It stops again and then cocks its hind leg and urinates over her. To give her credit, she doesn't budge an inch during this dousing, but stares stoically straight ahead.

A man appears walking slowly toward the lion. He's carrying a halter and what looks like the best part of a goat carcass. The lion meekly submits to having the halter placed over its head and is led off with the goat between its jaws. The band give another ta-ra as if the whole thing was planned.

As Thelma and her party are being shoo-ed and shoved out of the ring to a chorus of boos, one whole side of the tent suddenly lifts up and flaps madly in the wind. For a fleeting moment, I'm sure that I see Buzz running away into the darkness.

Despite the ringmaster's pleas to remain seated, the show is clearly over and people begin scurrying out of the tent. As I exit, I see a man with the remains of a Latvian toffee apple stuck to the back of his coat. He'll probably need a power tool to get it off.

Friday:

On my way to the paper shop I see Buzz and Thelma about to get into their BMW.

'Did you enjoy the circus?' I ask and then give my best impression of a snarl.

Thelma gives me a withering look and Buzz looks a bit shamefaced.

'I think you cut the tent ropes Buzz,' I say. 'I saw you running away. And I think you were somehow responsible for the lion's untimely appearance.'

'Why would I do a thing like that mate?' he says getting into the car.

''Cos you're a misguided little shit that's why,' I say. 'It's pure luck that nobody was injured and your stupid missus only got pissed on instead of being eaten. But then thinking about it, I imagine even a mangy old Latvian lion has got some discrimination.'

They roar off in the car and I feel quite brave and pleased with myself.

Saturday:

I spend some time reading the manual for the new washing machine. Any instructions that begin with the word "simply" are always unnecessarily complex and these are no exception. I'm also miffed by the pious bullshit about saving energy and water. What about the illuminated fountains in Trafalgar Square? They probably consume more energy and water in a day than I would use in three lifetimes, but I bet the mayor of London doesn't get lectured about it by washing machine companies. I might just go down to the river and bash my smalls on a rock.

Sunday:

I notice Toyboy arriving accompanied by another Adonis of about the same age. A little later, I see them on the lawn with Cordelia. She has her arms around both of them and is clearly very happy. Blimey, I don't stand a chance there. I resolve to give up lusting after Cordelia — it's a lost cause.

On my way to the car to go to the mini-market, I bump into Reg the caretaker. Forgetting my earlier resolve, I decide to pump him about Cordelia's love life.

'What's the deal with our new resident's love life?' I ask him in a man-to-man sort of way.

Reg taps his nose.

'That's for me to know and you to find out,' he says.

Cocky bugger.

Lord Lucan

Monday:

I get a letter from the Department for Work and Pensions trumpeting a rise of thirty four pence a week in my state pension. I won't let this windfall go to my head, however, and will continue to hunt down bargains for my now full to bursting freezer and to put low fat spread only on one slice of the bread in a sandwich.

A funny old day. I can't seem to settle. I try the crossword, but can't get anywhere with it. Truth be told, I'm bored. I need a bit of spice in my life, a certain *je ne sais quoi*, a bit of frisson. Thirty four pence a week won't do it that's for sure.

The flat's a tip, but I can't be arsed to clean it. I've run out of books to read and there are no gigs on the horizon. There's something eating at me, some unfulfilled desire or itch. It could be sex of course, since my love life has been on hold for a while. But aside from the fragrant Cordelia, no one has stirred my loins for some time. But then she's a lost cause, what with her Adonis Twins. I ponder and ponder and then it comes to me in a flash. I haven't been to Ireland for about four years. That's what I'm missing. For me, it's the only place on the planet where one can re-charge one's creative and spiritual batteries, quaff stout and re-tune a sense of the ridiculous. Besides, I'm from Irish stock and with the help of a sentimental American website, festooned with shamrocks, I have recently been able to trace my roots back to Brian Boru and beyond to the King of the Leprechauns no less.

I go on-line to a company I've used before and lo and behold they have a late cancellation and a discount price for a small cottage in West Cork starting this very Saturday. It's described as being in a very remote location, but with all mod cons plus an open fire.

Throwing caution to the wind, but remembering that I'm currently seventeen pounds sixty eight pence better off per annum, I book it. The deal includes a compact car and airfare. The only drawback is that the flight is from Stanstead with an airline that would charge for breathing if it could. The destination is Kerry County airport, rather than Cork, but no matter, now I have something to look forward to.

I can already taste the soda bread and smell the peat smoldering in the hearth . It would be nice if I were going with a significant other and for a while I consider trying a few ex-girlfriends, or even wives, but then I think that this could be an adventure just for me. Besides, I can practise the sax to my heart's content without worrying about disturbing anyone — and I won't get nagged about my Guinness consumption.

Tuesday:

Past experience tells me that, in general, airlines don't like a big saxophone case taken on as hand luggage, presumably because it looks as though it could contain a rocket launcher or a diminutive terrorist. Over the years, I've had no end of arguments over this and was once persuaded by a Canadian airline that they would take special care of my sax in the hold. As I sat on the plane when it landed, I watched in horror as my sax was flung from the hold, missing the luggage trailer altogether and bouncing on the runway. This seemed to amuse the moonlighting lumberjack luggage handlers no end and they made a game of trying to fling it back on the trailer, failing several times before it eventually lodged itself between some cases.

I contact the travel company who tell me that I can take the sax on board to Ireland, but I have to book an extra seat for it. I know that I've already whittled away the beneficence of the Department for Work and Pensions and my groceries for the next six months, but I agree to do so.

'What name shall I book the extra seat in?' asks the very helpful girl.

'Well, it's a saxophone,' I say, 'does it have to have a name?'

'Fraid so,' she says. 'Just think of anything that we can print on the ticket and boarding pass.'

I pause for a moment or two.

'Call it Lord Lucan,' I tell her.

'OK, that's fine,' she says, clearly not having heard of the missing peer.

Going on-line later, I discover that parking my car at the airport for a week is going to cost more than my airline ticket. Oh, sod it, I'm committed now. When I get back, I'll just have to re-activate all the cryogenically preserved mince and other animal parts in my freezer and cut down on Fair Trade Angolan Chardonnay.

Wednesday:

After some concentration, I manage to persuade the new washing machine to perform. I warily hook up the bungee line and hang my washing on it. My black T shirts are speckled with bits of undissolved washing powder and are still very wet. The machine clearly didn't rinse or spin properly. Oh well, when the T shirts are dry I'll run the hoover over them.

Thursday:

A visit to a local travel agent to get some Euros. I only need a modest amount, but the girl at the exchange desk wants to know my full name, address and also have some proof of identity.

'Why all this for such a small amount? I query.

'Money laundering,' she says, as if any fool would know that.

I tell her that I can barely programme my new washing machine to sluice through a few T shirts and socks, so laundering money would be a spectacular achievement for me. I also say that I find it slightly insulting to be treated as if I might be a drug baron or an international spiv. Like the mini-market embryo, she obviously has a secret buzzer and a manager type is summoned. She appears at my side, dressed a bit like a hostess from a no frills airline.

She goes into a long spiel about government regulations and the need for vigilance against international terrorism. It's this last bit that gets to me and I start to lose it. I fight against it for a moment or two as she drones on, but it's no good. A kind of mist envelops me and my head buzzes with all the bollocks about health and safety, the hectoring about saving energy, re-cycling to save the planet and the way in which we all seem increasingly to be spied on by a variety of government agencies. My response is wholly disproportionate, but I've lost it.

'Listen,' I say, 'I hardly think my five hundred Euros are going to trigger the computers at GCHQ and the CIA. I can't imagine that there will be any border alerts over such a piddling sum. And another thing: if we and our American masters weren't bombing the shite out of no-mads so that we can grab their oil, there wouldn't be any need for vigilance.'

'If you're going to be abusive,' the manageress says, 'then I'll have to call the police.'

'Don't worry,' I say, 'keep your Euros, I'll take beads instead.'

With that, I sweep out of the shop. Euro-less.

Friday:

For me, packing for a trip is quite an easy matter since I have very few clothes. I settle Lord Lucan in his case and pack some socks, pants and a sweater around him for extra padding and to cut down what I'll put in my cabin bag. I'm determined not to give the money-grabbing airline an excuse for charging me for excess baggage.

I do some last minute shopping for toiletries and things I probably won't need, such as anti-diarrhoea tablets and sunscreen.

Saturday:

My flight is at eight am, so I have to be up at around four. I double check that I've got all the necessary ID and tickets, various medications, a collection of CDs and a couple of books. Thankfully, the little Fiesta starts first time and I begin the schlep around the charming M25. Even at this early hour, this is a nerve-wracking experience as I'm passed on both sides by dirty great juggernauts from all over Europe. For a while, I'm stuck in the middle lane and at one point I look in my rear view mirror and all I can see is the name badge of a truck that seems to be only inches away from my bumper. After about two hours I arrive at Stanstead Airport and park the car. This is followed by a walk of about a quarter of a mile to the shuttle bus pick up point.

At the check-in desk the girl looks at my sax and tells me that it will have to go in the hold. I explain that I've bought an extra seat for it. She looks disappointed as if I've robbed the airline of the pleasure of smashing it up. Before I hand her my passport, she glances at one of the the tickets and suddenly becomes quite deferential.

'Thank you my lord, 'she says, almost curtseying, 'will you be re-quiring an in-flight meal?'

'No, I'm OK thanks,' I say. I point to the sax and add,

'He had a full English before we left, kidneys and all. He's a stickler for that.'

Once she sees my passport, the smile instantly leaves her face as she realises that it's the sax that's got the blue blood. I'm told that I should have called it "A.N Other" so that they would know that it's a musical instrument. I explain that I wasn't told this and after several tuts she grudgingly issues two boarding cards.

Next stop is the x-ray machine and the search for explosives disguised as shampoo. The sax goes through and I'm fully expecting alarm bells to ring because it could so easily be mistaken for a Kalashnikov or a grenade launcher. Nothing. Then my little cabin bag goes through and my traveller's cork screw is confiscated together with my nail clippers. This must be an example of the vigilance that the travel agent spoke of.

The flight is called and there's a walk of what seems a couple of miles to the plane. Once on board, the friendly cabin attendant invites me to put the sax in the overhead locker. I'm tempted to say that Lord Lucan gets claustrophobic, but think better of it. I decline her offer and I put him on the seat and fasten his seat belt. I wonder if he'll be offered an in-flight meal, or perhaps a free drink that I can quaff. Neither of these is forthcoming and I realise that the golden age of refined air travel is well and truly dead. We'll be lucky to get a slap on the wrist and a glass of warm water.

The first time that I flew to Kerry airport many years ago, it had a grass runway and a collection of sheds. Today it has a tarmac runway and a collection of sheds. I go to the car hire desk and the girl checks my voucher, runs my credit card through and hands me some keys. No fuss, no body search, no ID and a genuine smile.

'It's in line B in the car park' she tells me. 'You can't miss it, it's yellow and very small.'

I find the car and it's so compact that by the time I've pushed the driving seat back far enough for me to get my knees from around my neck, my head seems to be only inches away from the rear window.

So, off I go heading for the Beara Peninsula and my dream cottage. No juggernauts, no motorways, minimal traffic and spectacular scenery. On the way, I stop off in the lovely town of Kenmare to get some Euros and buy some groceries. At the bank, I'm not asked for ID or treated as if I were an anarchist, or a threat to world order. In the little supermarket, the Chinese girl at the deli counter and the Polish girl at the checkout are very helpful and speak with Irish accents. It'll only take a generation before their progeny will be totally absorbed, playing Gaelic football and fighting among themselves.

I have instructions to call into the post office in the tiny village of Ardgroom and ask for John Shea, the owner of the cottage. I arrive and discover that it's not only a post office, but also a petrol station, internet café, grocery store and quite possibly an undertakers. John himself is there right enough and after the best cup of coffee I've tasted in years, he invites me to follow him in his four-by-four to the cottage. We travel along a single track road for a couple of miles and then turn off onto a rugged track that winds up the side of a mountain for a further mile. All this is done at breakneck speed and I'm fearful that the little yellow car will rattle to death. *

Eventually, we arrive at the cottage and John proudly shows me round and explains how to use the various appliances, which include, joy of joys, a dishwasher. There's soda bread and bacon, eggs, sausages, white pudding, milk and butter in the fridge and a supply of logs in an outbuilding and slabs of peat in the hearth. John leaves and there I am, halfway up a mountain with just Lord Lucan and several hundred sheep dotted across the mountain for company.

It's a fine evening and I sit outside munching on soda bread and Galtee cheese, washed down with quite a nice chardonnay purchased in Kenmare. The views across the Kenmare river to the mountains of Kerry beyond are stunning and my old heart sings. Later, I light a peat fire and listen to some music, before tumbling into a very comfortable bed, whence I dream of someone called Another.

Sunday:

The drummer hasn't quite got it right. He rattles on for a bit on the snare, then stops, then speeds up and slows down. Every now and then there's a deep boom of timpani rolls and a clash of cymbals. I struggle to bring this to some order. After all, I'm a classically trained musician and a session man of long and bitter experience. Now, unbidden, the strings come in howling like banshees and the woodwind have started a staccato, unruly riff. I wave my baton frantically, but to no avail. Now the brass take up the chase, with the trombonists stretching their arms and puckering their lips to get to the lowest notes. A particularly loud roll on the timps brings me to consciousness and I realise that there's a storm raging around the cottage.

For many people, this would be a disappointment at the beginning of a holiday. For me, however, it only heightens a sense of cosiness, isolation and adventure. I've got plenty to eat, lots of fuel and Lord Lucan to put through his paces. I look out and it's raining stair rods and what trees there are on the mountain are bent nearly double in the wind. I can no longer see the Kenmare river or the mountains beyond. As I prepare a good old Irish fry up, I feel utterly at peace with the world and myself. I'm home.

Jubilee Jones

Monday:

The storm lasted for most of the day yesterday and I loved every minute of it. I lit a fire and the peat spluttered away in the hearth, I knelt before it to give it a bit of a blow and a sudden gust of wind came down the chimney howling like a train and blew clouds of soot into the room. Eventually, there was a nice fire going and I settled down for a read, my only concern being what to have for lunch and whether I could make it to the local pub in the evening for my first taste of real Guinness in an age.

As I was reading, I thought that I saw a figure flit past a window. I dismissed this as probably a bent over bush and continued reading. Then I saw it again. A head bobbed up and then disappeared. I got up and forcing the back door open against the wind, peered around. A disreputable looking border collie, bent low, scuttled out of sight behind an outbuilding. Then, out of the mist, walking slowly toward me with faltering steps came what looked like The Scarecrow from the *Wizard of Oz*. He had an old trilby on and a battered and ragged overcoat tied with string. There may even have been straw poking from under his hat. He was carrying a large shopping bag.

I'd like to say that I don't scare easily, but the fact is I do. So, there's me, with not a drop of stout having yet passed my lips, seeing things. I fully expected to see Cowardly Lion, Tin Man and Dorothy. Perhaps the collie was an updated version of Toto. Now I knew I wasn't in Surrey. I was about to slam the door and have a serious reality check when the scarecrow spoke.

'I'm Paddy, John Shea's father, just up to check on the sheep and to deliver a message. Will I have a cup of tea?'

I understood that this wasn't really a question and beckoned him in.

'God bless all here. It's a soft day, so it is,' he said taking off his hat and shaking the water out of it. 'But I see you have a nice fire going and plenty to eat no doubt. You'll be as snug as a bug until they get the road fixed.'

'The road? I asked.

'Yes, that's the message. The road between here and the village was washed away overnight, down by the little stone bridge. John will be up here tomorrow with some men to fix it — weather permitting.'

'But how did you get up here?' I asked.

'Why, I walked. I do it most days, except some Fridays when I cut the grass at the church.'

No wonder the English have never been able to subdue the Irish. Here's a man of at least seventy-five years old, who has walked two or three miles in a tempest to check on his sheep and tell me about the road. The womenfolk are an even tougher breed and I remember reading somewhere that they were once sent into battle first to frighten the enemy.

'So, John sends his apologies and hopes the enclosed will bring a little comfort until normal service is resumed. A little of the black stuff, if you'll pardon the expression.'

He plonked the shopping bag down on the table and I saw that it contained a dozen cans of Guinness. Not the same as a thoughtfully drawn pint, but most welcome.

Several cups of tea later and having given me his whole family history, Paddy left and I watched him pick his way down the mountain toward the village. The last thing I saw was the black and white tail of his collie disappear into the mist.

Some time later, I went to the bathroom and on looking in the mirror discovered that my face was completely black from the soot that had blown down the chimney. I realised that I had conducted the whole conversation with the Paddy while looking like a black and white minstrel and he hadn't commented. Not a word. Except perhaps to ask my pardon for his description of the Guinness.

Today, the storm has blown itself out, although it's still a bit blustery. The view across Kenmare bay to the mountains beyond has returned. After breakfast, I decide to take a walk to see whether the road repairs are under way. Eventually, I come across three men sitting on a wall. They are staring down into a gaping hole in the road. It's five feet deep, as much across and partially filled with water. We exchange greetings and I comment on the size of the hole.

'It's deep enough,' says one of them. 'Pat here swears he saw a kangaroo pop its head out of the water just a minute ago. But he's a powerful thinker at times.'

We all have a laugh and then a large tipper lorry arrives with John at the wheel. After some manoeuvring, he backs the lorry near the hole and tips a pile of rubble into it. Once this is done and the dust has settled, we all gather round the hole to see what effect this has had.

There are strange gurglings coming from the hole as the rubble finds its level about a third of the way up. I almost expect to hear a satisfied belch.

'It'll be done by this afternoon,' says John. 'If you drive over it later, get a bit of a speed up first.'

On this reassuring advice, I decide to walk on into the village for a pint or two and to buy some Shea soda bread.

By the time I arrive at the pub, I'm knackered and the Guinness is very welcome. I'm the only customer and the barman, who tells me he once worked in Slough, gets most of my history out of me before I've finished the first pint.

The walk back up the mountain to the cottage takes me the best part of an hour with frequent stops to admire the view and give the rattling in my chest time to settle down to an acceptable wheeze. I pass the road crew who are applying tarmac to the repaired hole.

'Give it an hour or two,' says one of the men. 'Or better still, leave it till the morning before you drive over it.'

It's a beautiful evening and I decide to practice the sax outside. The nearest house is over three miles away so I won't be disturbing anyone. I tootle a few high notes and I'm amazed to see all the sheep on the mountain stampede. When I stop, they stop. When I start, off they go again like lemmings. This amuses me for a little while, until I realise that they might come to some serious harm and I go inside to finish playing.

After my exertions, I have an early night.

Tuesday:

A lovely day. Not a cloud in the sky and the river sparkles and the mountains look imposing and majestic. The world, or at least this far-flung corner of it, is my oyster. So I jump in the little yellow car and rattle down the track. It's a bit like being in a tin can. Every bump, and there are many, causes an alarming metallic boom from the car. As advised by John, I increase my speed as I approach the former abyss and hit it at about fifty miles per hour. There is a sudden cessation of noise, a peaceful interlude, before I realise that I'm airborne. The little car clatters to earth some distance from the hole and it's all I can do to prevent it careering into the bog that borders the track. I stop the car and go back to inspect the repairs. What John and his crew have done is to create a perfect ramp rather than a level surface. I can imagine kids on skateboards having endless fun with it.

I fill up with Shea's petrol, have another cup of great coffee and a disgraceful cream cake, then drive out of the village. I'm heading for the Healey Pass, about which I've heard much. At the little village of Lauragh I see the sign for the pass and take the narrow road. It winds up and up, passing a few houses, meadows and hedgerows full of flowering fuchsias. The little yellow car struggles a bit, but I'm just able to overtake an intrepid cyclist, his legs going like egg beaters as he labours up the climb. After many bends, I reach the summit and the views are spectacular. I can also see the road snaking its way down to Adrigole on the east coast of the peninsula and I'm thankful that it's downhill all the way.

I pull into a layby where there is a little shop called Don's Mountain Cabin. ("Open 10am to 6pm — weather permitting") Behind the counter, almost hidden by stuffed toys, postcards and souvenirs of many hues, a man is seated. He has three strands of hair carefully arranged on his otherwise bald head. This turns out to be none other than Don, the proprietor. I imagine that it's a pretty precarious living running this establishment on the top of a mountain and I feel obliged to buy a coffee and a set of useless coasters wishing me the best of Irish luck.

As I'm going back to the car, a minibus pulls in and disgorges a bunch of elderly tourists. They are obviously American. The men all seem to be wearing check trousers and what look like golfing shoes. One of the men approaches me.

'Excuse me sir. Would you mind taking a photo of my wife and me?'

I agree and they position themselves with the views as a backdrop. I fiddle with their camera and then it clicks, so I presume it has worked.

'Take two or three,' he says.

So I do so and they thank me. As I'm about to get in the car, I hear the man say,

'Stupid Mick. He didn't even take the lens cap off.'

The road down to Adrigole is hairy but fun. Hairpin bend upon hairpin bend. The little yellow car doesn't seem to mind this at all. I have a pint of stout and an Irish ploughman's lunch at a pub in the village. The only discernible difference between an Irish and English ploughman's tastes seems to be the inclusion of a side order of very nice chips.

I can't resist re-tracing my journey in the opposite direction. When I reach the summit of the pass, the weather has changed dramatically. The wind has got up and there are dark and menacing clouds in the sky. I sit in the car admiring what I can see of the views and then the rain starts. I scuttle across to Don's Cabin and have another coffee. Don advises me to stay put until the rain eases up.

'It can be awful treacherous, particularly if the road gets washed out,' he tells me.

I just hope they don't get John's road crew up here to repair it, otherwise I could see coach loads of Americans plummeting to oblivion, cursing the stupid Micks on their way down.. The rain eases up and as I descend back to Lauragh, it starts to be a nice day again. Irish weather, like its people, is as unpredictable as the fate of Schrodinger's cat.

Back at the cottage, after having gingerly negotiated the ramp on the way up, I light a fire and settle down with a can or two of Guinness and listen to a CD of Jacqueline du Pre playing Elgar's cello concerto. Bliss.

Wednesday:

Another fine day. I decide to drive round the Beara peninsula. The very narrow road winds round the headland behind the village and in places the drop to the sea is several hundred feet. Only a low wall separates one from oblivion. Sheep amble across the road from time to time and then at one point the road is blocked by a very large cow that shows no inclination to give way. I honk the horn and bang on the car door.

The cow is unmoved, so I get out of the car and walk toward it making shooing motions with my arms. At this point the cow turns and looks directly at me with a quite venomous expression. It's then that I notice that where an udder should be there is instead the full male equipment of a bull. The distance between me and the car is perhaps fifty yards, but I cover this in record time. Once back in the car, heart pounding, I'm thinking that I might have to go backwards quite quickly just in case the bull decides to toss me and the little yellow car over the wall and into the boiling sea below. Thankfully, the bull hasn't moved, but is still staring at me with evil intent. Then with a toss of its head and a snort, it ambles off into a field, its massive balls swinging from side to side. I continue on my way and a little later see two men with sticks and rope, running down the road, presumably out to catch the bull.

After several miles and the most stunning views and challenging driving, I drop down into Castletownbere, an important fishing port and a nice little town. With Bantry bay on my right, I proceed along the coast to Glengariff and onward, heading for Kenmare. On the way, I come to the pretty village of Bonane and I'm surprised to see that it has a *chocolatier's* shop. I can't resist popping in, if only out curiosity as to how it comes to be there and how it can possibly make a living in this tiny village.

The shop is owned by one Benoit Lorge, a native of Lorraine in France and a renowned chef and chocolate maker who sells his products to all the best hotels. I buy a small selection which is packaged in an elegant little box. I'm not a chocoholic, but as I bite into these little creations, the taste and texture are simply marvellous. Ireland is full of such surprises. One more awaits me.

By the time I arrive in Kenmare, it's mid-afternoon. After scoffing all the chocolates, I'm not hungry, but I think a drop of the black stuff won't go amiss. I make to cross the road to a pub when I'm nearly run down by an ancient Rolls Royce. One of its huge wing mirrors brushes my arm sending me spinning to the ground. As I get up and dust myself off, the car stops and a uniformed chauffeur gets out to enquire after my health.

'I'm OK,' I tell him, 'I didn't see you.'

'Well that's understandable,' he says, 'it's a very quiet motor.'

The rear passenger door of the car opens and strange figure emerges, calling my name. He's portly, red-faced and wearing plus fours and a sort of shooting jacket. He's nearly bald, but has strands of red hair that lattice the top of his head, making it look like one of the decorative chocolates I've just eaten.

'Jones,' he says, extending his hand which I shake. 'Jubilee Jones. We were at school together. Don't you remember?'

I look puzzled and he moves a bit closer, as if not wanting to be over-heard by the chauffeur who's hovering at a respectful distance.

'Jubbles. That's what they used to call me,' he whispers. 'Jubbles?'

I pause for a moment to give the old data banks time to shuffle through this information. Then I remember a strange red-haired boy who took even less interest in lessons than me and always seemed to be in trouble with the teachers and was the whipping boy for the bullies. I also recall that he left under a cloud, never to be seen again, but after so many years, I can't remember what brought this about.

'Oh yes,' I say. 'How are you?'

'Sound as pound dear boy. So what brings you here to God's own country?'

'I'm on holiday,' I tell him.

'Married? he asks.

'Not at the moment.'

'Me neither. Tried it a few times, but they will answer back and try to get their own way. Won't do. Where are you staying?'

I tell him about the cottage.

' We're practically neighbours,' he says. 'I live out near Lauragh. Why don't you come for dinner tomorrow? My man here can pick you up. Come early so we can catch up with each other before my other guests arrive. Six-thirty suit you?'

I agree and start to explain to the chauffeur how to get to the cottage.

'No need sir,' he says. 'I know it well. I'll collect you about six fifteen tomorrow.'

I forego the pint I was planning and head back to the cottage. Later, as I sit outside sipping a nice Chardonnay, I ponder on Jubilee Jones. Two things strike me: he has acquired a middle class accent and he appears to be wealthy. It will be interesting to hear his life story tomorrow.

Thursday:

After another disgraceful breakfast, I take a walk up the mountain from the cottage. It's hard going and I'm not really equipped for it, having only my trainers on and a light jacket. It's a bit cloudy and there's a light breeze, but otherwise it's fine. After about an hour I'm at the top and the view alone is worth the effort. The cottage is a speck below me. I sit on a rock day dreaming and pondering on this evening's visit to Jubilee Jones.

After a while, I look down the mountain and I can't see the cottage anymore. A heavy mist is rolling up toward me, the wind has increased and there are a few raindrops. I thought that mist rolled *down* from mountains, but then this is Ireland. I know that I came up roughly in a straight line, so it shouldn't be too hard to retrace my steps. I start to make my way down and the rain increases and the mist thickens. It's not long before I can't see more than a couple of yards ahead of me and I'm completely disoriented. There's no shelter, so I have to keep on. I figure that if I continue in a downwards direction, I'll reach civilisation at some point. Within minutes, I'm having to jump across raging little streams that weren't there on the way up. Just when I'm beginning to think I'll die up here, I hear a dog bark and John Shea's dad appears with his collie by his side.

''Tis a fine day for a walk,' he says, 'if you know where you're going. You'd better follow me.'

I feel like kissing him. We set off in the opposite direction to the one I had been on and it's as much as I can do to keep up with him. He's like a mountain goat. We eventually arrive at the cottage and I thank him profusely and ply him with tea. When he leaves, I sink into a hot bath and count my blessings.

Jones' chauffeur arrives on the dot of six-fifteen in the Rolls. I sit up front with him as we make our way down the track. He talks ten to the dozen, giving me his family history, while looking more at me than the road. I'm conscious that we're approaching the ramp and I try to warn him.

'Look out,' I say. There's a nasty ramp ahe…'

Too late. He hits it at a rate of knots and the old car takes off. The fact that we're airborne doesn't cause the slightest pause in his chatter. We land with a clatter and there's not a bother on him as he skilfully brings the car under control while continuing his narrative.

At the village of Lauragh we turn off onto a narrow road and then up a long dark drive that is densely curtained with rhododendrons. The house is an impressively large mock-Tudor pile. The front door is opened by a butler, who looks like a wrestler. I'm shown into a library room where Jones is ensconced in a big leather chair. He rises to greet me. He's wearing slacks, a sports jacket and a cravat.

'My dear chap, welcome to my humble abode. I imagine a wee snifter wouldn't go amiss — am I right? Whiskey? Brandy?'

I say a brandy would be nice and apologise for being informally dressed in jeans and T shirt.

'You're on your hols old man. You can wear what you like. Bring this man a large brandy, Talbot,' he says addressing the butler. 'And top mine up while you're at it.'

The butler gives a small bow, but I notice a slight raising of one eyebrow as if he doesn't entirely approve of his master's alcohol intake. He goes to a drinks cabinet and returns with two enormous glasses of brandy.

'Take a pew squire' says Jones taking a large gulp of his drink. 'Chin chin.'

There's something that doesn't quite ring true about Jones' accent and his choice of words sounds slightly archaic, like a saloon bar bore in a provincial pub, or a cad from a Fifties film who fancies his chances with Diana Dors.

'So, what have you been doing for the last fifty years?' he asks.

I give him a potted history of my modest musical and academic career and tell him that I now live a fairly frugal existence in the very town where we both spent our childhood.

'There's a lot to be said for a frugal existence,' he says, taking another gulp of brandy.

I ask him what he's been doing for all these years and mention that he seemed suddenly to have disappeared from school and that I couldn't remember why.

'Do you remember a boy called Grudgeon?' he asks.

I confirm that I do and also that he was a terrible bully.

'Well he bullied me unmercifully. So I shot the vicious little bugger', he says.

'You shot Grudgeon?'

'Yup. I stole my dad's two-two air rifle. I hid up a tree and waited for him to come out of his house. I aimed for his head, but in the event I hit him in the shoulder. He went down like a sack of spuds, howling like a baby. I should have left it at that, but I clambered down the tree and gave him a good kicking as he writhed on the ground.'

'I met Grudgeon recently at a school reunion,' I tell him. 'He's a vicar now and a Queen's Chaplain.'

'I'm not at all surprised he was a first class shit. Well, he nearly met his future boss earlier than he was destined to do. I'd started to stamp on his evil little head, but I was dragged off by some neighbours. There was a court case and I was sent to an Approved School. Do you remember those? Charming little establishments where one was supposed to realise the error of one's ways in the company of psychopaths and sadists — and that was just the staff. My parents disowned me and never visited once. I spent six years there.

'Christ, it must have been awful,' I say.

'Yes it was. Probably worse than you can imagine, but it was the making of me, because I learnt to survive. I was far too puny and fearful to stand up to some of the bruisers in there, but I had a good brain and a certain amount of animal cunning. So I became a trader. I got friendly with one of the maintenance staff, a gardener, and persuaded him to smuggle in cigarettes, sweets, dirty magazines, you name it.'

'But how did you find the money to do that?'

'Sale or return to start with. Just a couple of packets of fags and a few sweets. I sold the fags singly at a great markup. I paid the gardener over the odds, so he was happy. I became untouchable, because nearly every boy there became dependent on me for something that they couldn't ordinarily get their hands on. Upset me, then no fags, mags, sweets or whatever.'

'A captive customer base and a mini empire.'

'Yes, in a way it was,' he says. 'I was never bullied again. In fact I had my own team of heavies who would collect debts, or put the frighteners on anyone who thought that they could take over my racket.'

'Eat your heart out Al Capone,' I say. 'That's amazing.'

'Indeed. Had I stayed longer, I could probably have had half the staff in thrall to me too. As it was, when I was discharged aged seventeen, I had stashed away around five hundred pounds. A small fortune in those days. I had no home to go to, so I headed for London. I've been a trader of sorts ever since, although mostly legitimately I hasten to add.'

I have so many questions that I want to ask, not least as to what he's doing here in Ireland, but we're interrupted by Talbot, the butler, who tells Jones that his other guests have arrived and are in the dining room.

Jones leads the way. I tip the remains of my brandy into a pot plant on the way out of the library. I have a feeling that I'm going to have to pace myself with alcohol tonight.

Jones introduces me to his guests. To my embarrassment, he tells them that I'm a long lost school friend on his uppers whom he found busking in Kenmare just yesterday. There's a local priest, Father Ryan, who is clutching what looks like a very large glass of brandy or whiskey. An Austrian couple, probably in their early sixties. They are Doctor Franz and his wife Gudrun. Then there is an intense looking young man of about thirty, who seems to be drinking water. Jones introduces him as his step-son, Lance.

The dinner is excellent and the wine flows. Jones seems to have an infinite capacity for alcohol and drinks copious amounts. He dominates the conversation and talks over everyone else. It's all quite convivial, if a bit one-sided. I ask Lance what he does, but before he can respond Jones steps in.

'What does he do? I'll tell you. Bugger all, that's what he does. Claims to be an actor, but like most arty-farty types, he's a fucking parasite.'

There's an embarrassed silence. Lance looks down at his plate. I notice that he's trembling.

'Come now JJ,' says the priest. 'Lance just needs a lucky break. It's a very precarious profession.'

Jones, with a sinister smile, turns to the priest.

'A bit like yours I suppose. Get caught out with a pretty young nun and you're consigned forever to a backwater like this, hearing the confessions of a bunch of Neanderthal sheep-shaggers.'

Now it's the turn of the priest to stare at his plate. Jones tells the butler, who has been hovering nearby, to bring out the brandy and port.

'JJ, I've told you that you must go easy on the spirits, says the doctor. 'Think of your heart.'

I'm waiting for Jones, or JJ as they call him, to start on the doctor. He looks too young to have been a Nazi, but I feel sure that Jones has probably got something on him too. Maybe I'm next.

Jones pauses. We're all staring at our plates now. He has gone red in the face and he points a finger at the doctor. His mouth opens, but nothing comes out. He starts to slide off his chair, but the butler catches him before he falls.

'Please help yourselves to a nightcap before you leave,' Talbot says as he carries Jones like a baby out of the room. 'Mister Jones will be retiring now.'

No one has another drink and the chauffeur is summoned to take me home. Just as I'm leaving, Talbot takes me to one side.

'You mustn't mind Mister Jones sir. He gets carried away sometimes. I know that he thinks very highly of you.'

'Have you known him long?' I ask.

'Oh yes, sir. We were once at a school together,' he says, showing me to the Rolls.

A strange evening. I have a nasty feeling that I haven't heard the last of Jubilee Jones.

Friday:

The Irish Tourist Board once had a slogan that read: "Ireland: Get Lost You Won't Regret It." Today I'll test this out by looking for green roads. These are unmapped lanes that differ from most other Irish roads in that they have a little more grass growing in the middle. I've done this before on previous trips and while I've occasionally ended up in farmyards or disused quarries, I've often found some delightful spots.

I take the road from Kenmare to Killarney. About five miles out I take a left turn into a narrow lane that winds up steep hills and down into wooded valleys. There are so many twists and turns that I lose all sense of direction — which of course is the charm of such a journey. I've struck lucky with this road and there are no dead ends, nor another car or a living soul. Every now and then, I get a glimpse of Ireland's highest mountain, Carrountoohil. After some ten miles, the road winds ever upwards until I reach a larger road and a sign that tells me I've reached the Glencar Highlands. I drop down to the village of Glencar where I have a nice pint and some cabbage, bacon and a pile of spuds at the Climber's Inn.

I continue on to the town of Glenbeigh on the northern part of the Ring of Kerry. In the past, I've spent many happy and mad times here staying at The Falcon Inn. Sadly, it is now derelict. I tip it a reminiscent wink as I pass by and carry on toward Waterville and Kenmare beyond.

On this, my last night in Ireland, I sit outside for one more time. It's a fine evening. The views across the bay are as enchanting as ever. I ponder on what it is that keeps drawing me back to this country. Aside from the landscape, the people , the Guinness and my own heritage, there's something else that I can never quite put my finger on.

Saturday:

And so back to the airport. I drop the car off and proceed to the check in desk. I'm expecting the same problem with the saxophone that I had at Stanstead, but the girl just issues me with two boarding cards and wishes me a pleasant journey.

Once on the plane, I give the sax the window seat since I don't like to see the wings shudder and flaps opening and closing. We're all set for take off, but one of the cabin crew appears to be counting the passengers. She looks puzzled and is joined by another crew member and together they count the passengers again. Finally, her colleague calls for our attention.

'Will Lord Lucan identify himself to a crew member please?' he says.

Gales of laughter from those passengers old enough to remember the Lucan case. I point to my saxophone and show the crew my tickets. They are not amused.

Sunday:

Back to grim reality, but I feel replenished and ready to face the day to day chore of staying alive in a woebegone country.

A-Barning We Will Go

Monday:

I get a CD in the post which includes the track that I did on the clarinet a few weeks ago. The clarinet is so far back in the mix that it could be mistaken for the plaintive cries of a distressed mouse. I see that I'm not credited on the album, which suits me fine.

When I was sixteen, I got a place at a prestigious music college in London. I was still playing in jazz bands, but my intention was to make a career as a classical clarinettist. I studied hard and for the most part enjoyed the experience. After about a year, I became friends with a highly talented Australian pianist called Bruce, who was several years my senior. Aside from his considerable musical skills, Bruce was also a prodigious drinker. He lived in Earls Court in London, which at the time was like a suburb of Sydney. It was full of Australians — perhaps it still is.

An afternoon student concert at the college was planned and I was asked to play the first movement of Mozart's clarinet concerto, accompanied by Bruce on the piano. I was very nervous and Bruce persuaded me to go for a pub lunch. In those days, pubs very rarely served food, so this meant only one thing for him. Alcohol.

While Bruce quaffed several pints, I stuck to lemonade — I was underage anyway.

'Listen mate,' he said, 'you need to loosen up. You're a bundle of bloody nerves. All the great players have a drink before they go on. I'll get you a stiffener for that lemonade.'

He went to the bar and returned with two glasses of rum. He poured one of the glasses into the remains of my lemonade and bade me drink up. I duly obeyed his instruction and almost immediately felt more at ease. Several more "stiffeners" followed and I was feeling no pain, but having a bit of trouble focusing.

We got back to the concert hall next to the college with only five minutes to spare before we were due to go on. I pieced together my clarinet and it seemed longer than usual. It also appeared to have many more keys than I remembered it having. I was staring at it with some curiosity, when we were announced and we both took to the stage to polite applause. My legs felt leaden and there was a strange whistling in my ears.

Bruce sat down at the piano and played a few arpeggios like a pianist in a cocktail bar.

'G'day,' he slurred, 'here's a little bit of Mozart for ya.'

He then went into the introduction at a hell of a lick. As he played the opening bars, I stared at the music on the stand in front of me. It meant nothing. Absolutely nothing. I might as well have been a chimp trying to decipher Sanskrit. However, I had rehearsed the piece and came in on the right notes and in the right place. I just scraped through the first part from memory.

There followed a short piano section where Bruce ratcheted up the tempo even more, chuckling demonically as he did so. During this, I started to feel very queasy. I didn't come back in where I should have, so Bruce played the preceding bars again. By now, I was no longer in front of the music stand, but had lurched to the edge of the stage. I desperately needed to be sick and have a good lie down. The whistling in my ears had reached a crescendo and the world was spinning before me.

I started to fall forward and, dropping my clarinet, desperately clutched with both hands at the nearest object, which happened to be the curtain on the side of the stage. I swung out over the audience and then back to the stage. On my second outward swing, the curtain started to rip and I slowly abseiled into the front row, knocking several horrified dignitaries from their seats. Then I threw up and passed out.

Bruce got a job playing on a cruise ship and I later heard that he had gone missing and was presumed to have fallen overboard in mid-Atlantic. So the drink got him in the end. I returned home in disgrace, all hopes of a concert career dashed. I tried to get some professional dance band work, but was told that I also needed to be able play the saxophone as well as the clarinet.

Tuesday:

Last night I had great difficulty getting off to sleep. At one point, I even tried counting sheep, but to no avail. In the early hours, one's problems always seem to be magnified. I've maxed out on my credit cards because of the trip to Ireland and my old car won't go on forever. Then there's the irregular heartbeat and. I try to think of something nice, something that won't make me feel anxious.

As a boy, one of my favourite books was Mark Twain's *The Adventures of Huckleberry Finn*. I imagine drifting down a mighty river on a raft just as Huck did with the runaway slave, Jim. My only problem is that I have no idea how to construct a raft. How does one lash the logs together? Will it float? Could I build a small cabin on it? In the process of trying to figure all this out, I fell asleep.

Today, I attend yet another funeral. If this keeps up, I'll soon be on nodding terms with all the local funeral directors. Perhaps they'll cut me a deal when it's my turn.

Wednesday:

Over breakfast, I listen to the clarinet track again and remain mystified as to why the group wanted it on their album. I listen to the rest of the tracks and realise that when taste and musical sensibility were handed out, this lot were at the back of the queue.

I continued to play the clarinet until I was in my late teens. This was mainly in traditional jazz bands and for very little money. At the same time, I did a number of menial jobs on building sites, or in factories. I was going nowhere, began to hate the music I was playing and thought of giving up altogether.

Around this time, I played a gig at a dreary working man's club and the resident band had a saxophonist who invited me to have a go on his sax. I put the sling on, hooked up the sax and took a few tentative toots. The fingering was different than that of the clarinet, but within minutes, I had grasped it. This was a moment of musical epiphany for me. With the sax player's permission, I played the next set with the jazz band on his saxophone, much to the disgust of the other members of the band who regarded the sax with the same disdain as folkies once viewed the electric guitar. I didn't care. I had to have one. Soon.

Thursday:

A quiet day. I check my lottery ticket and find that I have won ten pounds. I take the ticket to the mini-market to claim my prize.

'I won't let it change my life,' I tell The Embryo as she hands me the ten pounds. 'I'll still keep sending out the begging letters.'

For a moment, I fear that she's going to buzz the manager, but then she smiles. She actually smiles. Encouraged by this, I tell her that I can't decide whether to take a world cruise, or buy a yacht with my winnings. As I'm saying this, I realise that her smile is not directed at me at all, but at a spotty youth standing behind me, who is dressed entirely in black and has various bits of metal and chain threaded through his lips, nose and eyebrows.

'Allo Stef,' he says. 'This old prick giving you any trouble?'

'Nuffin' I can't 'andle Pete,' she simpers.

I suddenly feel very old and a bit defenceless as I shuffle away with my tenner.

Friday:

I have an appointment with my dentist. He's very ancient and should have retired years ago, but he doesn't bang on about dental hygiene, or charge too much. As I sit in the waiting room, I casually glance at the magazines which are decades out of date. One in particular has photographs of high class young ladies who have become engaged to be married. They seem invariably to have double-barrelled last names and their future spouses all appear to be officers of fashionable Guards regiments. Other photographs in the magazine show these types at various social gatherings, or shooting at animals. A common feature of these young things is that many of them have receding chins and ears that stick out. As I await my turn in the dentist's chair, I have a little fantasy about how this might be so and imagine an anthropologist giving a lecture...

I have recently discovered a very interesting tribal mutilation ritual among the British upper classes and royalty. It is called, Barning. It is always carried out in the greatest secrecy and very few people have ever actually witnessed it, save those directly involved and they are always sworn to silence.

It usually takes place in a rural setting far from prying proles. It can be a costly procedure and top barners can command a high price. Mis-barning or over-barning does sometimes occur, but generally a repeat, or reverse procedure can correct this and will be carried out for no extra fee. The extent of barning is always down to individual taste, but in general, full barning is preferred by royalty. Indeed, at one time, it was carried out exclusively on royals. These days, the rules have been relaxed somewhat and the 'full thwack', as it is known among the cognoscenti, is becoming the norm, particularly for those who can afford it. It is rumoured that Russian oligarchs and even wealthy Americans have begun to invest in it.

The procedure is deceptively simple, yet in the right hands, extremely effective. Its apparent simplicity has attracted amateurs and there have been reported cases of irreversible over-barning, or in extreme cases, barn-out, in which the recipient (or barn-ee) has been rendered permanently senseless. However, even in these isolated incidents, the barn-ee has generally been able to go on to attain lucrative directorships, honours and high office.

It is generally carried out on boys between five and seven years old, but there is a sub-procedure for females called barn-esse, or barnessing, (female recipients are called barnettes) which is more subtle, but equally effective. Pre-barned children of either sex are known as un-barns. They will be invited to nice parties, and pony club events, but until they have undergone barning, will not be eligible for country house weekends, eventing, the Proms, or the Henley Regatta.

The barning ritual is generally carried out as follows. Young Tarquin, for let us call him that, is driven down to the country, usually on a Saturday. On the way, his anxious parents will keep him distracted with I-Spy and organic muesli bars. Arriving at a remote farm, he will be led to a barn. At this stage, the barner and his assistant (called the under-barner) will not be visible. In the barn, nestling among bales of straw will be a ewe with a lamb, or a sow with some piglets. At a signal from the hidden barner, the parents will say, 'Oh look Tarquin, a lovely lamb (or piglets).' Tarquin will move forward to get a closer look.

Like a hangman assessing the weight of his victim, the barner, discreetly hidden from view, will make a fine judgment based on the child's height and cranial circumference. With the help of the under-barner, he will then swing the barn door with a finely calculated force directly into the back of the child's head. If the barner has calculated correctly, Tarquin will fall to the ground under such an impact, but should recover quite quickly.

There now follows a crucial series of tests to determine whether the barning has been successful and whether the barner will receive his full fee. (The barnpurse) While the little lad is still a little stunned, cali-

pers will be applied to his head to measure the exact extent to which his ears now protrude and how far his chin has receded as a result of the massive blow. These measurements in themselves will not guarantee that the full barnpurse will paid. Other tests will be carried out as he recovers and there will be a degree of tension between the parents and the barners as these are conducted. This is where the Barnbroker plays a crucial role. She (and it generally is a she) will give the standard pronunciation of key words, which the barnee will be invited to repeat. For example:

Barnbroker *'Now Tarquin, say after me. OFF.'*
Small Boy (still a little dazed) *'..er..er..ORF'*
Barnbroker: *'HOUSE'*
Small Boy: *'HICE'*
Barnbroker: *'GIRL'*
Small Boy: *'GEL'*
Barnbroker: *'CLAPHAM'*
Small Boy: *'CLAAM'*
Barnbroker: *'YES'*
Small Boy: *'EARS'*

Provided these criteria are met, then the full barnpurse will be paid. Tarquin will now be equipped to go into the world. And despite being permanently brain damaged from his little visit to the farm, will later miraculously pass the common entrance exam for Eton, or some such school, join a fashionable regiment, or City institution and may even become a member of parliament...

...I'm called into the surgery and require only one filling. The dentist asks whether I'm interested in rugby as he drills away. I can't answer of course, having a numb jaw and clamps in my mouth. He then gives me a blow by blow account of the latest match between England and France.

'Those Frogs might be cheese-eating surrender monkeys,' he says, 'but they play a good game of rugger.'

Saturday:

I've got a few gigs coming up so I practise the sax. After I'd tried it for the first time all those years ago, I knew that I just had to have one. I scrimped and saved and eventually bought a second-hand sax for one hundred pounds. It's the one I still play to this day. It's a Selmer Mark Six, considered by many, including me, to be the Stradivarius of saxophones.

I continued to play jazz, but this was at the dawn of the Sixties and a revolution in music was going on around me, of which I was more or less oblivious, or disdainful toward. This was soon to change.

Sunday:

I have an urge for a Sunday roast. Only a British person would understand this. It's hard-wired into most of us in some mysterious way. We might go for ages, eating nouveau cuisine, fondue, burgers, curries and chop sueys, but then a piquant itch will stir within and only a roast dinner will do. I drive out to a country pub and have the full works: roast beef and spuds, Yorkshire pudding, cabbage, parsnips, plus apple pie and custard to follow. I return home and have a little siesta.

Life's A Burger

Monday:

I think that my upright freezer needs to be defrosted. The interior now looks like a miniature polar landscape, with icy mountains, glaciers and vast expanses of snow. I half expect to see Oates giving a plucky wave to Scott before he walks off to oblivion between the dark shapes of long-forgotten frozen food.

The door no longer closes completely and I force it shut by wedging a squeegee mop between it and the opposite wall in the kitchen. I imagine that I just have to deprive it of power and it will defrost. God knows what I'll do with all the stuff that's in it while this is taking place.

During the night I go to the kitchen to get a glass of water. I trip over the squeegee mop and head butt the oven. Appliances ganging up on me again. As I drag myself to my feet and re-position the mop, I snarl at the blameless microwave that I hardly ever use.

Tuesday:

I'm awoken this morning by a knock at the door. I stumble from bed. My head is throbbing and my vision seems a little blurred. If it's the Jehovah's Witlesses they'll get short shrift from me today. All that bollocks about the elected few who will get to heaven. Surely God has made His mind up by now about who's in and who's out. So why does He continue to torture us with door- stepping crones?

There are some obvious candidates for elevation like Mother Theresa, Robin Hood, the Good Samaritan, Ebenezer Scrooge and W C Fields. If the downward, hell-bound candidates were subject to a vote, then my very long list would have to include Hitler (couldn't paint), Sting (whiny, up his own arse), Cliff Richard (sanctimonious posing and God-bothering), Margaret Thatcher (completely misunderstood the Good Samaritan parable), all Tories, most guitarists, bell ringers and all the executives from Rank-Hovis-McDonalds-Goldman-Sachs-

Wall-Mart-Tesco-Cable and Wireless-Microsoft-Burger King. Inc.

Grumpily, I poke my head round the door and see that it's the delectable Cordelia.

'Oh, I'm sorry,' she says, 'I hope I didn't get you out of bed.'

'No, it's OK, 'I've been up for hours,' I lie.

'Well, it's just that my nephew wants to learn the saxophone and I wondered if you could perhaps give him some advice.'

'Well I'd be happy to, but I don't give lessons I'm afraid,' I say, thinking it would be unwise to give her my standard advice which is to stick it in your gob and blow like a bastard. I keep the door half open, hoping that she won't see my tatty underpants and that I sleep with my Dennis the Menace socks on.

'He's coming to tea this Sunday. Perhaps you would like to join us around four o'clock? I know that he would be thrilled to meet a living legend.'

'I don't know about that,' I say, chuffed to monkeys, 'but yes, I'd be pleased to come.'

She smiles, a heart-stopping smile and I get the faintest whiff of a nice perfume. Little Voice, the one in my head that entertains lewd thoughts, is about to kick in, when she looks quizzically at me and says as she turns to go,

'Have you been in a fight?'

I close the door and rush to the bathroom mirror where I see that I have a black eye from my encounter with the oven during the night. I dig out my shades and go to the minmarket. The fact that it's raining will obviously make me look a bit silly, but perhaps The Embryo will think I've had a cornea implant. If she thinks at all.

Wednesday:

Once I had bought a saxophone in my late teens, I left the clarinet and trad bands behind and began playing in semi-pro modern jazz groups and crappy old dance bands. Then I got a call from a local group who had recently turned professional.

In those days sax players were in short supply and I can't recall being auditioned for the job. It was enough I think that I owned a sax and could blow a few notes. Having a jazz background meant that I had quite a good ear, so I was able to pick up the riffs fairly quickly. But my true education and delight was in the material itself.

This band, called The Stormsville Shakers, were playing black American r'n'b, by the likes of Solomon Burke, Ray Charles, Sam Cooke, James Brown and many others. I had never heard this stuff before and I took to it like a duck to water. All my prejudices about "pop" music fell away. I was also amazed at how many clubs and pubs there were throughout the country where this music was being played by bands such as Zoot Money, Georgie Fame, Cliff Bennett, Chris Farlowe, Graham Bond, Geno Washington, John Mayall and many others.

The centrepiece of all this was undoubtedly the Flamingo Club in Wardour Street London. We played there many times before a knowledgeable and critical audience, many of whom were black US servicemen. The Emcee was one, John Gunnell, who with his brother, Rik, owned the club and a booking agency. The Gunnells were a formidable pair. John had a long knife scar on his face and could generally silence a heckler with a menacing stare. Rik, a smooth character, who had at one time been a boxer, would, on occasions, condescend to thump a persistent troublemaker.

We often played a double gig at The Flamingo — the all-nighter as it was called. This meant playing from around eight-thirty in the evening until four or five in the morning. We took breaks of course and the tiny dressing room at the side of the stage would always be full with hookers and hustlers, other musicians and, if we were lucky, female fans.

Thus began my life on the road as a musician. We travelled the length and breadth of the UK and also in France and Italy. Despite the privations, lack of decent money and shitty hotels and boarding houses, it gets in one's blood. In this respect, musicians are like gypsies; rootless and forever seeking fairy gold. More than forty years on, I'm still easily persuaded on occasion to go off on money-less tours with other Peter Pans who are old enough to know better, but who can't resist giving it another crack. Maybe I'll grow up one day.

Thursday:

A bright, sunny day, which justifies my continuing use of sunglasses to cover up my black eye. I manage to complete The Times cryptic crossword, despite not having had a classical education. I also discover on a senior's web site that I have been over-paying council tax for the last four years. Apparently, I should have had a single person's discount of twenty five percent. A nice rebate awaits methinks.

I phone the local council office. Once connected, I'm cautioned that my call might be recorded for training purposes. Training what? Clematis up a trellis? Potty training? Shrew taming? Eventually I get through to the right department and I'm told that my call is very important and valued, but that there is a queue. In the meantime, I'm treated to a little Vivaldi, followed somewhat incongruously by Sinatra singing *Fly Me to the Moon*.

I know that many people regard Sinatra as a musician's singer and there's no doubt that his phrasing was unique and very clever. However, he gives me a headache. It reminds me of soulless airport lounges, shitty shopping malls and Sixties fondue parties.

Eventually, I get through to the tax department and explain my overpayment to a woman who sounds like a recovering narcoleptic, bored before she even got to the office.

'Yes, you are entitled to a discount,' she says.

'Oh good,' I say with some glee, 'do you want my bank details for the rebate?'

Ignoring me she continues,

'But you should have indicated on form WDC1798 stroke 6A that you were a single occupier. We cannot reimburse retrospectively.'

I feel like telling her that I can't whistle out of my arse either, but I just manage to stay in control of my temper.

'But I've been overpaying for four years,' I tell her.

She droningly repeats that no rebate will be forthcoming. I can feel myself losing it. And I do.

'But that amounts to around twelve hundred pounds of my money that you shouldn't have had. I suppose you've spent it on a new chain of office for that fat git of a Tory mayor, or you've blown it on a staff junket to Bognor, or a bonding day firing paint balls at each other. Or maybe it's been used to send fact-finding missions to Corfu or Disneyland. I don't suppose that the name Wat Tyler means anything to you, but I won't let this go. It's robbery.'

I'm quite out of breath in my rage. There's a silence at the other end of the line and then a tinny pre-recorded voice tells me that abusive phone calls are not tolerated and I may be reported to the police. The line goes dead. Shitbags.

Friday:

Today, I have a serious lapse of judgment. I go to the local DIY store to get a new head for the squeegee mop. The old one seems to have gummed itself to the freezer door. When I tried to remove it this morning, half of it remained on the door. So, I now have a dysfunctional freezer, the door of which is decorated with bits of blue sponge. I turn the freezer off and place several old towels around its base to collect the water.

On leaving the DIY store, I notice that a new branch of a hamburger chain has opened next door. I have never eaten anything from such an outlet, but for reasons that I can't fathom, I go in. It's teeming with screaming kids and grumpy mums. There's a faint odour of sweaty armpits, which I put down to the sheer weight of numbers crowded into the place.

The minimally-waged girl behind the counter asks me a series of questions, none of which mean a thing to me. I answer in the affirmative anyway. Some minutes later I'm presented with a very large bag and what appears to be half a gallon of cola. I take all this back to the car and look to see what's in the bag. Aside from a box containing the burger, there are also a lot of fries and some onion rings. I open the burger box and there's that odour again. It almost has me gagging. It reminds me of school changing rooms, or the *deuxieme classe* on the Paris metro before *egalite* and readily available deodorants kicked in at last in the late Sixties.

I nibble on the salty fries and have a few sips of the giant cola, which is so cold that it sets my old teeth on edge. I bite into an onion ring and it's like an elastic band in batter with undertones of those blue things that are put in gent's urinals. I should have stopped there of course, but nothing ventured nothing gained. I take a bite out of the massive burger. A layered, almost Proustian, experience. But this is no madeleine.

The bun has no substance and I can't believe any kind of grain was involved in its production. Then I hit what I think might be a slice of gherkin. This immediately reminds me of Christmases long past. Family rows, the Queen's speech and my tipsy Dad standing up for the national anthem. This is followed by what could be lettuce and tomato, although there's no taste to either. Then what I think might be cheese, but which could just as easily be a carpet tile, or medicated play dough.

Finally, I reach the burger itself. The centrepiece of this corporate creation. It was presumably once a part of a cow that was packed into a depressing truck one day, slaughtered and finely minced.

As it travelled to its doom, did this lowly cow gaze with big trusting bovine eyes between the bars of the truck and wonder about the world it was passing through? Perhaps it saw bleak out of town shopping centres, with Frank's dispiriting voice echoing through the malls. And super stores, Ikeas and used car lots with paunchy salesmen barking down their mobiles. Maybe it passed by great soulless office blocks, all glass and pointless ingenuity. And burger outlets that it would soon re-visit in a different form. Half gassed by traffic fumes, it might have turned to a hapless companion saying,

'Humans. Whatever will they think of next? '

As my teeth glide effortlessly through all this slurry, the sweaty armpit odour invades my sinuses and the gagging reflex kicks in. I spit the whole mouthful back into the bag. When I've recovered, I take a look at the burger. It looks like one of those things one used to patch one's shoes with. *Phillip's Stick-a-Soles*. Children are eating this stuff. It's madness. I bin the lot.

Back at home, the freezer is beginning to defrost and peering in my gaze is met by the beady stare of the halibut that I bought from Freddie the Fish Man. I'm feeling queasy anyway after the burger and this doesn't help.

Saturday:

The freezer finally defrosts. I quickly put the halibut in the bin before it can give me any more recriminatory looks. I look over the remaining contents, much of which I can't readily identify, and heave it all in the bin. I resolve that in future I'll label stuff before I put it in the freezer.

My black eye has almost disappeared. There remains only the faintest hint of a yellowish bruise. I think I would look a bit daft wearing sunglasses to the tea party tomorrow.

I spend the evening writing to my local Tory councillor. I quote the Magna Carta, the Peasant's Revolt and anything else I can think of to convince her of the injustice of me not getting a rebate on the council tax. I also claim to be a lifelong supporter of her party. Letter completed and spell-checked, I hit the tit on the printer. Out comes the letter in a sort of muddy brown, khaki colour. In this instance, the medium is not the message and will get a good kicking before too long.

Sunday:

I've been very nervous about today's little tea party at Cordelia's. In the event, I needn't have been concerned. It went swimmingly well. Her nephew was a charming lad of about thirteen. I took my sax along and he had a preliminary toot. I also played a few flashy riffs which I think impressed his aunt.

We had nice sandwiches and cakes and I recounted some of the less salacious experiences of being a professional musician. For once I was enjoying myself without the usual chaos that seems to surround many of my social endeavours. Cordelia, looking scrumptious, tolerated my flirting with her. All in all, it was a great success and I could envisage moving our relationship up a notch. Then the bloody Adonis Twins arrived looking bronzed, young and annoyingly healthy.

Cordelia hugged them both warmly and introduced them.

'This is my son, Richard and his partner, Charles.'

The penny dropped. They were a couple. Not rivals and not her toy boys. There's hope for me yet. A promising end to the week.

Stoats and Weasels

Monday:

The usual Monday junk mail. There's a premature invitation for me to sign up to an over-seventy's funeral plan and another to release the equity in my property. In each case the phrase "peace of mind" crops up and there's a picture of a helpful looking girl aching to receive my call. Insurance in any form is parasitic. It preys on people's fears and insecurity and is just another way to extort money from us. Lloyds of London is held up to be a venerable and vital institution, yet in reality is little more than a bookie's shop, or a semi-benign protection racket. Be-suited stoats, who might otherwise be pillaging Toad Hall, spend their days juggling odds, while their weasel cousins in the legal profession devise elaborate get-out clauses to be buried in the small print. Bastards. Come the revolution, they'll be among the first in the tumbrels, together with other bottom feeders and jackals like estate agents, politicians, bankers, Richard Branson and the former Amstrad tycoon, whose name I cannot utter without retching.

I meet Brint on the stairs. He tells me that Shards is pregnant. Bang goes the gene pool.

'Course, I'll have to put learning the axe on the back burner for a while. Ankle biters can take up a lot of time,' he says.

I congratulate him and can imagine the world of music heaving a collective sigh of relief that his artistic aspirations have been temporarily halted. Clapton and Santana can rest easy for a while.

Tuesday:

I walk into town and pause on the old wooden river bridge by the church. I used to trudge across this bridge on my way to and from school. Now, as I stare into the water, I try to remember what it was like being me more than half a century ago.

I was a skinny and sickly kid with weak lungs. My mother constantly pestered the local doctor to give me a tonic, something to build me up. She seemed in a constant state of anxiety regarding my health. Of course, I played on this and had many happy days off school. When I was in my late teens, it was found that I have an unusual blood group. I told my mother about this.

'I can't understand it,' she said defensively, 'I always looked after you properly.'

I leave the bridge and cross the park dedicated to the memory of a native son, Jack Phillips, who, as the radio operator on the *Titanic*, stuck to his post and went down with the ship while tapping out SOS messages to the last. There's a supermarket trolley in the memorial pond. Perhaps it's a piece of street art symbolising the demise of the great liner. The burger boxes and beer cans that litter the pathways are another matter. I wonder what the plucky young Jack would have made of it all. I'm sure that Kate Gym Slip and Leonardo DiCaprio were far too busy canoodling on the poop deck even to have noticed him as he vainly tapped away in the bowels of the sinking ship. I'm ashamed to say that I quite enjoyed seeing the smarmy Leonardo eventually sink beneath the waves.

Cordelia phones to say that her nephew is still keen to learn the sax and that she is willing to buy him an instrument. We arrange to meet on Saturday and go to the local music shop to check out what they have.

I was very lucky that my first sax was the Selmer Mark Six. At the time, I had no idea what a wonderful instrument I had bought. I honked away on it for perhaps twenty years before I realised that, like some of my wives and lovers, it had been patiently waiting for me to grow up. It can't be hurried or bullied. It can deliver a distinctive tonal quality that is deep and rich. These days, it has become a collector's item fetching many thousands of pounds, but I'd give up a kidney before parting with it, whatever the price.

Wednesday:

The Anorak finally pins me down. He phones and I agree to him coming to the flat tomorrow to discuss my valiant part in the musical revolution of the Nineteen Sixties. The very fact that he wants to interview *me*, one who played only a bit part in the mayhem and pretence, speaks volumes about the nature of his proposed book.

Far too much has been written about the Sixties and I don't want to add to the pile of waffle. Suffice to say that there was a kind of revolution, the seeds of which were sown in the Fifties with rock 'n' roll and a gradual rise in prosperity. Young people started to have spending power and challenged many of the old social conventions. Rebellion was in the air, although it was generally harmless and often laughable. It's often claimed that there was also a sexual revolution, but hand on heart I can honestly say that it was still very difficult to persuade girls to jump into bed, even though I played in a band — a supposedly glamorous and attractive occupation.

The rise in youth spending power was quickly seized upon and ruthlessly exploited by the world of commerce. It shouldn't be forgotten that The Beatles were a hard edged rock 'n' roll band before Lennon and McCartney were persuaded to become a latter day Rogers and Hammerstein. The producer, George Martin, is often credited as being the "fifth Beatle" for his so-called masterly arrangements. In reality, he was an an old fuddy duddy who sanitised much of their work and encouraged L and M to write what was mostly a load of mawkish crap, which he then adorned with anodyne strings. He's now a "Sir" as is Paul. John, probably the real rebel, must be content with his ashes drifting around Central Park in New York. Perhaps they have by now been fully ingested by generations of the emaciated chipmunks and squirrels that dart among the dying trees, used needles and tourists waiting to be mugged. Imagine that.

Every time that I see Sir Paul pull that wide-eyed, cheeky chappie, loveable Scouser face, with his thumbs up as if we're all mates together, I want to put my fingers down my throat.

When Punk emerged in the Seventies, I actually liked it — not the music, but the attitude. It was a piss take of all the preceding hubris and pretension of the Sixties. It's interesting that like rock 'n' roll, it first emerged in the USA. But then this is in turn became commercialised. Malcolm McClaren might have acted out rebellion, but at heart he was a sharp-eyed little shit on the make. He was lucky enough to find a group of guys, The Sex Pistols, who could be more outrageous than he would ever have dared.

I think that it was Mao Tse Tung, that other sharp-eyed shit and murderer of millions, who was once asked what he thought about the French Revolution.

'It's not over yet,' was his reply.

I feel the same way about the Sixties. Those of us who were silly enough to think that a great change would occur, that peace and understanding would prevail, that art and creative endeavour would at last be valued were, ultimately, sadly disappointed. The cold hand of commerce saw to that. Now we have the odious Simon Cowell who has turned creativity into a cruel spectacle, where he and his ignorant and talentless celebrity panellists and a baying audience of fast food poisoned no-hopers have become the arbiters of what is artistically worthwhile. I despair. It's a re-run of *They Shoot Horses, Don't They?* Come the real revolution, there will be tumbrels awaiting Simon and his ilk. Has the world gone mad?

And while I'm in rant mode, here's another cautionary tale.

The town of Farnham in Surrey has had a long tradition of professional theatre. In nineteen eighty-four a wonderful new theatre was built and named in honour of the distinguished actor, Michael Redgrave. Like most regional theatres, it struggled from time to time, but its productions were of the highest standard. In fact it's where I got my first chance to write music for the theatre in a brilliant production of *Cyrano de Bergerac.*

Then around ten years ago the local branch of The Worshipful Company of Philistines, Conniving Master Charlatans, Stoats, Weasels, a major supermarket chain and the council put their empty, but rapacious heads together and decided that they would tear the theatre down and replace it with a development including a new supermarket and luxury flats. Thus far this has not yet come to pass, because the Worshipful Company of Etceteras have apparently been squabbling among themselves over the spoils.

The theatre has stood dark and boarded up for over a decade. In the meantime, a group of professional actors and many local people have campaigned against the proposed development and for the theatre to re-open.. They have held raffles, murder/mystery evenings, concerts and dinners and many other events in order to raise funds. Each summer, the actors put on a three week programme of plays. These take place in a marquee in the grounds next to the theatre. These are well attended and very professional shows and I have been to many of them, but there we all sit on hard chairs under a sometimes dripping canvas, while a stone's throw away is a purpose built theatre that stands dark and unused, awaiting the wrecking ball of the Worshipful Company of Etceteras, once they can sort out who gets which share of the cake.

When the actors have taken to the stage and when they have taken their final bows in the little marquee, I've always been full of admiration for their bravery and determination to keep theatre live and alive, even under difficult circumstances. What does it matter? It matters a great deal. Art in all its forms is the lifeblood and metronome of a civilised society. Without it, we are infinitely poorer, like ravening stoats.

My old heart weeps.

Thursday:

The Anorak arrives. He's actually a nice man and I feel guilty for having given him the run-around. The mystery of why he wants to interview me is solved when he tells me that his book will concentrate only on the groups that emerged from around the area of my home town — where I still live in fact. He rattles off musician's names and venues that I had either forgotten, or didn't know in the first place. It's a pleasant hour or so and he's keen to hear anecdotes about life as a musician. Given the specific local nature of his project, it makes me feel that I was perhaps a big fish in a small pond, since very few of the neighbourhood players from that era went on to become professional. After he leaves, I feel quite chuffed for a while until I remember that in the early Sixties there was a nationwide explosion of bands all trying to make it, slogging up and down the new M1 motorway in clapped out vans. On a Saturday night, the Blue Boar Café at the Watford Gap services on the motorway would be full of tired musos counting their pennies to see whether they could afford a solidified egg and soggy chips. We all had high hopes, but very few went on to fame and fortune.

It's not easy being a footnote.

Friday:

This morning, I line up at the local surgery for the 'flu jab. Everyone seems to be so much older than me, until I realise that I went to school with at least half of the shuffling dafties that are presenting their arms in the production line. When my turn comes, I'm told to expect a small scratch, which is better I suppose than feeling a small prick.

This evening I watch a documentary about Bill Clinton, former president of the home of rock 'n' roll. He's a Southern boy who made good, studied his books, became a lawyer and said the right things in the right places to elevate himself up the greasy pole. He married a fellow weasel, who, at the time wore spectacles that looked like the bullion glass in a Dickensian sweet shop window. She and Bill produced a piranha-toothed child who looked like an orthodontist's dream and was called Chelsea. After the bridge I suppose.

Bill couldn't keep his pecker to himself and was caught out having had an affair with a young intern at the White House. With my track record, I can hardly pass judgment on infidelity, but when he looked his country and the world in the eye and said that he had never had sex with *that* woman, as if she were just a worthless piece of shit, I knew he was lying. Scale it down and he's no better than the Worshipful Company of Etceteras. He can't play the sax either. Hilary now wears contact lenses and Chelsea has had her teeth fixed. Now she only looks like a barracuda, rather than a denizen of the Amazon.

Saturday:

And so to buy a saxophone. Cordelia drives me and her nephew to the shop in her posh car. I've no idea what make it is, since I have zero interest in cars. This lack of enthusiasm has, in part, been compounded by having once watched a few minutes of a TV motoring show hosted by one, Jeremy Clarkson. He also writes a xenophobic column for a Sunday newspaper, as does his friend, the restaurant critic, A A Gill. Gill recently boasted that he had shot a baboon while on holiday in Africa, simply because he could. It is to be hoped that one day he might turn his gun on Clarkson and then in turn be shot by a police marksman. It's an interesting fact that these marksmen are such good shots that they can only ever kill, rather than incapacitate, their victims.

The brass section of the music shop is presided over by none other than the saxophone expert with whom I had words in the pub a few weeks back. Rather than being resentful at my having told him to fuck off, he is very deferential and tells Cordelia what a splendid musician I am as I try out some saxes. This will hopefully gain me a few points.

We settle on an instrument which costs around a thousand pounds. Cordelia pays without a qualm, which warms me to her no end. On the way back, we stop at a pub for lunch, which she insists on paying for. Perhaps I could become a kept man. Stranger things have happened.

Sunday:

I'm awoken this morning by Cordelia's nephew honking on the sax. It sounds like a cow in labour. I feel churlish for having said that I never give lessons, so I go down to offer a bit of advice. Cordelia is clearly pleased by this. More points I hope.

I'm delighted when she offers me some freshly ground coffee. A kept man, well supplied with decent coffee. Too much to hope for I think.

Later, I lie awake unable to get to sleep. I resort to trying to solve the problem of constructing a raft as a way of nodding off. I can't work out how one would lash the logs together and in my mind's eye see myself and raft sinking slowly to the bottom of the river. I could Google it I suppose, but that would be cheating and defeat the object, which is to put myself to sleep.

Anarchic Dafties

Monday:

Robin has left Adrian, *aka* VATman, and moved in with Reg the caretaker. Last night, while lying awake trying to figure out how to build a bloody raft, I heard a good deal of shouting and banging of doors. This morning I bump into Adrian as I go to get the paper. I wish him a good morning and he buttonholes me.

'I suppose you know Robin has left me for that bugger in the basement,' he says.

I deny any knowledge, although I had suspected this would come about after seeing all the comings and goings over the past few months.

'I wouldn't mind,' he continues, 'but he's probably thirty years older than her *and* he's a country music fan.'

I commiserate with him, not so much about losing a wife, as losing one to a country music fan.

'She'll soon get fed up with all those whining pseudo-cowboys,' I tell him.

I'm surprised to discover that the local newsagent has closed for good. A sign of the times I suppose. I expect Tescos will do their best to cram one of their express stores into his tiny premises. I sometimes wonder whether Tesco is controlled by aliens. What a perfect way to take over a planet. Monopolise food distribution. At a given point, the oily iguana who really runs the company could close all the stores for a day or two. The populace would be on their knees in no time, begging for re-formed turkey slurry, microwave-able ready meals and bread you wouldn't wipe your arse with. All will have to renounce any religious beliefs they might have had and bow before the great god Tesco. Meanwhile, the oily iguana and his confederates, like McDonalds, Burger King and Rupert Murdoch, will plunder what's left of our natural resources, fill our rivers and oceans with even more toxic waste and then move on to another planet. Tesco-ism will then be replaced by cannibalism.

(The names Tesco, McDonalds, Burger King and possibly even Murdoch are registered trademarks and used here without permission. I should also like to make it known that I have no tangible assets.)

I get my Murdoch-owned newspaper from the mini-market. I'm served by an eastern-European girl with a moustache... I'm served with a moustache by an eastern European girl... I'm served by an eastern-European girl who has a moustache. Syntax is a bugger sometimes.

Tuesday:

Following my success in gaining points with Cordelia, I'm determined to press home my advantage. I drop a note through her door inviting her for supper *chez mois* this Saturday. I also say that it would be nice if her son and his partner came too. I don't want her to think that I'm setting up a twosome.

I meet Shards on the stairs and congratulate her on her pregnancy. She blushes and I notice that she appears to have lost a lot of the hard edged, combative look that she generally has. In fact there's a glow about her that one often sees in pregnant women. It's as if they've received divine affirmation that the miseries of menstruation, having awkward plumbing, bouncy bits and having to lower lavatory seats after men, has had a meaning and purpose after all.

Cordelia phones this evening saying that she and The Adonis Twins would love to come for supper on Saturday. I immediately go into panic mode, having not thought about what I can serve up. As I lie awake until the early hours, this question replaces my recent efforts at constructing a raft. I finally drift off having mangled several recipes.

Wednesday:

I get a call from the Anorak seeking clarification on some minutiae. It's a shame that he seems so hung up on trivial details, because there are many tales that I could tell which might liven up his book.

Musicians love tales. They brighten the tedium between gigs and they are passed from band to band and generation to generation. In the long nights on the road, when the high of performing was rapidly wearing off, to be replaced by hunger and boredom, a small voice might break the gloom to say,

'Did I ever tell you about…'

And so a story would begin. We all knew in advance of the telling that it would have been embellished and we might have heard it before in one form or another, but we would sit back in the cramped Transit van waiting to be entertained. There are many such tales, but here's one that has always amused me.

There's a guitarist of my acquaintance called Dougo. Like me and many others, he's a footnote in the history of pop music, but he has paid his dues and is still gigging to this day.

Returning home late one night from a gig, he saw a note in the kitchen from his long-suffering wife saying "Dinner in the oven. Ten minutes at Gas Mark 5". He was tired and a bit hungover and decided to pass on the dinner. He got undressed and was about to get into bed when he had second thoughts, feeling a bit peckish after all. Completely naked, he returned to the kitchen and crouched down, opening the oven to see what the meal was.

In the corner of the kitchen, lying snugly in a basket, was a cute little kitten that they had recently acquired. It watched as Dougo stuck his head in the oven to check the meal. Its eyes narrowed to yellow slits and it slowly stirred, arching its back and extending its claws. It might have been a suburban moggie, but like its larger cousins in the Serengeti, it was attracted by movement. In this case, the movement in question was Dougo's manhood swinging between his legs as he peered into the oven. One could almost imagine a background soundtrack of jungle drums, tribal chants and chattering chimps.

Millions of years of evolution came into play as the kitten pounced, digging its sharp little claws into Dougo's scrotum. He quite naturally let out a piercing scream and in struggling to get to his feet, smacked his head on the oven and passed out. His wife, hearing the noise, rushed downstairs to the kitchen. There was a naked Dougo lying with his head half in the oven with a cat attached to his balls. His wife couldn't work out whether he was trying to gas himself or shag the cat. Or perhaps he *had* shagged the cat and was filled with suicidal remorse. He still walks with a slight limp to this very day. Dougo apparently walks almost normally.

The point of these stories is of course the humour, but there's another dimension. Musicians seem to attract a disproportionate amount of chaos and silliness in their lives, compared with say, librarians, or accountants. It goes with the turf, so to speak, as does a dislike of authority. (Hence some of my own various run-ins with officialdom) The stories confirm our collective membership in a confederacy of anarchic dafties.

Thursday:

I wake up early and somehow I just know that this is going to be what I call an "argh" day. Beyond grumpy. This is quickly confirmed when I foolishly listen to the *Today* programme on Radio Four. A group of politicians is engaged in a heated exchange of lies and platitudes, chaired by a cretin who hasn't the courage or the gumption to call them to account. I know that it's fashionable to knock politicians, but in general, they are a bunch of shysters. Argh!

Take our former prime minister, Tony Blair. We trusted a man with scary eyes and the smile of a snake oil salesman. He stood on the steps of Number Ten and said that his priority was "education, education, education". Now our kids are saddled with years of debt when they try to get the same education that he and his cronies got for nothing.

Without a shred of hard evidence and a pack of lies, Scary Eyes teams up with the smirking pygmy brain in the White House and squanders billions bombing the shite out of Iraq. For what? And when Scary Eyes moved on to the lucrative international lecture circuit, we got a one-eyed son of the manse, who talked like he had the remains of an illicit gobstopper in his mouth and printed worthless money faster than Mae West allegedly dropped her knickers. Argh!

Then there's health and safety. Kids are not allowed to climb trees anymore. They have to wear visors if they want to play conkers — that's if they know what a conker is and they're not glued to the telly or a game console, or shagging each other. The next thing'll be that we'll all have to wear hi-viz vests when we go out — just in case you get run down by the man in the little supermarket eco-van delivering shite to the masses. Argh!

I might be an anarchic daftie, but even I can recognise bullshit at a hundred paces. All this crap about how we are all in it together to save the nation's finances. Most of us had nothing to do with the profligacy and greed that went on as smart-arsed little spivs bet the farm on worthless securities. There's an oxymoron for you: "worthless securities". Argh!

I haven't got out of bed yet, but I'm seething. And there's another thing, one of my favourite hobby-horses. All the crap about "Your M and S", "Your Tescos". As if they are our friends. They must think we're complete simpletons. I drift into fantasy mode, which, but for my current grumpiness, might have involved Cordelia. I see Joe Public as Lennie Small in *Of Mice and Men*.

'Tell me again, Tesco Kid, about the spread we're gonna have. Where chickens and livestock will roam free across the rich green acres. Where every little helps, where a man can grow and gorge on barn eggs, grits and fresh-baked biscuits, maybe raise a family. Where we won't have to hide no more. Tell me again about how I can have a rabbit of my own to pet and get loyalty points. And how you'll always be my friend.' Argh!

(I would like to repeat that Tesco and M&S are registered trademarks and I have no tangible assets.)

Friday:

I go to the supermarket to do a big shop and to seek inspiration regarding this Saturday's supper. I'm actually not a bad cook, but the up-coming meal has a particular significance for me, as I appear to be falling in love and I would hate to ruin my chances with a botched offering.

I ponder on various options, but in the end decide on a simple beef casserole, followed by fresh fruit and cream. I buy the necessary ingredients, plus some wines and cheeses and proceed to the checkout. On the way, I'm waylaid by Little Owl, who looks disdainfully at my purchases.

'Well that lot'll kill you if nothing else does,' she snorts.

I watch a DVD of Vittorio De Sica's brilliant film, *Umberto D.* It makes me cry, perhaps because there are so many similarities between the life of the hero and my own. I don't have a dog though. Worse luck.

Saturday:

I get up early to begin preparations for tonight's little soiree. While the casserole is simmering in the oven, I try to persuade the vacuum cleaner not to be petulant. It doesn't do a very good job, but I marvel at the fact that all the dust, skin flakes, dead flies etcetera are sucked in and presumably end up back at the power station run by those nice energy company people who keep exhorting me to save the planet. I might write to them suggesting that they turn all this detritus into briquettes which could then be used to build affordable homes.

It's a very successful evening. For one who normally seems to attract disaster, I think I did a good job. The Adonis Twins were very funny in that anarchic way that gays so often are. The wine flowed and I think a good time was had by all. Around midnight, the Twins left and Cordelia offered to help with the washing up.

'No, it's fine,' I said, 'I'll just stack it up and do it in the morning.'

'Well, while you're stacking up, I'll fix us both a nightcap. Come down in about ten minutes,' she said. With that she wafted out of my flat and glided down the stairs to her own.

Ha ha. This one-time would-be serial womaniser, once a hopeful defiler of young maidenhood, Bluebeard of the Home Counties, lounge bar lothario. I immediately went into panic mode. Any man who thinks that he has "pulled" a woman, that this is somehow random, or a result of his charm and persuasive powers is sadly deluded. The woman decides on the progress of a courtship. No amount of posturing and derring-do on the part of the man makes a scrap of difference. Cordelia must have known for some time that I fancy her like mad, but she has kept her distance and has even been mocking at times. This in itself might have been a calculation to reel me in. However, I'd like to think it was my masterful casserole, the artfully arranged supermarket flowers in a milk jug and the occasional *bon mot* that might finally have tipped the balance in my favour. Who knows?

I thank the heavens that I'm not wearing tatty underpants or my Dennis the Menace socks as I descend to Cordelia's flat. I tap out a jaunty tattoo on her door, hopefully suggesting playfulness. She opens the door and whispers that she has a visitor. It's Robin, the recent abscondee to Reg's basement lair and wife of VATman,. She's sitting on a sofa, sobbing quietly and dabbing at her eyes with a tissue.

It transpires that Reg is not after all the man of Robin's dreams. He drinks too much and his dog, the detestable, Patsy *nee* Cline, has bitten her twice and chewed up her best shoes. There's no nightcap and I sit sipping a glass of water and find myself joining Cordelia in a head-tilting display of sympathy. The upshot is that Robin is offered sanctuary for the night and I'm sent packing with a peck on the cheek. Oh well, back to the raft building.

Sunday:

I get a call from Cyclops. She tells me that the Reverend Coot is very poorly and has asked if I might visit him again soon. She also runs through a litany of recently deceased schoolmates, which cheers me up no end.

'You could have amounted to something if you had put your mind to it,' she says before hanging up.

I finally finish the washing up from Saturday night's soiree. Although it's a bit chilly, I sit out on the balcony sipping some left over wine. It's not the nightcap I would have wished for a day ago, but such is life. I open my dog-eared copy of Chaucer's Prologue to the *Canterbury Tales* and read yet again the opening lines:

"Whan that Aprille with his shoures soote,.."
The droghte of Marche hath perced to the roote..."

It's written in an almost unintelligible Middle English, but the cadence and the rhythm of the verse still electrify me and Chaucer's portrayal of the pilgrims' strengths, foibles and weaknesses rings true across the centuries.

He would have hated Tescos.

Black Dog

Monday:

Today, the minmarket is selling chickens at three pounds each. They are very small, but I put three in my basket on the basis that should the snows return this winter and cripple the country, I won't starve to death. I could cook all three together and get something like an emaciated jackdaw with six legs, which might keep me going for a few days before the intrepid council workers on their bicycle mounted snow ploughs carve out a path to the outside world.

Proceeding toward the checkout, I daydream about the possible scene at the local council depot as the wintry skies cloud over...

The ploughists have made last minute adjustments to their machines, oiled their sprockets, honed their mini plough blades and checked their bells and cycle clips. They sit in a Nissen hut, sipping cocoa and engage in a light-hearted banter that belies the underlying tension of the situation.

As the skies darken further and a light snow begins to fall, they are put on red alert by the grim-faced depot manager, who's a hard taskmaster, but loved by the ploughists under his command. His faithful Labrador, dozes peacefully by the old stove that heats the hut and gives out an eerie light. He periodically lets go silent, but lethal, farts, which cause the occasional dispute among the ploughists as to their ownership.

Elsewhere, in a nerve centre deep beneath the council offices, seconded refuse collectors, town planners, rodent control operatives and other know-nothings on double time pretend to be meteorologists and study the latest weather reports, while slips of girls from the accounts department shovel marshmallows and meringues, representing snow fall, around a table map of the borough.

The mayor arrives in the bunker, fresh from a Round Table meeting, ostensibly to discuss the next town pageant, but actually to hammer out contracts with his fellow altruists to build substandard social housing and generally carve out their various fiefdoms in this piddling parish. He's wearing his chain of office, probably purchased with my council tax over-payments and is accompanied by his brassy wife, who was once, in the brief bloom of youth, a handmaiden to a carnival queen. The mayor, who at the time was a plasterer, made her pregnant during a hurried knee trembler behind the chip shop and they married in haste and have lived a happy life of mutual recrimination ever since.

The marshmallows and meringues are building up on the parish map at an alarming rate, suggesting at least a half inch of snow in places. This is a crucial moment. Only the mayor has the authority to launch the ploughists and the responsibility of this weighs heavily on him. His wife, in an unusual display of affection, mops his brow as he struggles with indecision. Finally, he pulls his pudgy frame up to its full height of around five feet one and gives the order to scramble. A boxful of little Lego men, representing the ploughists, is then tipped on to the map table to await positional reports.

At the depot, the order is received and the ploughists dash toward their bicycles, some of them falling over in the slush. They mount up, hi-viz jackets glowing in the dark. Some of them collide with each other as they wobble off on their missions. In the hut the Labrador, consumed with indifference, delivers his best fart of the day to an unappreciative void. Outside, the depot manager taps his pipe out against a "Shoes for Africa" bin and curses the gammy leg that has prevented him from taking part in tonight's sorties.

The ploughists fan out across the borough, their legs going like egg beaters as their mini bicycle-mounted blades almost clear some minor footpaths and the forecourt of the Conservative Club, wherein the mayor and his lady wife have repaired to keep abreast of the situation.

The ploughists appear to be fighting a losing battle against the light powdering of snow. Then the order goes out to deploy the ultimate weapon. Each of them is equipped with a small vial containing Sainsbury's "Taste the Difference Essex Sea Salt". They begin sprinkling this at important road junctions to absolutely no effect. In the morning, as ever, the town comes to a complete standstill.

Oh this sceptred isle in a sea of corruption, incompetence and amateurism. Did we really once have the greatest empire the world has ever known? And is there honey still for tea?...

'Ere, you gonna buy these chickens or not?'

It's The Embryo, impatiently drumming her fingers on the checkout counter.

'Oh, I'm so sorry,' I say, 'I was miles away.'

'Losin' the plot more likely,' she cackles to a colleague who is sucking on a bottle of cola, while dusting the fruit and veg.

I recently learnt that The Embryo's actual name is Steff, or Steph. It sounds like one half of a malevolent bacterium.

Tuesday:

I return to the Eventide Nursing Home to visit Coot. He's not in the day room as before.

'He very poorly. Stop eating.' the Slavic care assistant tells me. 'He die soon I think.'

Coot is in his own room propped up in bed reading. He looks smaller and even more sparrow-like than before.

'My dear boy,' he says, putting down his book. 'How good of you to come again.'

'It's a pleasure,' I tell him. 'I hear you've not been well.'

'Well, I've certainly lost my appetite for food of late, but not for a good book,' he says. 'I've just been chuckling over Swift's *Gulliver's Travels*. I particularly enjoy his visit to Laputa, where with the help of a magician, he is able to summon up and question any figure from human history. Monarchs, princes, nobles, courtiers, politicians and military leaders appear before him. Without exception, they each tell him that they were driven by a will for power and wealth at any price. They freely admit that they countenanced corruption, perjury, murder, infanticide, genocide, torture and many other inhumanities in pursuit of their goals. Sounds familiar doesn't it?'

'Yes, I'm afraid it does,' I say 'but humanity has progressed a little since those days. Perhaps the checks and balances of hard won democracy have tempered ruthless ambition.'

'Well, we no longer have the divine right of kings or holy wars, but these have been replaced by the divine right of the dollar and the idea of the just war. Corruption and inhumanity continue, but are cloaked in different, but equally spurious justifications. Nationalism, Free Trade, nation building and religion, to name but a few. One always needs to ask oneself who are the engineers and ultimate beneficiaries of conflict?

It's not the hapless soldier, or those slaughtered, or maimed by ever more ingenious weapons.'

'If we could hold a similar identity parade to that conducted by Gulliver, but drawn from recent history, we would find the same types of ruthless shits and charlatans that he found. The only difference being, I suppose, is that they would be politicians, bankers and captains of industry rather than monarchs and princes. Different players, but the same motives. It's no accident that when the Americans and their allies marched on Baghdad, the back markers in the convoy were the trailers and trucks of major hamburger outlets. And let's not forget those pious Calvinists, the Swiss, who have lent money to all sides in many wars, while remaining smugly neutral and subsequently enriched.'

I'm amazed that a man who appears to be at death's door can still summon the will and energy to rail against injustice and have the mental faculties with which to analyse its causes. Far more succinct than my rants against society.

'Do you know,' he says, 'I would very much like to go outside for a while. See if you can persuade my muscular carer, Ludmilla, to let you push me around the garden in a wheelchair.'

I go to see Ludmilla, who thinks this is a good idea and might restore his appetite. She fetches a wheelchair and easily lifts Coot into it. I notice that his legs are thinner than his arms.

'Maybe you like some favourite cake when you get back, yes?' she says, as she wraps him in several layers of blankets.

'That would be very nice,' says Coot and we set off for the garden.

It's a bright, autumnal day and the trees have begun turning to wonderful shades of pastel and a breeze sends leaves scudding across the lawns.

'I hope that I haven't depressed you with my chatter,' says Coot.

'It's a very bleak picture that you paint,' I tell him. 'Is there no hope for humanity?'

'Yes, I believe there is', he says. 'Alongside the ravening will to power that I spoke of, I think there is also in many people a will to good, by which I mean compassion, justice and equality. Each of these can perhaps be explained in evolutionary terms, but I think that the latter might one day prevail. The Sermon on the Mount summed it up beautifully. Unfortunately, we've been waiting for over two thousand years for it to come to pass.'

I continue to push the chair around the garden for some time and there's a companionable silence between us. Every now and then the leaves are whipped up into little vortices like mini tornadoes and a slight chill enters the air, foreshadowing the winter to come.

'Are you alright? I eventually ask. 'Do you want to go back in yet?'

There's no response and going round the chair to face him, I realise that he has died, flown like a little sparrow. He looks very peaceful and has a hint of a smile on his face. I wheel him back inside and tell Ludmilla that he has passed on.

'Bugger,' she says, 'I cut some of his favourite cake for him. You like to take it? Very nice. Is called angel cake.'

When I get home, I call Cyclops to tell her the news.

'I hope you didn't upset him,' she says.

Wednesday:

A reflective time. It's not every day that one finds oneself pushing a corpse around in a wheelchair. Of course, Archibald Coot's death was not tragic. He was a ripe old age and he wasn't a relative. Nevertheless, he has been a significant figure in my life. When I first challenged him all those years ago over the concept of God's omnipresence, it was the first time that I had openly rebelled against authority. I had form, as the police say, for lying about illnesses and for being a sullen and reluctant schoolboy, but my contradiction of Coot was of a different order.

In retrospect, I think that it was quite brave, since any transgression in the Dickensian madhouse was usually rewarded with a sound beating. Hence the hushed silence of my classmates when I spoke out. I was Oliver to Coot's Mister Bumble and it could only end in tears.

Many times since, I've tried to work out what it was that impelled me to rebel against Coot's dogmatism. When he was delivering his homilies, I was only half awake and dreaming of being Robin Hood. It would be easy and convenient to conclude that I was a smart young kid who wasn't easily taken in by mumbo-jumbo — a sort of cub crusader after truth. But this was not the case, because I was certainly taken in by Errol Flynn's portrayal of the obviously mythical Robin and I played around with reality with my fake sick notes and imagined ailments. I was a fantasist and a consummate liar when it suited me.

The truth is probably more prosaic. I was quite simply bored to death with school. I hated the numbing routines, the rote learning, the brutality and above all, the clamour of it all. I was a loner, happy with my own company and daydreams. When Coot prodded me in the chest with his bony finger to emphasise his point, he pressed a button that turned ennui to anger.

Now, I'm just a grumpy old fart.

Thursday:

I drive to an out of town M&S store to get replacement underwear and socks. Under normal circumstances, I would find this traumatic, but my misery is compounded by the fact that some two months prior to the event, they are already celebrating Christmas. Cardboard reindeer and a life-size inflated Santa adorn the entrance and carols blare out across the shop. I get what I need, but I'm feeling hot and irritable.

Next door is a Tesco twenty four hour mega-store. I'm very thirsty, so I go in to get a drink. I immediately get lost and find myself in an aisle selling Christmas decorations. There are fairy lights, inflatable Santas, plastic Christmas trees and other such junk. I wonder whether the hands that made these for a pittance in far off climes even know or care what Christmas is. If they start to get ideas above their station and demand fair pay and conditions, perhaps we'll bomb them all soon in the name of free trade and nation building.

I eventually buy a bottle of apparently fresh orange juice that says it has bits. Presumably this means bits of orange. What a surprise and how good of Tesco to include them. I might otherwise have thought that I was drinking llama piss.

Friday:

I've realised that I'm actually feeling quite depressed and I have been for some time. Coot's death, particularly as I was wheeling him around the rest home garden at the time, hasn't helped, but there's something else. Sometimes, I really do envy people who seem happy to accept the status quo, who don't get worked up about Tescos and all the things that seem to trigger my anger. Churchill, our still revered one-time national leader, suffered from depression and called it the black dog. Given his track record as a cynical political turncoat, alcoholic and gleeful architect of mass slaughter, I'm not surprised that he occasionally got depressed.

Saturday:

Another local pub gig with a blues band. They are very good, but the singer prefaces most of his lines with "Well". I remember reading somewhere that John Lennon claimed, falsely I think, that he and Paul always avoided the word "just" in their lyrics. I've never had the time or inclination to check this.

I drink too much and have to get a taxi home.

Sunday:

I walk to the pub to retrieve the Fiesta. As it stutters into life, I ponder on mine and it seems rather bleak this Sunday morning in a pub car park in the back of beyond. A man walks by with a dog with only three legs. I count my blessings and return home for a frugal breakfast.

Tonight, I watch *The Antiques Road show* on television. I'm fascinated by the facial expressions of the punters as they await the valuation of the object they have brought to be valued. In every case, they try to assume an air of nonchalance, as if this is the last thing on their minds.

I'm reminded of a wonderful Kurt Vonnegut story in which a group of Earthlings is abducted by aliens who put them in a zoo on their home planet. Each Earthling is told that they have a million dollars invested on the New York stock exchange. In their cage is a giant illuminated board displaying fictitious share prices. Unknown to the Earthlings, visitors to the zoo can manipulate these prices just to see how the abductees will react. They watch in wonder as the Earthlings' emotions run from joy to despair in a few moments and they marvel at how anyone could be so stupid.

Ho hum, as Kurt would say.

Scunthorpe Travelodge

Monday:

The Black Dog seems to have found another victim to torment, so I feel quite chipper today. I deliberately avoid listening to the *Today* programme and I even forego *The Times* crossword on the basis that my eye might accidentally glance over some news item that could lower my mood and trigger a rant.

In the flat below, Brint and Shards are having a blazing row.

'You, Brent, are an idle, good for nothing piss ant,' Shards screams.

'Why what have I done now?' Brint remonstrates.

'What have you done? What have you done? I'll tell you what you've done. Fuck all. That's what you've done,' she bellows, making me flinch and I'm not even on the receiving end.

And so on. She is clearly softening Brint up for fatherhood and its attendant responsibilities and duties. She then delivers lines that lift my spirits even further.

'I should have listened to Mumsie and married that taxidermist from Brissy. He had lovely hands. But no, I wouldn't listen and I've ended up with a galoot on valium.'

Brint will clearly have some grovelling to do before the day is out. I know the pattern well. Shards will inflict the ultimate female weapon on him for the rest of the day and perhaps into tomorrow. Silence. The deadly "No Speaks". I might be regarded as a traitor to my sex for revealing this, but men really hate it. They will claim, in the safety of the lounge bar perhaps that they care little about it, but they do. Oh, they do. They hate it more than the tongue lashing that usually precedes it.

Brint will hold out stubbornly for an hour or two, then he'll start to do a few jobs around the flat that he's been putting off for ages. He'll make her some coffee and perhaps even change the duvet cover on the bed. (A task most men, me included, find virtually impossible) In extreme cases, he might even do a little light dusting. If they had a lawn he'd probably mow it. Eventually, when a sufficient number of penances have accrued, Shards might decide to forgive him and he will swear to change his ways, without ever realising what he did wrong in the first place. Been there, done that.

I eventually succumb and go out to get the newspaper. I read that Paris Hilton has made an album on which she apparently sings almost in tune. It's nearly an argh! moment as I think about the cult of celebrity, but I don't want to go there and spoil my day. Instead, I imagine a miniaturised probe, a nanobot, being injected into Paris's brain on a fact finding mission to see what makes her tick.

As the nanobot glides through cathedrals of vast and vaulted emptiness, neural pathways randomly flicker dimly like a budget disco. Images momentarily appear. A cute little puppy, a much-loved pony, a half-completed colouring book, a nail varnish chart and a ra ra skirt. The nanobot explores many of these pathways, only to find cul-de-sacs or incomplete connections.

The probe goes deeper and deeper until finally it reaches the core of Paris's being, the central thingamajig. Here it finds a cob-webbed attic, wherein a fluffy pink gonk is rocking backward and forward saying, "Me, me, me, me, me..."

Given the intellectual vacuity revealed by the nanobot's probing, I'll be that Paris could, nevertheless, inflict some monumental silences if she had a mind to. But for an accident of birth and entitlement, she might easily have been called Scunthorpe Travelodge.

Tuesday:

And thinking of Paris, the city that is, not the singing hotel, I played there a lot in the Sixties. Parisians should never be confused with the French. They are a race apart and, indeed, consider themselves so. Most French people are casually rude to foreigners, particularly the English, as a matter of course. Parisians, on the other hand, go out of their way and put a good deal of effort into being downright nasty. Never believe that crap about them liking it if you at least have a go at speaking their stupid bloody language. Forget it — they hate you from the outset.

However, for a short space of time in the mid-Sixties, everything English was considered chic and cool in Paris. I played there often. It sounds glamorous, but we stayed in the cheapest hotels in the most run down areas. (The Hilton was beyond our dreams) We had very little money and were often on the brink of starvation. We did as many as five gigs a day at weekends, dodging across the city, playing in ballrooms and tiny clubs. To say that we were mercilessly exploited by our French agents would be an understatement. We had no work permits, so we were constantly just one step ahead of government officials who wanted to deport us.

In the early hours of the morning, we would go to raucous cafes and bars in the colourful Pigalle district, where our mangled French and longish hair amused the hookers so much that they would often buy us food and drinks. There was no question of any sexual relationship with these ladies of the night. After all, we were in the same business. Getting shafted for very little money.

Cyclops phones to tell me that Coot's funeral is on Friday.

'It's strange,' she says, 'he's requested that there shouldn't be a service, just a burial. Surely something ought to be said. A prayer or perhaps a hymn at least?'

'If that was his wish,' I tell her, 'then it should be honoured.'

'Well it seems odd to me,' she replies. 'He was a man of the cloth after all. Perhaps his mind had gone at the end.'

I think of Coot, even in his last hour, having a very acute and active mind — which is more than I can say for Cyclops.

Wednesday:

That thoroughly nice chap and national treasure, David Attenborough, is on television doing his usual thing of bonding with gorillas, creeping up on unsuspecting stone age tribes and speaking from windswept cliff tops for no particular reason. I met him once.

In the mid-Seventies, tiring of a life of debauchery (or lack of it) and a diet of alcohol and crisps, I abandoned music and went back to school. I got the necessary qualifications to go to university and got a place at the University of Sussex. This lies some four miles outside Brighton amidst rolling hills and parkland. In those days, it was regarded as a hotbed of radicalism and student protests of one kind or another were an almost daily occurrence. Being a lot older than most of my fellow students, I avoided these and became something of a swot.

After three years I got my degree and although many students shunned it, I was determined to attend the convocation where the degrees were presented. It seemed to me to be a vindication. A small, but satisfying victory over those teachers who had treated most of us kids as morons in the Nineteen Fifties. I duly donned my fur trimmed gown and mortarboard and went to the ceremony.

The Chancellor at the time was Richard (Dickie) Attenborough, Dave's brother. He was seated on a sort of throne. He wore a flowing gown and had a very silly hat on with feathers in it. He was surrounded by other worthies in equally silly outfits. Before the main presentations began, his brother, Dave, was to be given an honorary doctorate in zoology or for jumping out on chimps or something. His name was called and he came on stage wearing a gown and a silly hat.

The usual form would be for Dickie to rise from his chair and present the scroll to his brother. However, he remained in his seat, looking a little glassy eyed. Dave, ever the resourceful boy scout, took the scroll from his brother's limp grip and presented it to himself. Dickie had either lunched a little too well, or he was weighed down with planning crowd scenes for his up-coming film about Gandhi. Either way, he was not in the right state of mind to hand out all the other degrees, so Dave took over, presenting them instead. When it came to my turn, he shook me warmly by the hand and said "Well done". I felt like a Kalahari Bushman being given a roll of fabric. As I left the stage, I glanced across at Dickie. He was sleeping soundly.

Thursday:

Robin, having been away for a few days, has returned to Reg's basement lair. Her husband, VATman, has taken to wearing jeans and a T shirt at weekends and playing loud prog-rock until the early hours. Given a choice between that and Reg's whining cowboys, I think I'd prefer Mantovani.

Friday:

And so to the cemetery for Coot's burial. It's an overcast and blustery day with the occasional shower. Cyclops is waiting at the gates with non other than the odious Grudgeon, the school bully turned Queen's chaplain. We are, it seems, the only mourners and we have to await the arrival of the hearse before proceeding to the graveside. I pretend to have received a call on my mobile phone, so that I won't have to converse with Cyclops and Grudgeon. I walk some distance away holding an imaginary conversation. I even pace up and down and aimlessly kick dead leaves just to give my performance a touch of authenticity.

The hearse arrives and we are instructed to follow its stately progress to the graveside. The coffin is brought to the freshly dug hole and the pall bearers retreat under some trees, lighting up cigarettes and punching each other's arms. I spot a figure weaving toward us. It's Ludmilla, Coot's former carer from the rest home. As she gets nearer, it's clear that she's the worse for wear — utterly drunk. She trips over a couple of gravestones and by the time she reaches us, she's totally bedraggled and covered in leaves and mud.

'Where Archie?' she wails. 'Where my Archie?'

It's ok,' I tell her, 'he's here. You're not too late.'

'Where Archie?' she cries. 'Where Archie?'

'Well, he's in that box,' I tell her. 'In the coffin.'

'In my country we no close box until ready to go in hole,' she says and begins scrabbling at the lid of the coffin, trying to prise it open.

I pull her gently away and she calms down a little.

With that, Grudgeon begins intoning.

'May it please you, Almighty God, that your faithful servant, Archibald Coot...'

'Hey, just a minute,' I say. 'I understood that he didn't want any form of religious service.'

'He wasn't himself at the end,' says Cyclops, her pinprick eyes doing their usual circuits behind her jam jar-bottomed glasses.

'If he wasn't himself,' I say, 'what the fuck was he? A three-piece suite? You're going against his wishes.'

Ludmilla, who has been silently snivelling during this exchange, then begins chanting in a remarkably deep voice, crossing herself from time to time. I think that she might have been singing in Russian, but I can't be sure.

'Peristroika, oh balalaika. Trotskylenin-wodka-vinter palacski-kay-geebeeski...'

'You always were a troublemaker,' hisses Cyclops.

'That it may further please you, Almighty God.' intones Grudgeon.

'Bolshoi-checkov-wodka-wodka-icon-pravda-babushka-katebush-ki-samovar-Stanislavski,' Ludmilla continues, her voice rising in pitch as she begins beating her breasts with her fists.

'This is all wrong,' I shout trying to make myself heard above the intoning and chanting. 'It's not what he wanted. He'd stopped believing in all that religious stuff.'

'That's what you say,' screamed Cyclops. 'But then you always were a liar. I know for a fact that your brother wasn't mauled to death by circus lions. He's alive and well and living in Woking. He's on Facebook.'

'And his only begotten son, who died for us on the cross,' Grudgeon drones on.

'Oh fuck off four eyes,' I shout at Cyclops.

She takes a swing at me with her handbag, but I see it coming and duck at the last minute. It continues its trajectory and hits Ludmilla full in the face. She stops chanting and a serene and beatific smile spreads across her face. She then, quite slowly pitches headlong into Coot's grave. With some considerable difficulty and with the aid of the pall-bearers and ropes, we get her back to the surface and Coot is finally laid to rest.

As we leave the cemetery, Cyclops says,

'I'll never speak to you again. Ever.'

'That's too soon for me,' I reply.

I drive Ludmilla back to the rest home. On the way, she wets herself and throws up in the car.

'Thank you for nice time,' she says, as she staggers away covered in mud and leaves.

When I get home, I pour myself a large scotch and ponder on what Coot would have made of the day's events. I think he would have found it hugely funny. After a couple more scotches, I do too. Even a tiny sparrow...

Saturday:

I have a very weak stomach, particularly with regard to unpleasant smells. I know that I have to clean the car out after Ludmilla's puking and soiling. I spray a tea towel with aftershave and tie it over my nose and mouth before proceeding. I'm busy scraping up bits of carrot and tomato skins, when Cordelia stops by the car on her way out.

'I think you'll find the banks are closed on Saturdays,' she says

'Banks?' I ask, mystified

'Well you look as though you're about to rob one.'

I explain that someone has been sick in the car and I can't stand the smell.

'I hope she was worth it,' she says with an annoying little smile, as she hands me an earring from the passenger seat before gliding off to her car.

Bugger. Caught on the back foot again.

Sunday:

On my way out to get the newspaper, I see Little Owl and The Centaur being cordially welcomed into Brint and Shard's flat. I imagine they're there to begin teaching Shards Cherokee birthing grunts or something similar. No doubt Chief Running Bear will be brought in too, if he can be dragged away from his pursuit of beaver. Perhaps Brint will be instructed on how to howl in complicit agony with Shards when the time comes for the little ankle biter to be delivered. Before then though, he might need a few caffeine enemas to smarten his ideas up. Can't have a dozy galoot in the natal teepee.

Against my better judgment, I watch Scunthorpe Travelodge being interviewed on television about her new album. She reminds me of The Embryo. All eyeliner and very little brain. A primitive life form that sucks in nutriment from its environment. An evolutionary cul-de-sac.

Appalling Flatulence

Monday:

A bolt from the blue. Cordelia phones to ask whether I would accompany her to a wedding in a month's time. Apparently, one of her nieces is getting married in a castle in Wales.

'It will mean quite an early start on the Saturday morning,' she says. 'There will be overnight accommodation and we can drive back on the Sunday.'

For me, this is a no-brainer, as politicians with just such a deficiency are apt to say. "Overnight accommodation" conjures up many images and expectations, but I decide to be a bit cool about it.

'Well, I don't think I'm working. Let me just check,' I say.

I then noisily flick through the pages of my diary as if they're full of exciting David Essex tours, television appearances and modelling incontinence pads.

'Yes, that looks OK,' I say. 'I'd be delighted to come. I haven't been to Wales for years.'

This is a complete lie. I've been to Wales many times in recent years. "Come Back" tours usually start and often end there. When they aren't trying to rip each other's ears off on the rugby pitch, or dressing up as wizards, the Welsh have a great love of rock 'n' roll and R&B. Llanfairpwllgwyngyllgogerychwyrndrobwllllantysiliogogogoch Working Men's Club can be a riot on a Saturday night, once the bingo has finished. (What other language could have four consecutive "Ls" in one word?)

A couple of years back, I played at an R&B festival in Wrexham, North Wales, with a wonderful African-American soul singer called, Charles Walker. The band was accommodated in a guest house that had seen better days. The three brass players, of whom I was one, were crammed into a tiny room. The owner of the guest house was all of a flutter as she showed us to it.

'We've never had a rock 'n' roll band staying here before,' she said.

I adopted a puzzled air as I scanned the room.

'I'm a bit undecided,' I said.

'Well, it's the best we could do,' she said nervously. 'We're completely full.'

'No, it's not the room,' I said. 'I just can't decide which window to throw the television out of.'

Tuesday:

Not all Brummies (natives of Birmingham) have whiny voices. Not all guitarists pull agonised faces and not all bass guitarists are pedestrian. However, some of the members of the backing band for Charles Walker pretty much conformed to these stereotypes.

The band leader and backing singer was a Brummie. He actually had a very good voice, where his natural whine was put to penetrating effect. Offstage, however, he sounded like a kid cajoling his mum for a choc ice. The guitarist pulled some classic faces. He looked very Germanic which somehow made this funnier — a bit like watching a swinish SS officer taking a difficult crap. Like the Brummie, he had no discernible sense of humour. The bass guitarist looked like a wax works model of Jack Palance, the actor. The real life Palance made a speciality of very slow and deliberate movement. The bass guitarist did his best to emulate this. There was also a keyboard player who was an excellent musician. He had a curious loping walk like Jar Jar Binks in the *Star Wars* film. There was a plant-like quality to him too, as if he might have been more at home in the hothouse at Kew Gardens rather than on stage. In the course of two European tours with Charles, I never heard Jar Jar speak. Not once. Perhaps he was too engrossed in photosynthesis, or devising ways of ingratiating himself with Obi-Wan Kenobi.

Normally, camaraderie develops within a band on tour. There might be the odd dispute, but generally tales, banter and a few pranks are the norm. It's a kind of defensive measure against the vicissitudes of crappy hotels, long journeys, villainous promoters, cramped dressing rooms and poor food. This band, however, quickly divided into two distinct camps. On one side were the brass section and the drummer — an old mate and a seasoned trooper. While on the other, were the Trio of Doom: Whiner, the SS officer and Jack Palance. Jar Jar remained neutral, like a disinterested orchid.

Among the Continental gigs we played was the fantastic Porretta Soul Festival. Porretta Terme is a beautiful old spa town in the Apennine mountains south of Bologna. Each July, it plays host to a galaxy of soul stars. Such is the townsfolk's enthusiasm, that the park where the event takes place is called Rufus Thomas Park and one of the main streets is Via Otis Redding. I can't imagine this happening in the UK. Cliff Richard's Passage or Bono Boulevard don't have quite the same ring to them.

The Trio of Doom complained about the food, the hotel and just about everything else. They took no part in after-gig carousing and had early nights. The exception being on one occasion when The Whiner scoured the town in the early hours looking for Charles and the rest of the band. Being a control freak, he couldn't stand the thought of not knowing where we were, or the idea that, horror of horrors, we might be enjoying ourselves. Perhaps he thought we might be corrupting Charles, an innocent fifty-something who grew up on the wrong side of the tracks and cut his musical teeth in some of the meanest and toughest bars and clubs from Nashville through Chicago to New York. The Whiner finally found us eating and guzzling wine in a pizzeria.

'It's half-past two,' he gasped, winded by his efforts.

'It's ok,' I said, 'I've got a day off from the paper round tomorrow.'

It was bound to end in tears and finally did so in Switzerland when, unbeknown to us, one of the Trio made a disparaging remark about the brass section. This was overheard by the drummer — normally a peaceable chap. When I came into the dressing room, he had the three of them pinned against a wall, threatening dire personal injury. Like the rest of us, he'd had enough of the Trio of Doom. Besides, none of them had a tale to tell. And they didn't drink. Perhaps they were, like Jar Jar Binks, aliens or even Triffids.

Wednesday:

I set up my keyboard. I like playing the piano, but I'm not very good at it. I use it as a tool for arranging and composing, together with the clever software that's available these days.

My father, on the other hand, was quite an accomplished pianist and had at one time played in cinemas for silent films. He had a wonderful ear for a tune and could play virtually anything after hearing it once. But his style was very odd.

We always had a piano in the house and often had singsongs with neighbours and friends after the pubs closed on Saturday nights. My father would run through his repertoire of old music hall songs as well as popular numbers of the day. On songs with which he was unfamiliar, his right hand picked out the tune well enough, but his left hand would flick hesitantly across often unrelated bass notes in a rhythmic rather than harmonic way. A bit like an elephant's trunk seeking out a titbit. He called this vamping.

As the drink flowed and the evening progressed, my father's playing would start brightly enough, but begin to slow down inexorably until he slumped unconscious on the keyboard. He would be pumped full of black coffee and be good for a few more tunes, until once again the tempo would begin to get slower and slower, finally grinding to a halt as he again lost consciousness. This process might be repeated several times until the revellers realised that no amount of coffee was going to wake him up and the evening came to an end.

The Whiner would have hated him.

Thursday:

I buy some quite expensive "Duchy Originals" bacon from the min-market. "Duchy Originals" is the brand name for products that have come from the vast estates of Prince Charles, heir to the throne and over-barned twit. The range also includes sausages, biscuits, poultry, drinks and for all I know, or care, edible leaf mould.

The packaging trumpets the word "organic", as if this in itself is enough to justify the extra cost. I imagine Chas and his under-barned, once third-person-in-the-marriage, triple-eye-linered- gargoyle consort, Camilla, striding through pig shit in their designer wellies, somewhere in darkest Cornwall.

'Oh look, Cams. What delightful organic pig type things,' Chas says.

'Ears,' says Cams, smiling bravely. She's still feeling a little bruised from Chas's inept and noisy overnight fumblings. Below stairs on such occasions, the servants interrupt their gnawing at ferret gristle and guzzling mead, to nudge each other knowingly. 'Ah ha, the master be a-cam-shafting again.'

'Once I'm queen,' Cams thinks to herself, 'he can forget all that malarkey.'

'Just think, Cams,' he says, 'the meat from these animals will end up on the plates of honest everyday artisans. Thatchers, dry stone wall builders, Morris men, madrigal singers, swan uppers, fletchers, millers, canal diggers and homeopaths.'

'Ears', says Cams, her walnut brain struggling to cope with such a long sentence containing words other than pony, frock, or gymkhana.

I cook and eat some of the bacon and can't tell the difference between it and the BOGOF version at half the price.

Pass me my crossbow.

Friday:

On a whim, I have a look on Friends Reunited to see whether my first love might be on it. She isn't. Just as well really, otherwise I might have been tempted to send her a sloppy message. Her name was Helen Brown and I loved her with a passion that perhaps only a fourteen-year old can feel. She had raven hair, a beautiful face and deep, dark brown eyes. We would often cycle the countryside together and I would sometimes catch my breath as I watched her hair fly in the wind.

Helen's parents owned their own detached house in a leafy road in a better part of town. I was a council estate kid and although I hadn't met them, I think her parents disapproved of me. Helen felt that if they met me socially, they might come to like me. So she arranged for me to go to tea one Sunday afternoon.

The appointed day arrived. I walked nervously up the neatly paved garden path, past a well-trimmed lawn and formal flower beds. It was a world away from our front garden, which had the odd tuft of grass, some pram wheels and a rusty bike. After introductions, during which I felt Helen's mother's critical eyes giving me the once over, we went into the dining room. Her father, who looked a little like Oliver Hardy, said nothing apart from a gruff "hello". I felt about as welcome as a swine 'flu virus in a leper colony.

We sat down to dainty triangular sandwiches (no crusts), cakes on a tiered stand and tea in delicate bone china cups. To begin with, hardly a word was said. Food was passed politely and the only sound was the genteel tinkling of teacups and spoons. It was a far cry from the mealtime free-for-all I was used to at home, where there would usually be laughter, arguments, sometimes tears and every man for himself.

When Mr. Brown's first trumpeting fart broke the silence, I was taken completely by surprise and began to titter. Helen shot me a warning look. I stuffed my face with a cake and squirmed uncomfortably. She and her mother acted as though this thunderous emission hadn't happened and so did Mr. Brown.

In my house, farting, though not actively encouraged, was, nevertheless, seen as potentially comic. When I was about eight years old, I was ill in bed with a cold. My mother and brother were downstairs listening to the radio. My brother let loose a lengthy and whining fart that went "Muuuummmm". Whereupon my mother got up from her chair and shouted up the stairs.

'Ok, son, I'll be up in a minute'

My brother's fart became the stuff of family legend and brought laughter in the re-telling for many years. There was no such levity here at the Brown's tea table.

While Mrs Brown quizzed me about my background and future plans, Mister Brown said nothing, but continued to fart and occasionally belch at regular intervals. At one point, as I was telling her about playing the clarinet in a dance band and my plans to go to music college, he reached across the table for a fairy cake and let loose an appalling and prolonged fart. It was almost as if he and I were in competition with each other. My musical credentials versus his anal virtuosity. I somehow managed to quell the hysteria that was mounting within me. My family would have been in convulsions long before this. Mrs Brown rose from her chair.

'Has everyone had enough?' she asked

'Yes, thank you very much Mrs Brown. That was very nice,' I said, thankful that my torture was coming to an end.

'Let's clear these things away then, Helen,' said Mrs Brown briskly and they collected the dishes and took them into the kitchen.

I was now left alone with Mr. Brown, who hitherto had not uttered a word. He stared down at the table as if deep in thought, then looked up at me.

'I suppose the clarinet takes a lot of wind,' he said.

For me this was the *coup de grace*. I started to snicker. I coughed into my hand to try to cover it up, but it was no good. The snicker grew into a giggle. My shoulders began to shake and I started howling uncontrollably, clutching at my aching stomach and rocking back and forth in my chair.

Helen came back into the room looking puzzled. I tried to stop laughing, but I was past redemption. Helen's expression turned to thunder. This only made matters worse, because I found this wildly funny too. Her mother came back into the room.

'I think you might exercise some self-control young man,' said Mrs Brown stiffly and went back to the kitchen.

Helen ushered me out of the house still laughing.

'Why didn't you warn me,' I sputtered.

'You should have ignored him. We do. He can't help it.'

My expressions of regret between convulsions had no effect and she turned on her heel at the gate and went haughtily back into the house without a word. I had been tested in the crucible of her Dad's appalling flatulence and found wanting. I had blown it.

Saturday:

A last-minute pub gig of such awfulness that I can barely recount it without wanting to throw up, or turn my sax into a lethally spiked mace, specially crafted to maim guitarists. I realise that this is hardly fair, since I do know a lot of good ones. However, the one in question here, would have caused Gandhi to reach for a spear should he have been unlucky enough to be in the same room with him, let alone sharing a stage.

This cretin made The Gerbs Neanderthal strummer seem a paragon of restraint. He cut and slashed his way through every number like a runaway chain saw and at a volume level that made my teeth chatter. He strutted menacingly around the stage like a pantomime villain and had a cigarette permanently dangling from his lips. The concept of light and shade would, I imagine, be as alien to him as algebra would be to a gerbil.

On returning home, ears reddened and ringing, I listen to some Elgar, while imagining the guitarist slowly dissolving in a vat of acid.

Sunday:

I finish off the bacon.

Don't Mess with my Mum

Monday:

A bright autumn day. I awake in good spirits despite last Saturday night's ear bashing and a boring Sunday, during which I stared at the cobwebs and dust in the flat, wishing I had a housekeeper or a lady what does. I don't suppose Charles and Camilla have this problem, although I can imagine Chas in a Laura Ashley pinnie and little else dusting round Clarence House, while the eye-linered gargoyle languorously flicks a Cornish birch frond at his nethers. Organic S&M.

My mother hated the royal family, but then she hated authority in any shape or form. Top of her list was the local council, followed by anyone in uniform. My dad once got a job as the commissionaire at the local cinema. He was required to wear a stupid red uniform and a peaked hat. When he got home from work, he quickly got out of this outfit in case my mother mistook him for a Ruritanian army officer or an official of some kind and started beating him up. For some never explained reason, she also hated the Irish, which was strange, since she married a second generation Irishman and both her sons married Irish girls.

Although poorly educated, she was a very intelligent woman. She was from Welsh stock and had that nation's love of language and a story well told. She re-invented her past so many times that the truth is now lost in the mists of time and her skilful weaving. The one seemingly consistent fact, however, is that she was abandoned by her alcoholic parents while still under ten years old and left to fend for herself on the streets of London. She had various foster parents, but ran away so often I think the authorities gave up on her.

During the war, she and my brother and sister were evacuated to rural Surrey. She had no liking for the countryside and expressed bafflement as to why the open spaces weren't built upon. She also disliked country folk, describing them as "swede-gnawers".

She had a fearsome temper, particularly if she thought someone was taking the Mickey out of her or trying to take advantage. When I was around thirteen years old, I played the tea chest bass in a skiffle group. We had a gig at a local pub and my parents came to watch. Standing beside my mother were two Teddy Boys who seemed to find her presence among lots of teenagers amusing. As I tugged away at the bass, I could see what was happening and knew that there could only be one outcome. My mother had a fixed smile on her face — always a sign to run for cover. The Teddy Boys persisted in making remarks and generally taking the piss and in a flash she dropped them both and then resumed listening to the band as if nothing had happened.

She and my father would occasionally perform a mind-reading act around working men's clubs and pubs. I think they called themselves Albert and Violetta. It was a very good act and no one ever guessed its secret. I was in my teens before I was told how it was done and I was amazed at how simple it was. I am, however, still sworn to secrecy.

On one occasion, they were performing in a club and for some inexplicable reason my mother was dressed as a Polynesian girl, complete with a grass skirt and a flower in her hair. A drunken sailor, thinking he'd have a little fun, crept up behind her with a lighter and was about to set light to the skirt when she spun round and laid him out. Maybe she had read his mind.

Tuesday:

After breakfast, I decide to go for a drive. I have no destination in mind; I just feel a great restlessness and a need to be going somewhere. My mother was also afflicted with this restlessness, although she didn't have the opportunities to travel that I've had. In her seventies though, she went on a Mediterranean cruise. On her return I asked her about it.

'How was Haifa?,' I asked.

'It was OK,' she said, unenthusiastically. 'I was sitting in a market square when a shady looking Arab tried to persuade me to go down some alley to look at carpets. I told him to fuck off. They seem to understand that in any language dear.'

'And Athens?' I asked.

'It was alright I suppose, but those Greeks are a lazy lot of buggers. We cleared up our bomb damage years ago.'

On further questioning, I realised that she was referring to The Parthenon.

I chug along in the Fiesta, through pretty villages and an autumnal landscape, eventually arriving at the hideous seaside town of Little-hampton. By now, it's lunchtime, so I buy some fish and chips and sit in a shelter on the promenade to eat them. The wind gets up and it begins to rain. The grey sea, like me, is restless and unsettled.

Two teenage lads run into the shelter to get out of the rain. It's not long before they're nudging each other and giggling, obviously finding me amusing.

'Gissa chip Grandad,' one of them says.

'Yeah, gissa a chip,' says the other with a hint of menace.

'Here, finish them off,' I say putting the half-finished lunch on the seat and walking back to the car.

Had it been my mother sitting there instead of me, these lads might quickly have lost their appetites.

Wednesday:

I could be wrong, but think that Adrian, *aka* VATman and April, formerly Kevin the mechanic, have become an item. This morning I saw her getting into his car. He held the passenger door open for her as she folded her not inconsiderable frame into the seat. I'm reminded of the last line in *Some Like It Hot*, when Jerry, who's been posing as a woman, tells Osgood, his millionaire suitor, that he's really a man.

"Well, nobody's perfect."

Thursday:

No respite from the restlessness. I found it hard to sleep last night and even my imaginary efforts at building a bloody raft didn't help. I eventually dropped off, but kept waking up suddenly as if hit by a taser. I try to cheer myself up by having a cooked breakfast, but this seems tasteless to me. It's not until mid-morning that I realise that I'm having another visit from The Black Dog.

My mother suffered these visitations to a far greater extent than me and I suppose these days she would be described as being bi-polar and receive appropriate medication. In her day, however, there was little understanding of the condition and the standard treatment was the brutal and generally useless electric shock therapy, or being told to pull yourself together. When she had what she called one of her "funny heads", the rest of us in the house would be walking on eggshells. At these times she could be cruelly critical of everyone and everything around her. As a little boy, these episodes always made me feel that I had done something wrong to cause them and I would go out of my way to try to please her, generally to no avail.

Given her tough childhood, it's hardly surprising that she had demons, but despite these "funny heads", she remained an indomitable spirit to the end of her days. When she was in her eighties she had a stroke and went into a coma. I was at her bedside when she briefly regained consciousness.

'Are you all right Mum?' I asked.

'I'll be OK once I've had the baby dear,' she laughed and then slipped away. They don't make 'em like that any more.

Friday:

A printed card from Little Owl informing me and presumably the rest of the world, that in addition to giving colonic irrigation and caffeine enemas, she is now a Feng Shui consultant. My spirits are lifted as I imagine a scene where one of her victims lies helplessly tubed up while Little Owl re-arranges his furniture and garden.

I meet Cordelia on the stairs. Given that we're scheduled to spend the night together in Wales in a few weeks' time, she seems strangely distant and I realise that apart from fancying her like mad, I know next to nothing about her. I know that she works, but for whom and where? She has an expensive car and thought nothing of laying out over a grand for her nephew's saxophone, so she's not short of a few bob. Further inquiries needed I think.

A fleeting visit to the mini-market where I see The Embryo showing off an engagement ring to the rest of the staff. I imagine the lucky man must be the iron-mongered Goth I saw a few weeks ago in the shop. He seemed to have so much metal on or through him that I could imagine him constantly being forced to face north like a human compass. Perhaps they'll breed ball bearings.

Saturday:

I read a newspaper article about the supposed sexual promiscuity in the Sixties, particularly among musicians. There's an element of truth in this, but more often than not it's wishful thinking.

The first professional band that I played in comprised six hormonally charged and rampant young men with four principal priorities: sex, food, booze and somewhere decent to sleep. These were rarely achieved. Many promoters thought nothing of booking us all into a single dormitory-like room in some back street flea pit. This was hardly conducive to romance, but on the rare occasion when one of the band got lucky, a girl might have to be smuggled into the dormitory. In this case, there was an unwritten rule that the rest of the band had to maintain silence and pretend to be asleep. I've heard many declarations of undying love while pretending to be asleep.

One night, in the small mining town of Swadlincote in Derbyshire, one of our number sneaked back to the room with a girl. He and she tiptoed through the darkness and lay on his bed and were soon locked in a passionate embrace. Five pairs of beady and envious eyes slowly flickered open, straining in the gloom to see what progress he was making. He began snaking his hand up the girl's skirt. The technique is as old as the hills. An innocent caress of the knee as if it's the most amazingly erotic thing. Then a little further up the thigh. Then even further up the thigh. Whereupon this doughty Derbyshire lass slapped his hand saying,

'Eh up, tits first.'

The room exploded into mirth and the poor girl, realising for the first time perhaps that she was surrounded by the rest of the band, fled in horror. Another failure.

Sunday:

A quiet day. As I descend the stairs on my way to get the paper, I see VATman exiting from April's flat. At the foot of the stairs, huddled in a tatty blanket is Reg the caretaker. He has clearly been thrown out by Robin and has spent the night there.

Oh happy days.

Sprouts

Monday:

I have some leftover chicken from the weekend, so I decide to make a curry out of it. At the mini market, I buy a jar of some sort of curry sauce called Mystery of the East. On the label it has a picture of a grinning, turbanned Indian gentleman. I've hardly ever eaten curry — it's not something that appeals to me, but I'll give it a go.

I fry up some peppers and onions and then throw in the leftover chicken and curry sauce. I also cook some rice. I assemble this lot on a plate and start to tuck in. It takes only a few seconds for me to realise that I'm not eating a meal as such, but swallowing a torchlight procession. My head is on fire and my throat nearly goes into a fatal spasm. I rush to the kitchen and start guzzling water, but this seems only to exacerbate the extreme heat. After about ten minutes, the furnace that was once my digestive tract has calmed down a little. I take a look at the empty sauce jar and notice that it says "Seriously Hot" on the label. I wouldn't have been surprised if it had warned against spilling it on painted surfaces or non colour-fast fabrics. I worry that it has destroyed the lining of my mouth, my palate and possible my adenoids and that henceforth I might speak like Kenneth Williams. I bin the lot and have a cheese sandwich.

Tuesday:

The whole Christmas nonsense has started to kick in. The crappy town lights have been switched on by some nonentity who's playing Mother Goose, or Sinbad at a nearby theatre. The mini-market has tinny carols blaring out of the in-store speakers and the staff have begun decorating themselves. As I paid for my paper today, The Embryo, she of studied indifference, was wearing clip-on antlers. She looked at me uncomprehendingly when I asked if she might be Vixen or Blitzen. She shook her head dismissively and the antlers wobbled, making her look more like an aphid than a reindeer. Perhaps when she and the iron-mongered Goth embark on a fast-track breeding programme, as they inevitably will, the little ball bearings that they produce will gather around a magnet rather than a manger on Christmas Eve and sing along to Iron Maiden and Metallica

Wednesday:

I'm feeling distinctly unadventurous after the Bombay blow lamp episode, so I buy a pizza. I top it up with bits and bobs and it isn't half bad, but still a pale imitation of what a real Italian pizza tastes like.

I once spent a summer in Rome and at a seaside resort called Viareggio playing in an rock'n'roll band. It was here that I met and fell head over heels in love with a beautiful Irish girl called Sinead. She was a waitress at one of the clubs where we played. I was totally besotted and she likewise. This eventually led to me doing the worst gig I've ever done and losing two teeth.

After the summer, Sinead started a degree course at Manchester University while I returned to London. Anxious to be with her, I scoured the *Melody Maker* for a gig in Manchester. Finally, after a fruitless few weeks, I found one playing the clarinet in an oom-pah band in a bierkeller in the city centre. Each night I would have to dress up in lederhosen and wear a hat with a feather in it. The band was dire and was anyway only providing background music to the fighting which broke out on a regular basis.

I shared Sinead's tiny bedsit and apart from the nightly musical torture, life was blissful. She came from a large Irish family and told me that her parents were intent on her marrying a second cousin who ran a pig farm in Kerry. One night as we lay in each other's arms, the door was kicked open and two very, very big men entered.

It transpired that they were two of Sinead's brothers intent on rescuing her from a life of sin with an itinerant clarinet player. Before throwing me and my belongings down the stairs, they gave me a good thumping accompanied by dire threats not ever to make contact with their sister again. The two teeth that they dislodged in their persuasive efforts were, thankfully, not at the front, which would have been disastrous for a reed player. I don't know if Sinead ever married the pig farmer. Hearing even the faintest hint of an oom-pah band still makes my tongue travel to the empty spot in my mouth.

Maybe, before I die, I'll go back to Viareggio and sit on the beach like the doomed von Aschenbach in *Death in Venice*. As the sun sets and I begin to doze, an old lady will pick her way between the abandoned buckets and spades and Cornetto wrappers. She'll tap me lightly on the shoulder. And, looking up, I'll see that it's Sinead, much older, but still beautiful.

"Let's start again," she'll say. Then I'll know I've died and gone to heaven.

Thursday:

This morning The Centaur stops me on the stairs.

'You should ask Little Owl out for a drink,' she says. 'She's very keen on you.'

The thought of having a relationship with the beaded, blanketed manatee fills me with horror, but I try to be polite.

'I'm flattered,' I say, 'but I'm really not looking for any kind of relationship at this time.'

I've hardly got this out, when Cordelia emerges from her flat and to my surprise gives me an affectionate hug and a peck on the cheek before skipping toward her car.

'So I see,' says The Centaur. 'You want to be very careful there. She's not all she seems.'

'What do you mean?' I ask

'I don't know, but I've got a funny feeling about her that's all. She seems to go abroad a lot.'

'So would I if I had the money,' I say. 'Why don't you check with your spirit guide, Running Bear? Maybe he can shed some light on it if he's not too busy chasing beaver.'

The Centaur harrumphs and pushes her way past me and out of the block. As ever, her arse some distance from her considerable front.

Friday:

Christmas cards start to arrive and goad me into making a list of those I'll have send one to. I blame Prince Albert, Queen Victoria's consort, for this. Having been coerced into marrying a stumpy old frump who was apparently infrequently amused, he set about excusing himself from occasional and wholly unpleasant bedroom duties, by re-inventing Christmas. It is he, apparently, who is responsible for popularising Santa Claus, decorated trees and seasonal cards. If Queen Vic had been a ravishing beauty, then perhaps we might have been spared all the Yuletide Germanic crap and over-laden postmen, like sax players, wouldn't suffer shoulder problems in later life.

Saturday:

A visit to the superstore, as it's pleased and somewhat smug to call itself. At the main entrance is the usual band of seasonal suspects collecting for local charities. Carols blare out from some tinny speakers mounted on a van disguised as a sleigh. It's the local Round Tablers and Rotary, gripped by altruism and Yuletide spirit, all dressed as Santas and elves, rattling buckets at shoppers. For the rest of the year they are enthusiastic members of the Worshipful Company of stoats, weasels, charlatans, estate agents, dodgy builders, touts, snouts and property developers. But, once a year at this time they cast aside their rapaciousness and become yo-ho-ho-ing founts of benevolence. It almost brings a tear to my eye.

Inside the shop, more carols are playing. It's like a bear pit, with dozy husbands and screaming kids trailing behind harassed mothers. Why do they all have to go to the bloody shop? Why can't dozy take the kids to the park, or encourage them to play chicken on the by-pass?

In the veg section, a mountain of Brussels sprouts has collapsed and a heaving mass of zombie-like people tread them into the floor. A very fat woman, with bandaged legs slips and falls. She is nearly trampled to death as she flails around on the slimy floor like a beached turtle.

It was a serious mistake coming here and now I need to get out. I turn and push against the human tide making my way toward the door. The carols from outside and those from within compete with each other in different keys. I feel hot and dizzy. As I make slow progress through the zombies, I think that I might faint and not be found until the shop closes, indistinguishable from the squashed sprouts and perhaps the fat lady.

I emerge from the store feeling hot and ill. An elf, otherwise a local estate agent, I think, approaches with a collection bucket.

'Merry Christmas,' he squeaks.

'Piss off,' I reply, pulling his silly hat down over his eyes.

It's a long way from Bethlehem and still nearly a month before Christmas.

Sunday:

There's a chill in the air and a dusting of snow is forecast. Every time this happens it's as though those responsible for keeping the roads open are taken by surprise. '

'What, snow in December? Better order some Peruvian salt. It should arrive by spring.'

I imagine a leisurely llama train, led by colourfully dressed women in bowler hats, crossing the Andes with the salt, while the UK comes to a standstill.

To be on the safe side, I decide to panic shop with the rest of the population. I struggle up the stairs to my flat with bags full of part-baked bread, two cases of chardonnay and enough soups to have saved Scott's ill-fated Antarctic expedition. That's me skint for the week and I've got nothing suitable to wear to the Welsh wedding next Saturday.

Sir Galahad

Monday:

And so it snows overnight and the country comes to its customary standstill. It's almost endearing, as if there's something un-British about efficiency or forward planning: and it gives us all an opportunity to practice those twin national traits of putting a brave face on things and studious amateurism. This drives Johnny Foreigner mad, because we are also quite good at winning things from time to time — like some wars and the odd cricket match.

For the most part, the German Enigma Code was cracked during the Second World War by a bunch of eccentric crossword fanatics in a tin hut. When the Beagle failed to land on Mars and indeed disappeared, did we vilify the bunch of over-grown schoolboys who devised it? Not a bit of it. We loved them and ignored the fact that it cost millions. Tim Henman, the tennis player, was hugely popular precisely because he didn't win the Wimbledon trophy.

America is often described as having a "Can Do" culture, whereas our own might be termed "Could Do — but might not"

Tuesday:

The weather dominates the news and the television journalists have a nice time interviewing each other interminably. All the major airports are closed and thousands of motorists are stranded on the motorways. It's not as though we weren't warned some days in advance by the Met office to expect heavy snow. But as we are nationally obsessive about the weather, so we are also given to completely disbelieving the weathermen. This is allied to our innate mistrust of experts and our love of amateurism. The slicker the graphs and graphics are in the forecast, then the less we trust them. This is why thousands of people with minimal driving skills undertake unnecessary journeys in unsuitable cars.

Living high on a hill, I'm completely snowed in. Thanks to my panic buying, however, I've got plenty of food and I'm staying put.

Wednesday:

Cabin fever has started to set in and I'm spending more and more time staring out of the window onto the bleak landscape. I see The Centaur and Buzz vainly trying to get their BMW out of the snow. Lots of useless wheel spin and it's going nowhere. The Centaur slips on the ice and ends up on her back, arms and legs flailing, like an upturned toad. I'm sure that her spirit guide, Chief Running Bear would advise her to smother herself in moose fat and stay in her teepee until spring when beaver are plentiful. I imagine that Little Owl is probably hunkered down in a tie-dyed tent somewhere, scoffing unspeakable tofu and pulses.

Cordelia phones to ask if I'm OK

'I'm staying in London at the moment, but I'll be back on Friday night,' she says. 'My car is a four-wheel drive, so there shouldn't be a problem with going to Wales on Saturday.'

This reminds me that I really don't have anything to wear to the wedding and given that I'm trapped in my flat, little chance to rectify this before Saturday. Oh well, it'll have to be one of my old wedding suits. Maybe they've come back into fashion.

I make some soda bread and settle down to watch daytime television, which is marginally worse than the abysmal evening output.

Thursday:

No sign of a thaw. The weather continues to dominate the news. The prime minister has visited Afghanistan to hand out Christmas puds to the troops and have meaningful, nation-building talks with people from the Stone Age, whose idea of a good time generally involves public mutilation, centuries old vendettas, treating women as if they were less than goats and selling opium to the world. They also don't use knives and forks, preferring to eat with their hands — if they've still got them.

Friday:

I try on an old wedding suit. A bit tight round the waist, but I manage to squeeze into it. The last time I wore this, I was swearing undying love and fidelity and could climb stairs without wheezing.

Jeremy Clarkson is on the telly. If anyone personified what is called a "punchable face", it's him. Huw Edwards reads the news in that slightly whiny, hard done by, Welsh voice.

I fall asleep watching *Newsnight* with Jeremy Paxman. Paxo, as he's known to his friends, is apparently a probing, fearless reporter. To me, he's an Oxbridge establishment figure, like David Frost, John Cleese, Stephen Fry and Alan Bennett. They don't really rock the boat, but they'd like to think they do.

Saturday:

And so to Wales. We leave at seven in the morning and for most of the journey I'm gripped with fear as Cordelia roars along the icy motorway and careers round country lanes. To give her her due, though, she's a brilliant driver.

The castle where the wedding is to take place comes into view and looks very imposing in a snowy landscape. We have separate rooms, which is a bit disappointing, but hardly surprising since we hardly know each other. In my room a knight in full armour stands guard by a four poster bed. Very quaint.

The ceremony takes place and then there's a reception afterwards in a great hall, with serving wenches and minstrels. Then to completely ruin the medieval atmosphere there's a disco. I have a particular loathing for discos and an equal amount for the DJs who run them. Their choice of music is almost always inappropriate and too loud. Also, they seem to think that they are in some way creative, that it's they and not the music they play that are the attraction. Bah!

Cordelia tries her best to get me to dance, but I have seen far too many men make fools of themselves on the dance floor to be persuaded, although I do have a final smoochy dance with her before we go to our rooms for the night.

'I've ordered some champagne,' she tells me. 'Why don't you join me in about ten minutes?'

I skip back to my room and check on my deodorant levels and have a shave. I change out of my suit into jeans and a T shirt. Just as I'm leaving the room, I'm struck with a bit of inspiration. I remove the helmet from the armoured knight and put it on. I stumble to Cordelia's room, because it's hard to see my way through the narrow slits in the helmet.

I knock at the door and when she opens it, I give an elaborate bow.

'Sir Galahad at your service my queen,' I say in a rather muffled voice.

'Ooh, brave knight,' she coos, 'I hope your intentions are honourable.'

'Never less so madam, ' I say.

She lifts the visor and gives me a very passionate kiss, which, had I been wearing one, would have split a cod piece.

'Let's have some champagne,' she says leading me to a sofa. Through the slits in the helmet, I can see that she's wearing a silk robe and I catch a glimpse of lacy underwear beneath it as she sits down. This does look promising, but what I have planned can't easily be done wearing a metal helmet.

But I can't get it off. I try not to panic as I tug at it while Cordelia pours the champagne. When I put it on, it opened at the back, so I fiddle around over my shoulder trying to get it to open again. Nothing doing. I confess my difficulty and she seems to find it highly amusing. She caresses the armour, flapping the visor up and down.

'Oh Sir Galahad, I love your helmet. Be gentle with me dear knight,' she says between giggles.

When it becomes obvious that the helmet is not coming off, she becomes very businesslike and says that we have to go to the nearest casualty department for help. While she enquires of the castle receptionist where the hospital is, I tiptoe past and wait for her by her car. As we drive to the hospital, she glances at me from time to time and hoots with laughter.

It's the early hours of Sunday morning and the casualty department is full of the drunken debris from Saturday night. I try to be inconspicuous as I pick my way through the crowd, but this is difficult if one is wearing a knight's helmet.

'Christ, it's the man in the iron mask,' shouts one wag. This starts Cordelia hooting again.

As we sit waiting to be seen, no end of people seem to find my condition amusing and I'm treated to various remarks and jibes. One particularly obnoxious drunk with a fat lip and a black eye starts to sing the Tin Man's song from The Wizard of Oz and this is taken up by several others. Even the policemen and ambulance crews that pass in and out snicker and nudge each other. I've been holding the visor open in order to converse with Cordelia and see my way, but now I let it snap shut and try to adopt a dignified pose.

Finally, we're called into the treatment room, where a fearsome looking nursing sister with legs like Mills bombs and arms like hams tries to wrestle the helmet off my head. All she succeeds in doing is to half throttle me and twist the helmet out of alignment. Worse still, the visor will no longer open, so that I'm in fear of suffocating. I try to tell her this, but my voice is muffled and she can't understand what I'm saying.

'I think this is a job for the fire brigade,' she tells Cordelia, as if I'm not there, or incapable of taking it in.

They both enjoy a little chuckle and I'm sent back out to the waiting room, where a loud cheer goes up from the assembled drunks. The Tin Man songster is being led out by two burly cops.

'I should leave it on mate,' he says as he passes. 'When they do yet another re-make of Robin Hood, you'll be all ready for a bit part.'

The fire brigade arrives with sirens blaring. Half a dozen of them assess the situation and between laughter decide that they'll have to cut me out of the helmet. I'm taken back into the treatment room and they produce a frightening looking device with a long serrated blade. Just as they're about to switch it on and begin hacking at my head, a junior doctor walks by.

'Wow,' he says, 'a Plantagenet battle helmet. Don't damage it. These always have a secret clasp that releases it.'

He fiddles around at the back of the helmet and bingo, it opens.

'There you go,' he says and swaggers off.

I'll bet he had a pencil box at school.

We drive back to the castle and the moment for amour has well and truly passed. We go to our separate rooms and I replace the helmet on the knight. Thank God I didn't put the whole suit on.

Sunday:

At breakfast this morning, Cordelia breaks into periodic giggles as she recalls the night's events.

'You do make me laugh,' she says on the drive back. 'Let's go out for dinner soon, but please don't wear fancy dress.'

There's hope yet.

Undercover Police

Monday:

Driving back from Wales yesterday, I asked Cordelia what work she did.

'Oh just a boring old civil servant,' she said.

'What department?' I asked

'I'm sort of attached to the Foreign Office — just statistics really, you know, that sort of thing.' she replied.

'Gosh, you're not a spook are you?' I said. 'MI6, that sort of thing?

'Oh, so you'd fancy a bit on the side with a spy would you?' she laughed. 'Nothing so glamorous I'm afraid. I'm just a pen pusher and a number cruncher.'

Today the usual junk mail plus a pile of bills. I really must try to get a few more gigs to make ends meet. I go on-line and search for "sax player wanted" adverts of which there are precious few. One does catch my eye, however. It's for a band who all dress up as Elvis and perform on stilts. It says that the ability to ride a monocycle would be an advantage. I check further to see whether this is a wind-up and sure enough, they really do exist. I can imagine waiting in the wings to go on, teetering on the stilts and sweating in an Elvis outfit and bling, to be told,

'You're on after the seals.'

Tuesday:

The snow has all but gone. I walk into town, over the old wooden river bridge and through the Phillips Memorial park. I pause at the plaque that celebrates Jack's heroism. As the stricken and doomed *Titanic* was slowly sinking, amidst all the panic, shouting, prayers and vain promises to God, this young man, who was actually an employee of Marconi who had a monopoly on radio telegraph at the time, continued to tap out the SOS message. He went down with the ship. Legend has it that the ship's band continued to play and also perished. Most of the musos I've ever worked with would have been busy dressing up as women and children — me included. Two years after the sinking of the *Titanic*, the pointless blood bath of World War One began, wherein hundreds of thousands of brave young men, just like Jack, needlessly lost their lives on the whims and machinations of blimps and braggarts.

Marconi died in his bed in Rome in 1937. He was an avid supporter of fascism and Mussolini, who had just slaughtered hundreds of thousands of Abyssinians on a whim. Strutting like a braided, self-decorated puffed up peacock, this short-arsed monster would go on to add to this tally many times over when he allied Italy with Germany when it decided to go on a European tour. To their everlasting credit, most Italians showed an extreme reluctance to be senselessly heroic and eventually strung the peacock and his mistress up on a lamppost in Milan.

As I continue to read the dedication to Jack, a fragment of newspaper flutters rounds my feet. I pick it up and see a picture of a smirking George Bush Junior. He has apparently written (sic!) an autobiography in which he seeks to justify the slaughter in Iraq that so many of his pals profited from. He's wearing a flying jacket and I'm reminded that he managed to avoid the draft to Vietnam by doing his national service in a Ruritanian outfit called the Texas Air National Guard who presumably daily risked their lives crop spraying and mapping out potential oil wells, further to enrich the Bush dynasty in their continuing struggle to bring democracy to the world.

O brave new world. That has such people in't.

Argggggh! These people are still there. The ones who will vow to fight to the last of other people's sons. Who bow their heads at cenotaphs dedicated to the "glorious dead", yet treat with arms dealers and despots. Those for whom the words freedom and justice are portmanteau words, carrying many shades of meaning, all of which suit themselves and their interests. I'm reminded of the interchange between Alice and Humpty Dumpty in *Through the Looking Glass*.

'I don't know what you mean by glory,' Alice said.

Humpty Dumpty smiled contemptuously. 'Of course you don't—till I tell you. I meant there's a nice knock-down argument for you!'

'But glory doesn't mean 'a nice knock-down argument,' Alice objected.

'When I use a word,' Humpty Dumpty said, in a rather a scornful tone, 'it means just what I choose it to mean—neither more nor less.' 'The question is,' said Alice, 'whether you can make words mean so many different things.

"The question is," said Humpty Dumpty, "which is to be master that's all."

I carry on into town and buy books and gift tokens for my nearest and dearest for Christmas. This is a cop out I know, but I'm past struggling to think what to buy and this at least gives them the option to choose rather than trying to understand why I would have bought oven gloves, impossible cook books, or fondue sets.

Returning home, I pass by my old primary school wherein so many years ago I had the confrontation with the late Reverend Archibald Coot, tried my hand at country dancing and fell in love with all the girls. There are Christmas decorations on the windows and I can hear the strains of *Away in a Manger* being sung by infant voices. I'm tempted to peek in one of the windows, but I'm reminded that it wasn't so long ago that an entirely innocent paediatrician was almost lynched by an ignorant mob on a council estate in Portsmouth. I move on. Climbing the steep hill back to the flats makes me puff and pause a lot. I must be getting old.

Wednesday:

I read in the paper that human fat is a rich source of stem cells that could potentially be used to grow new organs and even limbs. This would apparently circumvent the current ethical issues regarding the use of foetal tissue. Of course, it also puts obesity in a completely new light.

Currently, people who are overweight are treated with opprobrium and constantly hectored and lectured, almost as if they are enemies of the people and a drain on resources. However, this could now all change and they might henceforth be regarded as public spirited in providing a source for the stem cells. Guilt-free fat donors could happily munch on cream buns and no end of junk while being tapped like rubber trees. No niggardly digestive biscuit for them, like that offered to blood donors. They'll be encouraged to live short, but merry lives of bacchanalian and epicurean excess. These Buddha-like figures will hardly have settled their considerable bulks onto a park bench, before they'll be offered food by reverential passers-by and small children. Ducks and pigeons will become extinct.

Wealthy X-rays, like Victoria Beckham, or Scunthorpe Travelodge might actually have their own live-in fatties, just in case they need to grow a new ear, or pep up their pouts. Perhaps the new body parts might be grown *in situ*, rather than in laboratories. I can envisage the fatties waddling around, their considerable midriffs festooned with developing eyeballs, lungs and other body parts. At the appropriate time, these would be carefully harvested like caviar or truffles.

O brave new world...

Thursday:

No sign of Cordelia. I've tried phoning and calling round, but to no avail. She's obviously off somewhere doing her number- crunching. Although I buggered things up in Wales, I don't want the trail to go cold.

Friday:

The front page of the local rag carries a story of police laying siege to a house in which they suspected an armed man was holding out. There's a photograph. In the distance one can just make out a bungalow, but this overshadowed in the foreground by an abandoned washing machine. No sign of a policeman. I dash off a letter to the editor praising the intrepid reporter's valour in getting to within a mile of the house and I also marvel at the cunning of the police in disguising themselves as a washing machine. I should have left it there, but I continue saying that I'll never look at fly-tipping in the same light again. Those abandoned piles of rubble and junk one see occasionally on the side of the road might well be the police laying siege or lying in wait. I don't expect publication, but it was fun writing it.

Saturday:

At my secondary school, we had a history teacher called Miss North. She was an eccentric, but inspiring teacher. She would often act out historical dramas to the class, playing all the parts herself. Her rendition of the Battle of Hastings and the death of Harold was particularly moving. She was also drop-dead gorgeous.

In one winter term, when I was thirteen, Miss North devised an ambitious version of the Nativity that perversely combined Greek myth with the Gospel story. It was all very confusing and chaotic. It began with the opening of Pandora's Box and went downhill from there. The three wise men were dressed in academic gowns with mortarboards on their heads. Mary and Joseph were a Teddy Boy and Teddy Girl and the setting was not a stable, but a coffee bar. I was cast as Hermes, messenger of the gods. For the night of the performance, Miss North had arranged for a real donkey to be on stage, presumably as a nod toward the more traditional version of the story. What a donkey was doing in a coffee bar with two Teds, three pocket-sized academics and Pandora, was never fully explained.

Like most of the boys, I was madly in love with Miss North, which might explain why she was able to persuade a normally cynical young lad like me to wear the outfit she had devised for my part as Hermes. I wore a short skirt and sandals, plus a flying helmet and goggles. Silvery cardboard wings were attached to the sides of the helmet and the sandals. The sandals belonged to my dad and were several sizes too big for me, causing my feet to flap like flippers as I attempted to walk. I looked like a mixture between a cross-dressing Biggles and Coco the Clown. Miss North played the part of Pandora. She was dressed in a flowing diaphanous gown and her hair was piled high on her head and topped with a wreath of laurel leaves. She looked magnificent.

The performance took place in the school hall. It had no stage, but the caretaker had put together a makeshift arrangement of milk crates with sheets of plywood on top. The coffee bar was called "The Traveller's Rest" and there were some chairs and tables and a counter also constructed from milk crates. Pandora's box was centre stage and decorated with skulls and luscious looking fruit. We were using a nearby classroom as a dressing room, with a curtain to shield our entrances and exits from the audience.

The winter of this year was particularly harsh. It had been snowing all day and the temperature plummeted. The dressing room was unheated and we all shivered as we got into our outfits. The donkey was led in from the outside by its owner, a local woman who was even dottier than Miss North. Its back was covered in snow and as Miss North began decorating its ears with holly and ivy, it shook itself covering her in some of the snow. This soon melted, making her gown even more diaphanous — much to the delight of me, the Teddy Boy and the three wise men.

The audience arrived in the candlelit hall and the school choir began singing *In the bleak midwinter*. They were accompanied by the school harmonica band. Only a few days earlier, I had gotten a detention for pinning a notice on their rehearsal room door saying "Welcome to the Wizards of Wheeze"

It came time for Miss North to make her entrance to start the play. She led the donkey onto the stage via a small ramp. The audience gasped and then broke into applause. Whether this was due to the presence of a real donkey, or Miss North's damp dress that clung seductively around her thighs, is debatable. She tethered the donkey to the coffee bar counter and began warbling about all the good and evil in the world. She then opened the box. Lights flashed and the caretaker, who was off-stage, flapped a sheet of tin to simulate thunder. This was my cue to enter. The plan was that I should run back and forth across the stage with my arms outstretched like wings and shout, "I bring tidings from the gods, tidings from the gods." I pulled down my goggles and launched myself. I made the first pass across the stage without a problem, but because of the difference in temperature between the cold dressing room and the hall, my goggles steamed up. For my second pass I was completely blind and slipping on my over-sized sandals, I crashed into the coffee bar.

The donkey, which until now had been entirely placid, reared up on its hind legs, baring its yellowy teeth and letting out a loud bray. It then charged off the stage demolishing what was left of the coffee bar and dragging several milk crates in its wake. The audience scattered as the terrified donkey rampaged through the hall. Several people sought sanctuary by climbing up the exercise bars on the walls. The whole scene looked like a Yuletide version of the Pamploma Bull Run. The donkey was eventually captured by its owner. The performance was abandoned. The Wizards of Wheeze played a few more carols and then the shell-shocked audience trudged out into the snowy night. My last glimpse of the fragrant Miss North was when I saw her being beckoned into the headmaster's office. She didn't return to the school after the Christmas holiday and was replaced by the odious Miss Vine, she who confronted me recently at the school reunion.

Sunday:

In keeping with the season, I buy a poinsettia and twine some fairy lights around the bungee straps that serve as my washing line. I switch them on and of course nothing happens. I spend the next hour or two twiddling with the bulbs until they eventually light up. They look quite festive.

I settle down for some wine and a bit of cheese. There's a knock at the door and Reg the caretaker is standing there.

'You're not allowed to decorate the outside of the building,' he says. 'It's in the rules.'

'Oh really?' I say. 'Do the rules also mention shagging other men's wives, playing unspeakable cowboy music and having mangy dogs?'

'I'll have to report it to the management,' he says and turns on his heel.

'Why don't you get Christmas banned altogether?' I shout after him.

Miserable sod. Bah!

Away in a Manger

Monday:

Anyone who says that they don't fear death is a liar. We're hard-wired to fear and avoid it all costs. Thus far, and to my certain knowledge, no one has come back from the grave and said,

'You know what, it's not so bad, really it isn't. It's just like learning to ride a bike. You're scared shitless at first, but then you get the hang of it and before you know it you've got a newspaper round.'

According to some of the theories, if you've led a reasonably blameless life you'll be able to look down on your nearest and dearest after you die, but they won't be able to see you. What kind of torture is this? You see your bright daughter, the apple of your eye when you were alive, planning to marry a feckless schmuck. Or you see your widow being twisted out of the pittance you've left her, by a smooth talking shitbag. And you're powerless to stop any of these things.

The reason for my morbid thoughts is that when practising the sax this morning, I got a nosebleed. I couldn't stop it for some time. I immediately went on-line to see what might be the cause. I wish I hadn't. The list of possibles includes brain tumour, diabetes, meningitis and other scary ailments. Blowing like a bastard on the sax wasn't mentioned.

I have to admit to being a bit of a hypochondriac. I blame my mother for this, because she had a morbid fear of any illness. She also had an incomplete idea about human anatomy. I remember her telling my sister that if she continued to suck her hair, it would eventually wind around her heart and kill her.

It's not just illnesses that worry me. I also have a phobia about snakes and can barely watch when they're shown on television. If an interrogator wanted me to spill the beans he could dispense with the electrodes and water board and just threaten me with a picture of an adder. And it's not just snakes to worry about; there are lots of other nasty things out there. There's the candiru fish.

This little chap, also known as the toothpick fish, lives in the Amazon and happily swims into the gills of other larger fish and gorges on their blood, often killing them in the process. It finds its way there by being able to detect minute amounts of urea and ammonia excreted by the gills of its prey. Too bad for Amazonian fish one might think, but this vicious little sprat can't differentiate between a piranha and a penis. So a bloke taking an innocent tinkle in the world's second longest river is not immune from the toothpick's attention. (The juxtaposition of" toothpick" and "penis" already has me wincing) This intrepid little critter, attracted by the ammonia in the man's widdle, can swim up the Niagara of urine and enter the hapless pisser's old chap. Once inside, it releases spikes that fix it in position so that it can then begin feasting on the blood of its new host, who is, at this stage, writhing in agony and wondering why his pride and joy is throbbing like a hammer-struck thumb.

Since I live some four thousand miles away from the Amazon, one might say that my fears about this fish are groundless. However, there are a lot of anoraks and nerds in the UK who delight in keeping exotic pets. Ken Livingstone, when he wasn't trying to turn London into a version of the Paris Commune, was very fond of newts and salamanders. I'm sure that Ken and many others of his ilk are responsible owners, but there are others who fancy the idea of having say a tarantula, puff adder or box jellyfish for a pet, but tire of them when they won't fetch a thrown ball or sit up and beg. They then release them into the wild or flush them down the loo. (I can imagine an RSPCA car sticker saying, "A funnel web spider isn't just for Christmas".)

Apparently, our countryside is now alive with various exotic species. The Norfolk Broads are infested by giant hamsters called coypu and pumas apparently stalk Surrey and Bodmin Moor. So, it's not beyond the realms of reason to imagine a nerd in Neasden flushing a school of under-performing toothpick fish down the bog. They will probably have a happy time of it in the sewers picking off rats and Orson Welles, if he's still hiding there, but they'll breed and begin to infest domestic plumbing.

I imagine a scene where an estate agent, Nigel, is happily tra-la-ing in his shower, anticipating another day of staring out of the office window. Lurking just below the plughole the toothpicks are circling. (Cue *Jaws* music) The most daring thing Nigel ever does in his miserable, conformist little life is to piss in the shower...

I think I'll start peeing off the balcony.

Tuesday:

It's very near to Christmas now. I wonder whether the Messiah, whose birthday is approaching, could have had any idea just what industry, wars, inquisitions, burnings, rackings, thumbscrewings and ludicrous somersaults of logic and abandonments of reason his advent and grisly demise would spawn over the centuries.

Imagine it. There you are in a stinking, fly-blown stable surrounded by farting livestock. You've got a mum and dad, but the latter has apparently played no part in your conception.

Three saddle-sore wise guys from Taiwan or wherever, enter, offering you frankincense, myrrh and gold. You're too busy mewling and puking to take this in. You spend the next thirty years or so trying to learn carpentry and abandoning childish ways. Now and again, the frankincense and myrrh are used on high days and holidays, but of the gold there is not a trace or mention.

In between out-smarting the rabbis and chucking the money changers out of the temple, you live a very frugal life. The gold might have come in handy, if only to drive a harder bargain for the loaves and fishes. Wholesale maybe. And you might have started a little business knocking out kitchen units or scroll holders instead of annoying the Romans. The whole course of subsequent human history might have been completely different. No Crusades, or pogroms, no *Thought for the Day*, no happy-clappies, or Jehova's Witlesses.

So I've got this theory. I reckon that the innkeeper trousered the gold while Joe and Mary were busy trying to keep the flies away from the baby. They didn't discover that it was missing until they were back in Nazareth and by then it was too late. This innkeeper was called Hilton and from small, but dishonest beginnings, he founded the hotel empire that eventually spawned Scunthorpe Travelodge. If you think this is just another whacky conspiracy theory, then consider this. There's a Hilton Hotel in Bethlehem and numerologically Paris Hilton equals six. Two more of these and she'd be the Antichrist. I rest my case.

The poinsettia looks distinctly unhappy and is already shedding its leaves. My illuminated bungee display is holding up though.

Wednesday:

No sign of Cordelia. Even her answer phone has stopped responding. I know she has a mobile, but I don't have the number. I call on Reg, the caretaker, to see if he has it. I should have known that he wouldn't cooperate.

'That's confidential information mate,' he says. 'Have you taken those fairy lights down yet?'

'No I haven't,' I say. 'They're not on the building, but within my meagre balcony. Look, I'm worried about her. If you won't give me the number then at least call her yourself to see if she's ok.'

'I can't get involved in the love lives of tenants,' he says pompously. 'Maybe she doesn't want to take your calls.'

'Well you've been doing quite well so far in involving yourself where you shouldn't,' I tell him, referring of course to his cuckolding of VAT-man.

I try knocking on Cordelia's door, but there's no answer. I can see through the glass that there's a pile of mail inside that hasn't been picked up.

Thursday:

I get a very strange Christmas card. It's one of those clever ones where one can choose all sorts of images and captions. It has a cartoon picture of a knight in armour playing the saxophone. The unsigned message inside reads, "A parfit gentil knight. Remember we had Wales." It's clearly from Cordelia, but why wouldn't she sign it?

A boring visit to the minmarket. The Embryo is now in full Santa attire, but still dispensing her very own brand of gloom. Phil Spector Christmas songs are blaring out of the in-store speakers. His famous "wall of sound" does nothing to diminish the utter banality of the material. In Phil's day, he really did use five grand pianos, four hundred violins and a cast of thousands to achieve his sound. These days, it can be done on a laptop at a fraction of the cost, but it's still mostly crap.

Friday:

More snow is forecast. The weather man on the telly, who looks like an anally retentive undercover tax man to me, says that the Met Office has issued a severe weather warning for the Cairngorms and central Scotland. Wow! I'll bet that'll surprise the Scots. Snow in December north of the border. Whatever next? Airports as far south as Gatwick and Exeter are closing in sympathy and supplies of salt have already run out before a plough has stirred.

Saturday:

I attend a wonderful performance of *Wind in the Willows* by the local professional thespians who are still trying to raise funds to avert the demolition of the Redgrave Theatre by the Worshipful Company of Philistines, Stoats, Etcetera.

Also taking place within the same venue is a fair displaying and selling military memorabilia. There are lots of overweight men wearing combat gear selling Nazi helmets, bayonets, handguns, and all the paraphernalia of warfare and man's inhumanity to man. The families going to the *Wind in the Willows* have to pass by this. If I were a better writer, I could perhaps juxtapose it with the innocence of picnics by the river, life on the open road and simply messing about in boats.

Sunday:

Knowing that some little nerd will check up on it, I have to admit that the Bethlehem Hilton is actually in Bethlehem, Pennsylvania USA. However, the fact remains that Hilton, the shady innkeeper, while salaaming with the Taiwanese, probably pinched the gold. Anyway, there's a Hilton in Jerusalem.

Cargo Cult

Monday:

I think I'm being followed. As I set off in the old Fiesta to get my paper this morning, I notice a man and a woman in a black car parked outside the flats. They trail me to the mini-market and even go in and saunter around after me. I've got nothing better to do, so rather than heading back home, I drive out into the country to see whether they follow. I quite like this, it makes me feel that I'm part of a spy drama. I take all sorts of twists and turns, but the black car stays a little distance behind me, which is hardly surprising given that I'm driving a beaten up old Fiesta. I finally lose them by jumping the lights at a level crossing, just as the barriers are coming down.

It's the best fun I've had in ages, but I do wonder who they might be. Then it dawns on me. They're probably undercover agents from the council checking on my claim for a rebate on the council tax because I live alone. Sneaky bastards.

Tuesday:

The countdown to Christmas continues. Turkeys fill up most of the cooled shelf space in the mini-market. Norfolk Bronze they are called. I wonder whether they spend the last few days of their miserable lives under sun lamps, blissfully unaware of their impending doom. Or perhaps they are shipped off to Barbados in early December to finish off their tans.

'This is the life,' they'll gobble, as they toss back pino coladas and cranberry cocktails by the pool.

'Yippee! Next year, let's try Bermuda. Last one to the beach is a mince pie.'

Bronzed and invigorated, they'll return to Norfolk's icy wastes. Then they'll be herded into a truck for the short journey to the slaughter sheds.

'Where to now?' they'll ask each other as they bump along a farm track, their wattles quivering in anticipation.

'Maybe it's Acapulco this time, or the Riviera.'

At least they won't have to suffer the Queen's speech, or yet another repeat of *The Great Escape*.

Wednesday:

In the early 1920s, an itinerant bootlegger by the name of George Hensley founded the Holiness Church in Grasshopper Valley Tennessee. George and his pals, who probably made the baddies in *Deliverance* seem like jolly nice chaps, specialised in handling deadly snakes during their church services. Their theory was that if one was free from sin, then the good lord would give his protection. They also went in for glossolalia, or speaking in tongues. The church still exists in several southern states of the USA and over the years many worshippers have been exposed as sinners by succumbing to snake bites. George himself fooled around with a deadly cottontail snake in 1955 and slipped this mortal coil. His followers later claimed that he had suffered a heart attack. I'm thinking of this piece of trivia because this morning a leaflet came through my door announcing that there's to be a special candle-lit service at the parish church on Christmas Eve to which all faiths are welcome.

No doubt there'll be the usual suspects like Baptists, Presbyterians and various shades of non-conformity. Despite their slight doctrinal differences, I'm sure that the congregation will all behave in a civilised manner as they pray to the same suburban Jehova. There might even be minced pies and mulled wine in the church annexe afterwards. However, I think the vicar, in his ecumenical enthusiasm, could be taking a risk here. News of this all-faith service could spread via the internet, like the whereabouts of an impromptu rave, or a teenage party. I imagine the following scenario.

As he stands at the church door on Christmas Eve greeting the congregation, the vicar is amazed and temporarily gratified to see not only his usual flock, but also a procession of ganja-trumpeted Rastas, Druids, Jedi knights, whirling Dervishes and Voodoo priests with goats and chickens. Sting, taking a break from tantric sex, might turn up with some of his Amazonian chums with CDs in their mouths and there could also be an appearance of grass-skirted Cargo cultists with blow pipes and spears.

This latter group inhabits some of the most remote Pacific islands. During World War Two, army supplies were sometimes parachuted to the wrong islands and the natives, glad to receive this bounty, began to believe that it came from a great spirit in the sky whom they now worship. For reasons that are not entirely clear, some of them also believe that the Duke of Edinburgh is a deity, rather than a boring old fart.

Last to arrive are the good ol' boys from the Holiness Church, carrying baskets which the vicar mistakenly thinks are picnic hampers.

The service gets under way and apart from an occasional un-English 'hallelujah' and the insistent throb of voodoo drums, all goes smoothly until the good ol' boys get their snakes out of the baskets and begin twirling them about their heads and moving among the stunned parishioners. Not to be outdone, the voodooists slaughter a goat and a couple of chickens and the Dervishes begin a furious whirling dance up the aisle. As the vicar appeals for calm, the snake handlers begin speaking in tongues. This is all gibberish, but something one of them utters is, by complete chance, a huge insult to the Cargo cultists and they begin indiscriminately to blow pipe the congregation with poisoned darts.

The snakes escape their handlers and headless chickens run to and fro. High in the belfry, the bell ringers, unaware of the carnage below, begin their customary cacophony, as people are crushed in the stampede for the exit.

I think I'll give it a miss. Sting bores me and I'm terrified of snakes.

Thursday:

I listen to a radio programme about the late, great, saxophonist, Charlie Parker. It's narrated by Kenneth Clarke, a prominent Tory and hardly a libertine. I find it hard to reconcile the dissolute life of Charlie and the admiring tones of Ken, as he now likes to be known. As far as I know, our new cuddly Ken has never put a foot wrong — apart from being a Tory. Opposites attract perhaps. Personally, I've never been a great fan of modern jazz, although Charlie's saxophone technique and improvising skills always leaves me awestruck.

In the early Sixties, I played in Paris for the first time and was full of myself about it. On my return, I went to a local pub, a well-known haunt of bearded, beret-wearing modern jazz fans. I was holding forth about my trip when one of the beardies asked if I had been to the Blue

Note, a famous jazz club in Paris. I hadn't been near the place, but in my arrogance claimed to have been several times.

'Who was on?' asked one of the beardies.

I dredged my memory and came up with the name of an obscure sax player.

'But he's been dead for five years,' said the beardie.

'Yes, I know,' I said, 'he was rather faint.'

I fled the pub with my tail firmly between my legs. Oh, boastful Toad.

Friday:

A recording session at a local studio. I'm relieved to find that there's no committee of experts present, just a girl singer and the engineer. All the backing tracks have been completed, so it's just a case of dubbing on the sax. I'm only asked to play some solos which is very nice, but I can hear other places where sax parts would sound good. So, I end up dubbing and over-dubbing sax sections with harmonies. It takes far longer than I've been asked to perform, but it's a real pleasure to exercise some latent skills, rather than just honking out solos. Besides, I'm grateful for a couple of hundred quid and for the fact that they are using a real player rather than a sample.

Saturday:

Sounds of the Sixties on Radio Two this morning. I listen with masochistic fascination to dire performances from the likes of Joe Brown, Marty Wilde, Billy Fury and Cliff Richard. The sheer amount of crap that was churned out in the Sixties means that Brian Matthew, the presenter of the show (who calls himself "your old mate") can probably keep this up ad infinitum, or at least until he pegs it and joins Billy in the afterlife, where they'll hopefully be rogered on a regular basis with a Southern Comfort bottle by Janis Joplin.

Sunday:

I get three calls on my mobile phone. When I answer, there's no response. I check my landline and there's a funny buzz on it and a series of clicks. I can't believe it. The council is tapping my bloody phones, just to see whether someone other than me answers or makes calls. Maybe they've been checking my purchases at the mini-market to see whether

I've been buying for two. I can imagine the grilling I'd get under the lamp at their offices.

"So, why did you buy a twin pack of digestives and an Indian meal for two?"

When I think of the profligacy of the council, with their overseas junkets to twin towns that nobody has ever heard of or cares a fig about and their rubber-stamping of hideous building projects, it makes my blood bubble that they're hounding a pensioner who's only trying to claim what is rightfully his. I'm looking forward to leading their undercover agents a merry dance. I might buy some sanitary towels or lipstick the next time I shop.

Spooky

Monday:

Before rising, I lie abed pondering on my idea that the innkeeper might have trousered the gold during the Nativity and how the course of human history might have been changed by such small variations. I call this the "What-If" theory of history. There could be a book in this or an afternoon play.

There are some obvious examples. If Guy Fawkes had succeeded in blowing up parliament, we might have been spared centuries of waffle and duplicity and trudging about in mud on November the Fifth. Or, if Harold hadn't been hit in the eye by an arrow at Hastings and had defeated the Normans, we might not have French knickers and French windows. Letters would be Saxon rather than French and might not split just when you're depending on them. Free of the Norman yoke, in the just and merry England that followed, there would have been no need for a Robin Hood and Kevin Costalot-Costner wouldn't have inflicted his dire *Robin Hood Prince of Thi*eves film on us, or have been so splendidly up-staged by Alan Rickman.

If Helen of Troy had suffered from halitosis or appalling flatulence and had a face like a smacked arse, then it might have been a measly couple of coracles that were launched, rather than a thousand ships. The Trojan War wouldn't have happened and some of our brave boys wouldn't have escaped from Stalag Luft III using the old wooden horse wheeze. And if a film version of this hadn't been made and little Johnny Mills hadn't had a starring role, he might have fallen upon hard times and become a circus midget, or a jockey. We would then have been spared his over the top portrayal of an idiot in *Ryan's Daughter*, or plucky sailors in crappy war films.

I could while away a lot of time on this, but I'm out of eggs and bread. So, I get up and visit the mini-market. Lo and behold, the council spies follow me there and pretend to be shopping while watching me the whole time. They are either complete amateurs, or they actually want me to know that they are snooping. Having nothing better to do, I lead them on a tour of the local countryside. I park at a beauty spot as do they. Thinking I might as well confront them regarding this shameful waste of council tax, I approach their car, but they drive off at high speed.

I've realised that Johnny Mills wasn't in *The Wooden Horse* film, but who cares?

Tuesday:

Still no sign of Cordelia. Reg, the caretaker, finally agrees to phone her mobile, but it goes straight to voicemail. I realise for the first time that I really am enamoured of her and I'm now quite worried. After much cajoling, Reg uses his master key and we enter her flat. There's a pile of mail by the door. I'm dreading finding her half alive or decomposing, but there's no sign of life or death. The flat is neat and tidy and there's even a Christmas tree in the corner awaiting decoration.

'She's probably just gone away for the holiday,' says Reg, as he locks her door. 'Sunning herself on a beach somewhere with one of those strapping young men I've seen her with. You didn't stand a chance mate.'

I don't tell Reg that these young men are in fact her gay son and his partner. What a mystery.

Wednesday:

I meet Brint on the stairs. He tells me that he and Shards are thinking of going back to Australia for the birth of their child.

'No offence mate,' he says, 'but we don't really want a Pom in the family.'

'None taken,' I tell him and wish them well.

So Little Owl and The Centaur will be denied a chance to practice their arcane birthing rituals after all and Chief Running Bear can continue undisturbed in his pursuit of beaver.

'Pity we never had a chance to jam together,' he says. 'I'm beginning to get the hang of the old guitar.'

I try to look crestfallen.

Thursday:

I decide to confront the local authority head-on over this business of me claiming a single person's discount on my council tax. I go to their offices and finding the right department and demand to see the person in charge. After a long wait, during which I can feel my temper rising, my neighbour, Adrian, aka VATman, now living with April, formerly known as Kevin, appears.

'Oh hello Adrian,' I say. 'Are you here to complain about this shower of shit too?'

'Oh no,' he says, 'I'm in charge of this department. I no longer work for Revenue and Customs. What seems to be the problem?'

I explain that I've applied for a discount and a rebate on previous overpayments, but have had no response. He promises to look into it and reassures me that living in the same block of flats, he knows that I don't co-habit or have a lodger.

'Well, that's a relief,' I say, 'perhaps you'll call your dogs off now. I'm fed up with being followed around.'

He looks mystified, so I tell him about the sinister couple who've been following me and the suspicious buzz on my land line. He tells me that the council never uses such tactics and that I must be imagining it. I'm unconvinced, but thank him anyway.

Friday:

I'm leaving the mini-market car park with my morning paper and a couple of croissants, when I'm grabbed from behind and pushed up against the old Fiesta by two burly men in dark suits. Over my shoulder, I recognise one of them as the male half of the pair that have been tailing me for the past week or so.

I try to break free, but they've got me pinned against the car.

'So, it's come to this has it?' I scream. 'The fucking council employing bully-boy tactics on a pensioner. Christ, Orwell was right all along.'

'We'd like you to come with us and answer a few questions,' says one.

'Oh yes, I can just imagine it,' I shout. 'Some bunker at the council offices where no one will hear my screams. Why can't you get it into your heads that I live alone?'

They look puzzled, but retain their grip on me and start dragging me toward their car. I dig my heels in and scream for help.

'We can arrest you, or you can come quietly,' says one.

'Oh, I see,' I say, 'council flunkeys now have the power of arrest do they?'

They both produce police warrant cards.

'No, but we do,' they say in unison.

'What's the charge then?' I ask, while still struggling to get away.

One of them fishes about in the pockets of my battered old Crombie and produces a small plastic bag containing some white powder.

'How about possession of a class A drug?' he asks sarcastically.

'You just planted that,' I say. 'I've never used that stuff in my life.'

They bundle me into the back of their car and we drive off. Despite my ranting, they remain tight-lipped on the short journey to the local police station where I'm taken to a room in which a rather distinguished looking man of middle age is seated at a desk.

'Ah,' he says, 'our musician friend. Do take a seat.'

I'm pushed into a chair and the two thugs remain standing behind me. I begin loudly to protest my innocence of the possession charge, but he interrupts me.

'That might be a misunderstanding,' he says. 'We'd like to know about your relationship with Cordelia Cooper.'

'Why, what has she done?' I ask. 'Have you got her?'

We're working on that,' he says. 'We know you were lovers and we know all about your dirty weekend in Wales.'

'If you know so much,' I say, 'then you would know that we never actually slept together. What's this all about?'

He ignores me and shuffles through a file. He takes out a photograph and hands it to me.

'Do you recognise this happy couple?' he asks.

It's a fuzzy image, but I can see Cordelia with a man. They seem to be on the deck of a large yacht. He has an arm around her waist and they are both looking sun-tanned and happy. I can't make out the man's face very well.

'If you think that's me with Cordelia, then you're wrong,' I say.

'Oh, we don't think it's you,' he says with a chuckle and the thugs join in the joke, 'but we do think it's an old friend of yours. Have a closer look.'

I look at the photograph again and it dawns on me who he is. It's Jubilee Jones, the old classmate who I met briefly on my trip to Ireland earlier this year.

'Jubilee Jones,' I say, flicking the photograph back to him. I'm shocked. I can't think how there could be a connection between Jones and Cordelia.

'Bingo!' he says and the thugs giggle. He hands me another photograph. This time it's one of me talking to Jones in the street in Kenmare, Ireland after his Rolls nearly ran me down.

'How did you get this?' I ask, but I know it's a stupid question. These guys aren't cops, they're spooks from MI5 or something similar. They're definitely not from the local council. He ignores me and resumes looking through the file. He hands another photograph to me.

'This is a good one,' he says. 'It's you dressed up as knight at an A and E department in Wales with our Cordelia. Looks like some kinky sex went wrong there.'

All three of them have a good laugh.

'What do you know about Mister Jones?' he asks.

I trot out the little that I do know and conclude by saying that he seemed to be a wealthy trader of some kind. I also add that despite trying to woo Cordelia, I know next to nothing about her and that I certainly don't know how she could know Jones.

He stares into space for some time, before closing the file. I think he has realised that I'm not implicated in whatever it is he's investigating.

'Let me tell you a little about your old school chum,' he says. 'Jones is a trader, you're right about that. He began his career as a petty crook flogging mainly stolen goods or laundering money from robberies. Nothing of interest to us. But then he went international, selling fake and mainly useless drugs to Third World countries. In recent times he has specialised in weapons of all sorts, small arms, rifles, mines rocket launchers and even tanks. He often sells to both sides in a conflict.'

I'm flabbergasted. I just can't square what I'm being told with my recollection of Jones as a slightly ridiculous figure in plus fours, who seemed wedded to the brandy bottle and lives in a far-flung corner of Ireland.

'But where does Cordelia fit into all this?' I ask. 'She's been missing for over a week. Was she one of your people, whoever you are?'

'I can't help you with that at the moment and I've probably told you too much already,' he says. 'Right now we want to know her whereabouts and that of Jones.'

I spend the next hour or two going over every little detail of my brief and unconsummated relationship with Cordelia. Finally, I'm told I can go.

'What about the drug rap?' I ask.

'Oh that,' says my interrogator. 'Turns out to have been talcum powder. Our mistake.'

One of the thugs takes me back to my car at the mini-market. By now, it's late afternoon and I'm starving. I buy a crappy ready-meal and some wine.

Saturday:

Now that I know that I'm not being followed by the local council, I'm far more relaxed. My land line still has a funny buzz on it, so I guess MI-something-or-the-other are still tapping it in the hope that I might get a call from Cordelia that they can trace.

I dig out an old school photograph and there's Jubilee Jones smiling back at me across more than half a century, as if butter wouldn't melt in his mouth.

Sunday:

It's not often that one has a brush with the world of spooks and spies, so I keep turning over Friday's events in my mind. Cordelia clearly isn't a pen pusher and number cruncher as she claims. But where is she? Has she gone native and run off with Jones? I guess I'll probably never know. What I do know is that I fancied her like mad and I think we might have had a lot of fun together. Maybe she'll return and all will be explained.

The World Turns

Monday:

A promising start to the week. There's a gift-wrapped parcel on my doorstep. It's a bottle of absinthe from a mail order company. I thought that absinthe had been banned many years ago, because it drove people mad. Poor old Vincent, famed on canvas and in song, swore by it, as did the vertically challenged Toulouse-Lautrec — although I think the latter was probably born a short-arse, whereas Vincent only went mad on sunflowers in his middle years.

There's a printed card attached to the bottle which reads, "Keep on Rockin' Sir Galahad".

This can only have come from Cordelia and clearly refers to the embarrassing episode with the knight's helmet in Wales. My judgment might be clouded by ardour, but I can't believe that Cordelia is a traitor. And even if she is, so what?

Governments of all stripes routinely lie to us, taking us into unjust wars on spurious grounds and they use thugs and crooks like Jubilee Jones when it suits them. They snuggle up to tyrants and despots, while trumpeting their own commitment to democracy. So what price loyalty or patriotism?

Tuesday:

This morning, a team of men in white overalls is giving Cordelia's flat the once over. As I go down the stairs, one of the thugs who arrested me last Friday is standing guard at her door. He taps his nose and winks at me. I'm not sure what this means, since I don't follow detective or spy programmes on the telly.

'Any news?' I ask him.

'Shergar's still missing and so's our little bird,' he says.

This mystifies me still further.

As I reach the ground floor, Little Owl sweeps in with a weedy looking man in tow. I wish them good morning and Little Owl introduces him.

'This is my fiancé, Wesley. We're going to be your neighbours soon. We're moving into Chardonnay and Brent's flat when they go back to Australia.'

I shake Wesley's limp hand and wonder whether he's fully prepared for a life of marital bliss in which he might regularly be colonically irrigated and force fed caffeine up the rear end. Maybe that's his thing. The thought of them becoming my near neighbours has me checking my will to live. I can imagine incessant Apache drums and Wesley's muffled screams.

There are only three days to go to Christmas and the mini-market is crammed with shoppers who are buying everything in sight, as if we're all about to be encircled by Mongol hordes, bent on starving us into submission. Turkeys, sack loads of sprouts, mega packs of crisps, mixed nuts, pickled eggs, onions, gherkins, Yule logs and great tins of chocolates are flying off the shelves.

I fight my way through the scrum to get a newspaper and some croissants. I've already stocked up with wine, but I might venture out on Christmas Eve to get some nice cheese and pate, if there's any left. That'll do me. Christmas day is spoken for with my nearest and dearest, so no need for a turkey or sprouts. When I get back home I see that the spooks are still at it in Cordelia's flat. The thug on the door has been replaced by another, who stares menacingly as I pass.

The bloody bell ringers are at it tonight. No doubt inspired by the Christmas spirit, they surpass themselves in their manic cacophony. I have a Ken Russell moment in which I imagine the bell ropes attached to their thrusting nethers as they writhe naked in sexual ecstasy in the belfry.

The truth is probably more prosaic. They're all tone deaf Tories, with sensible pension plans, paid off mortgages and only have a small sherry at Christmas as they listen to the Queen's speech in front of log-effect electric fires. They're the flag-waving, monarch-saluting, Daily Mail-reading middling order, who want to bring back conscription and public executions. Or perhaps they're crazed Guardian readers, who went to Sussex University, where demos and sit-ins took precedence over lectures and tutorials. Either way, it's a God-awful racket.

Wednesday:

I walk into town across the old wooden river bridge, past the parish church and the memorial to our brave son, Jack Phillips, hero of the Titanic disaster. In the park, young mums and dads push their kids on the swings, as I have done in the distant past. I pass my old junior school where I locked horns with the Reverend Archibald Coot nearly sixty years ago and where I danced my Monday mornings away while he tortured my classmates with a theology that he would come to renounce in his dotage.

In the High Street, many of the shops are still boarded up. I pass a bank where they have a poster in the window with a group of multiracial staff members grinning to camera. The slogan reads: "We're here to help". Buzz and the Centaur's New Age shop has notices on the windows announcing a closing down sale. I'm sorry to see this, even though I think they're bonkers.

The Worshipful Company of Stoats and Weasels — otherwise known as the Round Table, Rotary or whatever are out in their Santa outfits shaking collection buckets at passers by. A Salvation Army band is playing carols under the arches of the old town hall. I put a fiver in their bucket and glare at the Santas. Given my views on religion, I probably won't make it as a sunbeam, but I might have need of a soup kitchen one day.

I buy some gift wrapping, sticky tape and festive labels. I meander round the shops and at one point stop briefly to admire a window display of female mannequins in scanty underwear. In the reflection of the window I can see an old man in a crumpled old overcoat and realise that it's me. I start to move on, when a voice behind me says,

'Turning into a dirty old man, are we?'

It's Cyclops. She's arm in arm with Grudgeon, the school bully turned Queen's chaplain. He's not wearing a dog collar and now looks as menacing as he did at school. I presume that he has renounced the cloth in favour of a life with the myopic gargoyle. I say nothing and head for home, pondering on how things might have turned out if Jubilee Jones had succeeded in killing Grudgeon all those years ago.

As I trudge up the stairs, April, formerly Kevin, and Adrian, the ex-VATman, once husband of Robin, emerge from April's flat. We exchange festive greetings and they skip and giggle down the stairs like newlyweds.

Back in my flat, I switch on the television for the early evening news. There's the usual litany of man's inhumanity, lying politicos, the odds on a white Christmas and most importantly, of course, the state of the Footsie 100. Just as I'm about to switch it off and concentrate on my first proper drink of the day, there's a late item of news.

'The well-known international financier and philanthropist, J J Jones is believed to have perished when his luxury yacht sank in the early hours of this morning, seventy miles south of Cork in the Irish Republic. Fishing boats in the area reported seeing a bright flash and hearing a loud explosion. There are no signs of any survivors'

The report is accompanied by aerial pictures of debris floating amidst a large oil slick in the sea. There is also old footage of Jones shaking hands with various heads of state, inspecting guards of honour in banana republics, opening schools and hospitals in Africa and having a medal pinned to his chest by a grinning Idi Amin, who is weighed down with self-awarded insignia. There's no mention of arms trading or dodgy medicines. The final shots show him in conference with rifle-toting men in beards and turbans. At his side, there's a woman in a headscarf taking notes. It's Cordelia.

Christmas Eve:

Despite a generous amount of Merlot, I found it hard to get to sleep last night. It seems certain to me that Cordelia would have been on Jones' yacht. I'll probably never know whether she was in cahoots with him, or was working undercover. What I do know is that I'll miss her. She was feminine, but feisty and challenged me in a mocking way that I found irresistible.

Shards and Brint call round to say that they're going back to Australia on Boxing Day, before she gets too pregnant to fly.

'If you're ever down our way,' Shards says, 'look us up. I know Dad would love to see you again. He thought you were bonza.'

I thank them and wish them well.

There are some days in our lives when we get a definite sense of the world turning, of time passing and a shift from one reality to another. For a fleeting moment, perhaps, we glimpse the interconnectedness of events and players. But the pageant moves on and as we get older our part in it becomes diminished. For me, today is just such a day. With a heavy heart, I spend it wrapping a few presents and tidying the flat. I even look in the oven with a view to cleaning it, but abandon the idea as pointless.

In the early evening, I go down to the mini-market to get some cheese and bread. Handel's *Messiah* is blaring from the speakers outside the shop where the usual group of sullen teenagers is gathered. Inside it's deserted. There's hardly a thing left on the shelves. I manage to get some cheese and some part-baked baguettes. Suddenly, I'm skittled off my feet by the teenagers rampaging through the shop grabbing bottles of wine and packs of beer.

The next thing I know is that I'm being helped to my feet by The Embryo, who is wearing her reindeer antlers. The manager brings a chair for me to sit on and tells me that he has called the police and ambulance. The Embryo gives me a bottle of water and brushes off my overcoat. Despite feeling dazed, I notice that she's not wearing her engagement ring and comment on this.

'Nah, I dumped him. He's a wanker. Anyway, I'm leaving here after Christmas. I might do some travelling, see a bit of the world.'

Jason, the community cop, arrives, out of breath and, as ever, wreathed in technology and a stab vest.

'The ambulance is on its way,' he says. 'I'll need to take a statement from you.'

I rise unsteadily to my feet and tell him that I don't need an ambulance.

'Health and safety,' he says, like a mantra, 'we have to cover ourselves in case you have some underlying injury.'

'Oh, shove health and safety up your arse, I'm going home,' I say.

The Embryo laughs at this. I wish her a merry Christmas and good luck on her travels. She gives me a hug and one of her antlers nearly takes my eye out.

'Take care,' she says.

My, my. How the world turns.

Back home, I open some chardonnay and pick at some bread and cheese. There's nothing that I want to watch on the telly, so I put on a CD of Elgar's violin concerto. I decide to give the absinthe a try. I pour a cautious measure, because I notice that it's over eighty percent proof. I add ice and water and take a sip. It tastes like Pernod with a bit of a kick. I make a silent toast to Cordelia, wherever she may be.

It's a chilly night, but I go out on the balcony to get some air. I look down on the little town where I was born, spent my boyhood and now live out my age of bewilderment.

Lights twinkle below and there's a faint hum of traffic. In the far distance, a rocket cuts through the night sky before exploding into a thousand multi-coloured stars.

* * * * * * *

Acknowledgements

My heartfelt thanks are due to my old friend and brilliant singer/songwriter, Phillip Goodhand-Tait. Without his encouragement this would never have been written. My thanks also to the wonderful comedian, thoroughly nice chap and national treasure, Arthur Smith, who offered welcome advice and cheer.

Thanks also to Brenda Longman (Soo the Panda), Pauline Scott, Michael "Dougo" Douglas, Kirk Riddle, David Apps, Tony and Lesley Leach, Phil Kemp, John and Linda Mitchell, Mark Ackerman, Bob Garrett, Richard Ashworth, Dennis Reeve, Ann Lavell-Jordan, Nick Harms, Richard Allen, The Sheas of Ardgroom, Sev Lewkowicz, John and Sue Bradney, my brother, John, Betty Sherrington and all those who followed the original blog, on which this book is based.

Sadly, my editor, Ophelia Rear-Otter, disappeared under mysterious circumstances prior to publication. Therefore, any errors and omissions are my own.

Sláinte!

About the Author

David Sherrington is a saxophone player, arranger and composer. While training as a classical clarinettist, he noticed that girls seemed more attracted to sax players and took up that instrument in his mid-teens, embarking on a career as a professional musician. He has also been a teacher, copywriter, washer-up, filmmaker, scriptwriter and an occasional burden on the state. He lives in Surrey, England.

You may contact the author at: DavidSherrington@aol.com

Lightning Source UK Ltd.
Milton Keynes UK
UKOW021928181111

182289UK00001B/80/P